DOING RESEARCH IN BUSINESS
AND MANAGEMENT

DOING RESEARCH IN BUSINESS AND MANAGEMENT

An Introduction to Process and Method

Dan Remenyi, Brian Williams
Arthur Money and Ethné Swartz

SAGE Publications
London • Thousand Oaks • New Delhi

ISBN 0-7619-5949-1 (hbk)
ISBN 0-7619-5950-5 (pbk)
© Tech Times Limited 1998
First published 1998
Reprinted 2000, 2002 (twice), 2003, 2005

SAGE Publications Ltd
1 Oliver's Yard
55 City Road
London EC1Y 1SP

SAGE Publications Inc
2455 Teller Road
Thousand Oaks
California 91320

SAGE Publications India Pvt. Ltd
B–42 Panchsheel Enclave
PO Box 4109
New Delhi 110 017

British Library Cataloguing in Publication data
A catalogue record for this book is available from the British Library

Library of Congress Control Number: 98060955

Printed on paper from sustainable sources

Typeset by Tech Times Limited, Reading, Berkshire
Printed and bound in Great Britain by
Cromwell Press Limited, Trowbridge, Wiltshire

Contents

Foreword

How to do research is a dilemma that confronts most business and management students at masters and doctoral levels. My experience is that the majority of research students are generally uncertain about research methodology, and unclear about what good academics will regard as good research practice. Outside of North America, the majority of business schools still don't provide formal training in research methodology, and frequently leave it up to students themselves to discover, by trial and error in many instances, how to do research.

Doing Research in Business and Management primarily addresses the 'how to' of research for masters and doctoral students. It shows clearly what students will face from the beginning of their research degrees, and guides them through all the important concepts and decisions that they will encounter.

The book provides extensive coverage of all the main methods of research that can be used in business and management, and allows the student to compare and contrast a range of research strategies, from theoretical to empirical, and from positivist to phenomenological. Perhaps even more important to the student, the authors discuss how work in the form of dissertations and theses at the masters and doctoral levels are evaluated. This is a practical book which graduate-level students in business and management will find invaluable while navigating their way through the research maze. Most students enter this labyrinth with uncertainty as to what constitutes sound research methodology and what the 'best' research approach is – this text will be of significant benefit to them in ironing out these issues.

The contribution of the authors to this challenging and much-overlooked area is to be welcomed. Research is a voyage of discovery which I for one enjoy taking – I think that guided by this book, students, and of course fellow academics will also find that journey an exciting and rewarding one.

Leyland Pitt
Professor of Marketing and Strategy,
Cardiff Business School,
University of Wales

Preface

Research methodology, especially in the business and management studies domain, is a life-long study which is continually evolving and for which it is not possible to write a fully definitive text. The evolution in this subject has mostly been a movement away from the methodological techniques originally borrowed from the physical and life sciences, such as physics, chemistry and physiology, towards concepts developed for the human or social sciences, such as sociology and education. As this evolution progresses so the field of research methodology for those studying in the field of business and management becomes an increasingly rich, but sometimes bewildering set of choices. This book will help the reader cope with some of these choices by plugging a number of knowledge gaps that cause problems for business and management researchers. Specifically, the book brings together in one place a wide range of issues that are important for a researcher to understand in order to be able to obtain the best results from his or her work, including:

1 a description of the different research methods, strategies, tactics and tools which are available to help with conducting sound research, as well as an explanation of the philosophical underpinning of these methods;
2 the different stages in the research process, both from a positivistic and a phenomenological point of view, emphasising the rigour with which academic research needs to be conducted in either of these differing traditions;
3 the different approaches to evidence collection that can be used by the business and management researcher;
4 techniques for the analysis of both quantitative and qualitative evidence;
5 the ethical issues with which the researcher in business and management studies needs to be familiar;
6 the range of degrees on offer to the business and management researcher and the different approaches required for each degree type together with how these different degrees are actually evaluated by examiners.

Because some students find research methodology issues quite daunting the book has been written in an accessible way, explaining the research methodological concepts and processes which need to be understood if a research degree is to be obtained.

Doing Research in Business and Management has primarily been written for senior students or research associates engaged in the research process for the purposes of a masters or doctoral degree in business and management studies. It will be useful to MBA students, MPhil students as well as PhD and DBA students. The book will help anyone already engaged in research as well as those who are considering the possibility of undertaking an advanced degree and who would like to know in some detail what is actually involved in obtaining a research based degree.

Furthermore, as an increasing number of institutions require some independent research work from their senior undergraduate students, *Doing Research in Business and Management* will also be useful to these students and it is a useful text for members of the academic staff working with them.

Dan Remenyi
E-mail: Remenyi@compuserve.com

How to Use this Book

Some books are read from cover to cover. Some books are read non-stop with only the shortest breaks for sustenance and rest. Some books are used for reference to particular topics and ideas. The intention in *Doing Research in Business and Management* is to provide the reader with a comprehensive guide to research at the masters or doctoral degree level.

For those who have had little or no prior exposure to academic research it might be useful to read the book all the way through. For others who have already started on their research, or have had some previous exposure to research it could be used as a 'dippers'' book. So, for example, to read about the issue of generalisation and research findings look at pages 116, 168 and 283. To learn about laboratory research read page 56, or to know about evidence sample sizes read Chapter 11, pages 191–204.

Doing Research in Business and Management is not intended to be read 'non-stop'. The issues covered range from the fundamental philosophical debates underlying different research strategies to practical tips on how to structure and write the final dissertation. Research methodology is a vast subject and all the issues and techniques addressed can be explored further by reading specialist books on each of them. This book is intended to help the reader understand how these issues and techniques fit into the greater mosaic of research in the field of business and management studies and how they relate to masters and doctoral degrees.

Many of the concepts discussed in *Doing Research in Business and Management* are quite demanding and the student will want time to think about them and to discuss them with his or her supervisor and colleagues. Like doing research itself, learning research methodology is best achieved by debate and discussion. Thus the ideas in the book are primarily offered to stimulate this type of debate and exploration. It is hoped that research candidates will enjoy the process of learning how to do the research required for their masters or doctorate degree.

Layout of the Book

Doing Research in Business and Management is arranged in chapters, a number of which have sections in common. For example there is a discussion on evidence collection in Chapters 5, 6, 7, and 8 and there is a discussion on research validity in Chapters 6 and 9. This has been done deliberately so that the topic is covered with the correct orientation for the particular chapter.

The book starts with a discussion of the nature of masters and doctoral degrees and points out the type and level of research that is required by universities and business schools. From this point the book proceeds with a discussion of the philosophical underpinnings of the various research strategies and tactics that are available to the researcher in order to obtain a masters or doctoral degree. When the student understands the essence of this discussion he or she will be in a position to select a research strategy and will know what the implications of such a selection are.

A detailed look at the positivistic approach to empirical research and a careful consideration of phenomenology, as another and increasingly important tradition, follows. These represent the two main strategies of research that all researchers need to be aware of, and know when the one is more appropriate than the other.

Chapter 7 addresses fundamental process issues relating to all types of research and how research often begins with narrative descriptions which are developed into formal paradigms, theories or hypotheses. This is a very demanding chapter which provides some of the insights required to grasp the nature of the research process fully and the student should take as much time over it as he or she needs.

Evidence collection, including the use of case studies, is discussed in some detail culminating in a close look at the design and implementation of questionnaires as a measuring instrument. It is important to note that the chapter on case studies contains both a practical guide as to how to use this technique as well as a discussion on the more philosophical nature of the case study story and its place in research. The ideas here are also central to the understanding of the research process.

The issues related to sample size and statistical analysis are then addressed. The book outlines some of the important issues, principles and techniques of statistical analysis, and the reader is directed to an Appendix for references to more detailed and extensive books on mathematical statistics.

As research for university degrees needs always to be conducted in an ethical way, consideration is given to some of the important ethical issues that must be thought through carefully when carrying out such research. A careful study of Chapter 13 and the application of the guidelines suggested therein will help to avoid any unfortunate arguments about whether the research was conducted in a proper way.

Finally, *Doing Research in Business and Management* addresses the practical issues related to the production of the dissertation before it is presented for examination, and consideration is given to the way in which the dissertation will be evaluated and examined. Detailed checklists are provided to help the prospective candidate achieve the result he or she requires.

About the Authors

Dan Remenyi PhD, started his academic interest in economics and political science before going into business. After a few years' business experience he undertook an MBA, joined the information systems industry and worked in a number of different capacities. Eventually he returned to academe to read for a PhD in management, completing the degree in 1990. Since then he has worked as much in the field of research methodology as in his original discipline of information systems management. In the past 12 years he has authored and co-authored more than 20 textbooks on a variety of subjects in the information systems domain was well as writing numerous academic papers on both information systems and research methods. Formerly Professor and Head of the Department of Information Systems at the University of the Witwatersrand in Johannesburg, South Africa, today he is an associate member of faculty at Henley Management College in the UK and a Visiting Professor at Chalmers University of Technology in Gothenberg, Sweden.

Brian Williams PhD, although originally a physicist, is the Director of the Epidemiology Research Unit in the Department of Health in South Africa. Before taking this post he worked at the School of Hygiene and Tropical Medicine at London University. Prior to this appointment he was a Visiting Research Fellow of the Royal Society at the Zoology Department at Oxford University. Before he transferred his interests to epidemiology he had a long and distinguished career as both a teacher and a researcher in physics specialising in crystallography in which he obtained a PhD at the University of Cambridge in 1972. His work has been published extensively in many outstanding academic journals. As well as his role as a director of a research unit, he is a Visiting Professor in the Department of Zoology at the University of Pretoria in South Africa.

Arthur Money PhD, is Director of Studies specialising in doctoral research at Henley Management College where his main area of interest is supervising a wide range of business research topics, both in the UK and abroad. Since obtaining his PhD in 1972 he has assisted several hundred postgraduate students as a supervisor or mentor. He has published extensively in the field of quantitative methods as well as in the measurement of information systems benefits. He regularly conducts seminars and workshops on research statistics in the UK and elsewhere.

Ethné Swartz PhD, is senior lecturer at Leicester Business School, De Montfort University where she supervises dissertations at postgraduate level and teaches various subjects: strategic management and small firms and entrepreneurship at both postgraduate and undergraduate levels. In 1994 she obtained her PhD, based on research into information management in small firms, from Manchester School of Management at UMIST. Her basic research philosophy is that of the phenomenologist and her current research activities include information systems management in small firms, business continuity planning in the UK financial sector and female entrepreneurship. She is currently engaged in establishing the Centre for Business Continuity Planning at Leicester Business School.

Acknowledgements

The authors would like to acknowledge the many helpful suggestions and ideas they have received from the large number of colleagues and students with whom the topics and concepts in this book have been discussed during the past seven years. Without the advantage of these many different perspectives and philosophies this book would not have been possible.

Prologue

A book with the title of *Doing Research in Business and Management* invites the question, 'What is different about research in business and management studies or is it just the same as any other social science?'

In answering this question four important issues need to be addressed.

First of all the stakeholders who have a direct interest in business and management research are different from those with interests in areas such as anthropology, education, sociology, psychology and other social sciences. There is a wide range of stakeholders who include management, unions, financiers, employees, shareholders, management consultants, academics (including students, supervisors, examiners and professors), etc. Each of these stakeholders will idiosyncratically have his or her own agenda and this will influence not only what is researched, but also the way the research is conducted, how the research is funded and to what use the research is eventually put.

Second, whatever stakeholder group is being considered in business and management studies there is a strong emphasis on the application of knowledge rather than on the creation of knowledge for its own sake. In fact business and management studies used to be referred to in some universities as applied economics. This name is no longer fashionable due, at least in part, to the fact that it is now realised that the scope of the subject is much broader than economics alone. The issue is that business and management studies does not usually lend itself to enquiries which might be considered basic research. This field of study, particularly at the masters and doctoral degree levels, most frequently seeks to find answers to real problems. And these answers are often reduced in masters or doctoral degrees to management guidelines that can be put into practice. In fact, the best business and management research will directly lead to knowledge which will allow management to change the way things get done in order to be more efficient and/or more effective. Some examiners will expect students to have validated the conclusions of their masters or doctoral research by having practising managers endorse their findings. An example of the problem-solving nature of business and management research can be seen by contrasting two studies – the management research into teams conducted by Belbin (1981), and the sociological research on teams by Gersick (1992) (see Chapter 6). These two studies of working in teams, have very different goals, approaches and outcomes. In the case of Belbin the goal was to understand better the team process in order to enable managers to operate more effectively when a disparate group of people are thrown together. In contrast, Gersick's research was not focused on solving an immediate management problem; indeed, she explains the initial vague focus of her research where the initial goal was merely to document what was being observed and then to theorise in a general way about the underlying processes. The fact that business and management studies seek to find solutions to practical problems does not in any way make this type of research easier, nor does it undermine its rigour. If anything, competent business and management research is extremely demanding and even complex because of the large number of interrelated issues and variables which are inevitably involved in the context of any real life business situation.

The third issue which makes business and management research different from other subjects in social science is the very broad nature of this field of study. Business and management studies range from enquiries into stock markets to debates as to how to display merchandise on the shelves of supermarkets. Topics including how to pay for efficient worker performance on the shop floor, how to fund research and development activities, how to depreciate assets in balance sheets most effectively, how to minimise cost expenditure on end-user computing and questions such as how political power struggles among the board of directors can be resolved, are all relevant to this field of study. There are probably few areas quite so broad in scope, with the result that there are many different research tactics and research tools available. Thus, one business and management student working towards a masters or doctoral degree might choose a laboratory experiment to pursue an investigation into how policies are made using decision support systems, while another may opt to use large-scale survey techniques to examine how investors respond to stock market changes. Yet another researcher may use ethnographic techniques to study how relationships develop and change over an extended period of time among senior managers as their organisations grow through a policy of corporate acquisition.

This wide range of possible research topics leads to a panoply of research tactics and tools and this book explains what the options are and gives some guidance as to how they can be applied and what the implications are of these different approaches. The issues covered also give the student in business and management studies a broader understanding of the research process. To some extent at masters level, but especially at doctoral level, degree candidates are expected to be aware of, and be able to evaluate the appropriateness of various research strategies, tactics and tools.

The fourth important issue that distinguishes business and management research is the context in which the research takes place. The fast pace of change in both the theory and practice of management creates a challenging context in which to conduct research. For example, in strategic management, a move away from the design school approach to the resource-based view of the firm took place in just a few years. The changes in thinking which included total quality management (TQM) and then business process re-engineering (BPR), etc. all occurred, in what for other social science subjects would be considered a very short period. Although these new ideas do not always represent fundamental revolutions in thought, the changes in thinking clearly have a significant impact on organisations, as well as on the research agenda.

In the final analysis, the answer to the original question, 'What is different about research in business and management studies or is it just the same as any other social science?' should highlight that business and management is a field of study within the broad scope of the social sciences, and thus the research methodologies available to students in business and management studies will be drawn from those also available to other social sciences.

Dan Remenyi
E-mail:Remenyi@compuserve.com

I CONTEXT AND PROCESS

1

Business and Management Research
in Perspective

If politics is the art of the possible, research is surely the art of the soluble. Both are immensely practical-minded affairs.

(Sir Peter Medawar, 'The Act of Creation', in *New Statesman*, London, 19 June 1964; from *The Art of the Soluble*, Oxford University Press, 1967)

1.1 Introduction

Many universities offer advanced degrees and it is useful to think of these as falling into two major categories which are the traditional research degrees gained by dissertation[1] or thesis and the more modern approaches, based on the American system, which combine course work and a dissertation or research report. The MBA (Master of Business Administration) was the first masters degree offered with a major course work component but today there is an increasing trend towards this type of degree, especially at masters level, and it is likely that doctorates based on course work and dissertations will become increasingly common.

1.2 Traditional Research Degrees

Traditionally, universities have offered two major research degrees in the pursuit of scholarship: the masters degree and the doctorate. The title of the masters degree has varied among universities as well as among faculties within universities, being referred to as Masters of Philosophy, Science, Commerce, Engineering or Arts. The doctorate has generally been called a Doctor of Philosophy and referred to as a PhD although some universities refer to their Doctor of Philosophy as a D.Phil.[2]

1.3 The PhD Degree

For nearly all universities the most advanced degree offered under direct supervision is the PhD.[3] This degree, for which it is often necessary to have already completed a masters degree, is regarded as the highest of all degrees.[4]

To obtain a PhD a candidate needs to have undertaken a substantial programme of original research and in so doing to have produced a material dissertation that makes a valuable and significant contribution to the body of knowledge.[5] For this degree to be awarded it is essential that the contribution made by the researcher is regarded by his or her examiners to have added something of value to the discipline which is being researched. The contribution made to the body of knowledge may in fact be quite small and indeed it is often said that a PhD adds only a few grains of new knowledge to an already established mountain. However, this does not detract from the value of the degree, which owes as much to a demonstration that the candidate has mastered the research process and the self-development of the degree candidate as it does to the actual result achieved.

While the PhD dissertation needs to be original, such originality (Howard and Sharp, 1983) may have one or more dimensions. Originality can be based on the fact that a new theory is being developed; it can be related to a new or novel research methodology that has been developed in the research programme, or it can be because the domain in which the theory and the methodology are being applied has not previously been studied in this way.

A PhD candidate will work under the supervision of one or more supervisors (Lumley and Benjamin, 1994; Wood-Harper et al., 1992). The amount of supervision that is given varies enormously. In some cases the candidate may see his or her supervisor every day and will in effect work with the supervisor throughout the whole period of the degree. In other cases the supervisor can be remote, with the candidate being given little access to him or her and virtually no help (Phillips and Pugh, 1994; Rudestein and Newton, 1992). Whether or not there is extensive access to the supervisor, the candidate is considered to be working on his or her own and is entirely responsible for preparing him or herself for the research work, as well as for the production of the dissertation (Easterby-Smith et al., 1994; Philips and Pugh, 1994; Howard and Sharp, 1983).[6]

A PhD candidate is expected to be fully familiar with all the literature appertaining to the subject area that is being researched as well as having a broad knowledge and understanding of the discipline in general. The candidate has to show he or she has understood and critically assessed all the main issues in the field of study. Arising out of this critical assessment he or she will then extend the body of knowledge by developing a new dimension of the discipline. To achieve this it is essential that the researcher be fully conversant with the wide range of research methodologies available. This is because the researcher's claim to have made a contribution to the body of knowledge needs to be justified by demonstrating that a sound approach has been taken to the research. Some universities offer a course in aspects of research methodology but this does not constitute a formal part of the PhD.

The following is a short extract of the requirements for a PhD or a DBA from the rules and regulations for Brunel University in the UK and indicates the breadth of knowledge that needs to be demonstrated by the doctoral candidate.

> In his/her thesis, the candidate is required to show ability to conduct an original investigation, to test ideas (whether his/her own or those of others) and to demonstrate a broad knowledge and understanding of his/her discipline and of appropriate cognate subjects. He/she should also demonstrate a knowledge of the research techniques appropriate to his/her discipline and show that they have been successfully applied. The thesis should make a distinct contribution to knowledge and provide evidence of the candidate's originality by the discovery of new facts or the exercise of critical power. The candidate is required to show appropriate ability in the organisation and presentation of his/her material in the thesis, which should be satisfactory as regards clarity of expression and literary form. It should be in the English language, and should be suitable for publication, either as submitted or suitably abridged.

The PhD degree usually requires a minimum of two years full-time registration at a university, although most candidates require between three and five years to complete. The time required tends to vary among different disciplines and depends on whether the study is theoretical or experimental and whether it is based in the laboratory or in the field. Although increasingly unusual, there are still occasional examples of PhD students requiring 12 to 15 years to conclude their degree, but such protracted registration would usually imply that the candidate has been registered on a part-time basis and may have been working full-time as a member of staff in the university.

A PhD degree will be examined by a panel of experts in the field being researched, as well as experts in the research process itself. It may be examined by the document being read and commented on in writing, or there may be an oral examination. An oral examination, sometimes called a *viva voce*[7] (but generally known as a viva), from the Latin for 'the living voice', is generally regarded as the most challenging form of test for the candidate. In the UK and the USA the viva is normally conducted in private but in some continental European countries the viva is a public affair which may be attended by a large number of people.[8] During this examination the candidate needs to demonstrate clearly a full understanding of the subject area, as well as a complete command of all the research methodology issues involved with the work.

1.4 The Masters Degree

In many ways the traditional masters degree by dissertation is a direct preparation for a doctorate. This degree has many of the same attributes as the PhD, but the subject is studied in less depth and with a reduced scope. Thus a masters degree by dissertation requires the candidate to demonstrate a mastery of the subject area being researched, as well as a comprehensive understanding of the research methodology being used. The work does not have to be original in the way that a PhD needs to be and requirements on both the scale and the scope are substantially less.

The following is based on an extract from the rules for a Master of Commerce and a Master of Economic Science degree, and illustrates the typical requirements for such a degree.

The candidate is required to show acquaintance with the methods of research in that he or she:

1   understands the nature and purpose of the investigation;
2   is sufficiently acquainted with the relevant research literature;
3   has mastered the necessary techniques;
4   has acquired a thorough understanding of appropriate scientific methods;
5   is capable of assessing the significance of the findings.

The main feature distinguishing a masters degree from an undergraduate or bachelors degree is that the candidate is expected to work alone and to demonstrate an independent ability to produce high quality work. Of course there will be a supervisor, but the help provided will be in terms of advice concerning the direction of the work. A masters research project should be designed so that it can be completed within a year of full-time study. However, as in the case of the PhD, not many candidates complete their masters degree in the minimum time.

1.5 New Masters and Doctoral Degrees

Since the 1960s, with the popularisation of the MBA degree, which was started at Harvard University at the turn of the century, there has been a growing trend to incorporate more course work and reduce the amount of research in masters degrees in the UK and elsewhere. In some parts of the world the masters degree by course work is now so popular that the masters degree by dissertation is virtually becoming obsolete. This has also begun to happen in the UK in the 1990s for doctorates, with several universities now offering the Doctor of Business Administration (DBA) degree which contains a substantial amount of course work and which has proved to be popular.

1.6 Course Work and the Doctoral Degree

Universities in the USA generally require PhD candidates to undertake a period of intense course work before they can commence their research dissertation. In many cases there is a requirement for two years of course attendance with corresponding examinations. This period is seen as preparing the candidate by ensuring that he or she has acquired all the appropriate background required in the subject area and associated disciplines to be able to cope competently with the research work ahead. Thus the course work will focus both on the subject matter as well as on issues of research methodology.[9]

The main advantage of this system is that the institution takes some of the responsibility for preparing the candidate to undertake the work required for the research degree. Thus, when the actual research period begins the candidate is in a much stronger position than his or her British counterpart. In recognition of this, dissertations from universities in the USA are sometimes less extensive pieces of work than they are in Europe. None the less, the basic requirement that the PhD represents a body of research leading to original ideas which add value to the body of knowledge still apply.

With the introduction of the DBA at several universities and business schools, this trend of formal courses has now begun in the UK.

1.7 Course Work and the Masters Degree

There is an even stronger trend for masters degrees to be based largely on course work. The rationale for this is that these course work masters degrees are intended to prepare individuals to take a more specialist or in some cases a more distinguished role in their profession. These masters degrees are sometimes referred to as mid-career development degrees. Between 50 per cent and 75 per cent of the time for which the candidate is registered is frequently devoted to course work. Thus the research component, although still present, is relatively small.

Although there is considerable debate as to how rigorous the research for a combined course work and research masters degree should be, it is generally agreed that it should go some way to meeting the standards laid down for a dissertation required by the more traditional masters degree. Thus a candidate for this type of degree will still have to be familiar with some of the research methodology issues as well as show a firm grasp of the subject matter being studied.

Of course the exact research requirements for this type of masters degree not only vary from university to university but also from one department or faculty to another within the same university. Different supervisors will also have varying views of what is required from the research component of a masters degree by course work. Thus candidates need to be familiar with precisely what is required of them by their own institution.

1.8 Research and the Undergraduate

Increasingly, senior undergraduate students are required to undertake a substantial piece of work on their own in order to help prepare them to be self-sufficient in the work environment. This type of project also allows undergraduate students to make contacts in the business world, which may subsequently lead to employment opportunities.

The main way in which this is achieved is for students to produce a substantial term paper or research report. Although at this level the student is not expected to add substantially to the body of knowledge in the chosen subject area, he or she is expected to be familiar with some of the ideas of research and its methodology, and be able to apply them in a manager–practitioner environment (Jankowicz, 1995). This type of research is directly linked to the course work the student is following, and therefore the content and the scope of the research project will most likely be defined by the staff.

1.9 Commercial Research in Universities

From time to time most businesses will investigate some aspect of the environment in which they function. Such investigations are frequently referred to as commercial or market research, and involve the collection of facts and figures from a wide variety of sources. Although commercial research is sometimes undertaken by universities, and especially by business schools, it is fundamentally different from the academic research described above, as it simply compiles already known information into a more appropriate form for use in business decision making. The authors do not perceive this type of research activity as scholarly research. It does not make a contribution to the body of knowledge, but rather re-formats existing knowledge. The methodologies necessary for this type of research are relatively straightforward and are not the subject of this textbook.

1.10   Summary and Conclusion

A wide variety of research is undertaken by universities in the area of business and management studies, ranging from work which seeks to generate original ideas which add value to the body of knowledge, to routine commercial or market research activities for business organisations. The extent to which attention should be directed at issues of research methodology varies enormously depending on the nature of the research being undertaken.

Although this book is primarily aimed at candidates for advanced degrees in business and management studies, any student pursuing a research interest may find the concepts addressed herein useful. Thus this book has relevance for undergraduates, postgraduates and those pursuing research for commercial reasons.

Suggested Further Reading

Barry, C.A. (1997) 'Information skills for an electronic world: Training doctoral research students', *Journal of Information Science*, 23 (3): 225–38.

Cryer, P. (1996) *The Research Student's Guide to Success*. Open University Press, Milton Keynes.

Easterby-Smith, M., Thorpe, R. and Lowe, A. (1994) *Management Research: An Introduction*. Sage Publications, London.

Howard, K. and Sharp, J.A. (1983) *The Management of a Student Research Project*. Gower, Aldershot.

Lumley, J. and Benjamin, W. (1994) *Research: Some Ground Rules*. Oxford University Press, Oxford.

Phillips, E. M. and Pugh, D. S. (1994) *How to get a PhD*. Second Edn, Open University Press, Milton Keynes.

Rudestein, K. E. and Newton, R. R. (1992) *Surviving your Dissertation: A Comprehensive Guide to Content and Process*. Sage Publications, Newbury Park, CA.

Notes

[1] In some academic circles the document produced by the candidate as a result of the research is referred to as a thesis. In other circles the term thesis is reserved for the theoretical conjecture or the theory formulated as a result of the research itself. It is important for the researcher to understand the way this term is used in his or her particular environment.

[2] This refers to the system prevailing in most of the English-speaking countries. In continental Europe the degree structures can be quite different and Appendix A provides a brief discussion of university degrees on a more general basis.

[3] Most universities also offer a second-level doctorate that is sometimes referred to as a 'senior doctorate'. The title of this degree varies enormously, but includes names such as 'Doctor of Science'. This degree is usually awarded for a significant and original contribution to the body of knowledge. However this degree is not supervised and often takes the form of a series of papers or books that have already been published by the recipient of the degree.

[4] Research degree funding arrangement are changing this practice of having to have obtained a masters degree before embarking on a PhD degree in the UK and thus increasingly PhD candidates only hold bachelors degrees.

[5] It is not easy to say what precisely constitutes a 'contribution to the body of knowledge'. Some academics would argue that provided the research reveals something that was not known before but which is interesting and important, it is sufficient even though the findings may be quite modest. The present authors suggest that a contribution to the body of knowledge should include one or more of the following: extending our ability to understand phenomena, new ways of applying existing science

or theories, creating new theories, rejecting invalid theories, providing unifying explanations for events and circumstances.

[6] This may lead to problems if the candidate does not have adequate access to the supervisor; it is important for the degree candidates to ensure the supervisor makes him or herself available at least to read a draft of the dissertation before it is submitted for examination.

[7] The *viva voce* is sometimes referred to as the oral examination, or in the USA it is called the defence of the dissertation.

[8] The public defence of a dissertation is the approach in Scandinavia where the university appoints a dissertation opponent who speaks about the work before a panel of judges as part of the PhD examination. In the Netherlands the PhD candidate faces a panel of opponents who question him or her as the final stage of the degree examination.

[9] Some UK universities have required PhD candidates to attend some courses in research methodology and statistics and in some cases even insisted that students pass examinations in these subjects. However the programmes offered to PhD candidate in the UK have not been as intensive as in the USA.

2

Philosophical Background to Research

I was thrown out of NYU in my freshman year ... for cheating on my metaphysics final. You know, I looked within the soul of the boy sitting next to me.

(Woody Allen, doing stand-up comedy in front of a college audience, *Microsoft Bookshelf*, 1997)

Philosophy is like trying to open a safe with a combination lock: each little adjustment of the dials seems to achieve nothing, only when everything is in place does the door open.

(L. Wittgenstein, *Personal Recollections*, 1981, said in conversation in 1930)

2.1   Introduction

The aim of this chapter is to discuss some of the philosophical issues that should be considered when undertaking academic research into business or management. This chapter also considers the available research options or paradigms and suggests ways in which a researcher can make an informed and sensible decision as to how to proceed. A discussion of philosophy is essential before embarking on a research project because, as was said by Hughes (1990),

> Every research tool or procedure is inextricably embedded in commitments to particular visions of the world and to knowing that world. To use an attitude scale, to take the role of a participant observer, to select a random sample ... is to be involved in conceptions of the world which allow these instruments to be used for the purposes conceived. No technique or method of investigation is self-validating ... they operate only within a given set of assumptions about the nature of society, the nature of human beings, the relationship between the two and how they may be known.

The starting point in all research undertakings is to focus clearly on the fact that the ultimate purpose is to add something of value to the body of accumulated knowledge and in this case accumulated business and management knowledge. This means that an unanswered question or unsolved problem will be identified and studied and that the researcher will attempt to produce a suitable answer to the question or a solution to the problem. Of course the focus here is on difficult problems to which the solution is not obvious and which when solved will add material value to the subject area being studied.

2.2   Philosophical Questions

There are at least three major philosophical[1] questions that should be addressed at the outset of the research. These are: Why research? What to research? and How to research? It could also be argued that Where to research? and When to research? although of lesser philosophical importance, also deserve attention. In addition there is the question of research ethics which is discussed in Chapter 13.

It is important to understand why it is necessary to be concerned with these philosophical questions. A researcher has to be able to convince an audience of the value and relevance of his or her research efforts.[2] This audience, which may be composed of examiners, funders and colleagues, is likely to be critical. In addition, the academic researcher needs to explain why his or her research should be considered important and needs to be able to point out precisely what was found and what use the findings are to the community. The researcher needs to be able to argue convincingly that something new and of value has been added to the body of knowledge. Sound answers to these questions rely on the philosophical underpinning of the research process.

For completeness, academic research into business and management issues needs to be contrasted with commercial research or intelligence. Unlike the former, the latter is about accessing already established knowledge and presenting it in a more accessible manner for the purposes of routine decision making. This type of research, although conducted by many business schools in order to earn money, may have virtually no scholarly or academic merit.

2.3   Why Research?

There are two levels at which the question Why research? should be considered. At the first level, which is rather obvious, the need for research is related to the fact that there are many issues and subjects about which we have incomplete knowledge. Although there are examples of this in every discipline, in business and management studies there are perhaps even more unanswered questions than in many other areas of study because of the fast changing nature of the subject. The relationships between markets and products, between financial structures and corporate performance, between individuals and their dislike of their work, and between individual performance and corporate structure; client satisfaction and after-sales service; men's and women's remuneration; middle managers' reluctance to change; and the relationship between information technology and effectiveness are but a few areas which need exploring in order to enhance general comprehension. In fact, business and management studies is sometimes said to lack a rigorously formulated body of knowledge and this view is clearly supported by Pascale (1990) who suggests that,

> Even today's most careful students of organisations will readily admit that they lack adequate models to predict[3] corporate success. Recall how widely we celebrated such New Age cultures as People Express, Atari, and Rolm. Ardent supporters include academics, consultants, business journalists, and seasoned executives. Our former enthusiasm becomes a source of embarrassment[4] when we hold ourselves accountable for predictive accuracy.
>   It is no longer permissible to dismiss these reversals lightly, acknowledging once again that 'management is an art', and excusing ignorance by giving it another name. The sobering truth is that our theories, models, and conventional wisdom combined appear no better at predicting an organisation's ability to sustain itself than if we were to rely on random chance.

Wiersema (1996) is even more disparaging about what American business organisations seem not to know about how to manage their affairs:

> In the 1970s and the early 1980s many companies had to admit that they didn't know how to make durable goods or deliver reliable services. Defect rates as high as 20 or 30 percent were common, and apathetic service was the norm.

The second aspect of the need for research is related to *Homo sapiens'* compulsive need for growth. There appears to be an endless requirement for increased performance in all aspects of life. Bigger and faster aeroplanes are required. Greater athletic performance is demanded of sports people. Better health care is actively sought. More profits are demanded of business houses, etc. In a similar way society understands that knowledge is power and therefore there is the need continually to break the frontiers of knowledge through the research process. In fact it is hoped that the acquisition of more knowledge will directly or indirectly lead to the greater good of the society at large. Thus billions of dollars or pounds are spent annually on research into a wide range of subjects affecting the daily lives of the population.[5]

Of course academic research may be conducted to obtain a degree, which may be an end in its own right, or it may be a means to acquiring a qualification for a particular employment opportunity. Research is sometimes conducted by university teachers in order to be confirmed in their posts, as well as to satisfy a need to be at the leading edge of their subject.

There is however a dark side to research. As knowledge is power, it can be misused and there seems to have been a considerable amount of suspicion about what knowledge could lead to. According to Rider Haggard (1995) writing in 1887:

> Too much wisdom would perchance blind our imperfect sight, and too much strength would make us drunk, and over weigh our feeble reason until it fell and we were drowned in the depths of our own vanity.

There are many examples of controversial research. Although genetics can help cure many diseases it can also be used to identify the sex of the unborn in order to allow the termination of unwanted foetuses. Genetics can be used to help resolve paternity or maternity suits, and in the hands of oppressive regimes this type of knowledge could be used for unacceptable racial classification. Knowledge of information systems can be used to help organisations become more efficient and effective, but it can also be used to impose punitive work regimes on the staff. Information technology can enrich certain parts of the society while putting many thousands of white- and blue-collar workers out of a job. Science, which is sometimes regarded as nothing more than another word for knowledge, has been described by Collins and Pinch (1994) as a *Golem*. A *Golem* is a powerful but clumsy slave who should be used with considerable caution. Dr David King (1996) has said that 'Knowledge is a hand grenade', while Professor Lewis Wolpert (1996) claims that 'Knowledge is value free' and therefore does not constitute the type of danger suggested by Dr King. Perhaps in the final analysis Sullivan (1952) is right when he says 'The ultimate justification of any intellectual activity is, it appears, its effect in increasing our awareness or degree of consciousness.'

Research certainly generates controversy but there is also no doubt that research is an exciting, stimulating and rewarding activity which many masters and doctoral students report as being the best part of their educational experience. Of course how the research is used is an entirely different matter and some of the important ethical issues in this respect are addressed in Chapter 13.

2.4   What (and Where) to Research?

The questions What to research? and Where to research? are closely related. Clearly it is not sensible to expect an institution at which there is little or no expertise in a particular discipline to support a research initiative in an area or field of study that relies heavily on that discipline. Indeed, it is important that the aspirant researcher look for an appropriate location at which to pursue his or her scholarly work.

Assuming that an institution with adequate competence in the business and management environment, and with expertise in the relevant disciplines is found, the answer to the question of what to research may at first seem obvious. In business and management the main focus of research should be on issues related to improving the efficiency and effectiveness of the business and management process. However this is too general to be of much value to an aspirant researcher.

Every would-be researcher will previously have studied a particular subject or discipline in some considerable depth. This may have been achieved through an undergraduate degree in economics, sociology, psychology or accounting, to mention only a few possible options. It may also have been achieved without a degree, through many years of working experience, especially where the individual has made a definite effort to keep up with the latest thinking in the field by reading the appropriate literature. These studies and/or experiences will have provided a strong base on which to build a research programme. However, as well as having in-depth knowledge of the subject, the aspirant researcher should also be widely read in order to put the research into context as well as to identify and draw on interdisciplinary linkages and connections.

None the less it is generally considered advisable, although not essential, for an aspirant researcher to work on a topic that is closely allied to the original discipline studied. Although some people do change disciplines, such a change will demand a substantial amount of work before the candidate becomes fully up to date with the subject matter and acquires sufficient familiarity with the relevant body of academic thinking (Gummesson, 1991; Howard and Sharp, 1983).

In addition to the researchers' own competence there is the issue of the expertise of the chosen institute and potential supervisors. Few aspirant researchers have a high degree of freedom as to where they will do their research. Usually personal finance, convenience of location, the nature of the proposed research or the candidates' previous academic pedigree restricts the institutions that will accept the researcher. With these constraints in mind it is vital for the aspirant researcher to get to know the faculty in order to establish their research interests as well as their strengths and weaknesses. In addition to these relatively objective issues there is the question of personal chemistry between researcher and supervisor. It is usually sensible to have some degree of empathy between these parties. In fact, there is a school of thought that suggests the aspirant researcher should primarily concentrate on finding a suitable mentor, and be prepared to accept a research topic recommended by him or her.

Whether or not such a personality oriented approach is adopted, it is most important for the student to find a research field in which the faculty has expertise and interest. This process can take time and it certainly should not be rushed. Far too many researchers begin with the notion that they would like to study a subject which is of no interest to any member of the faculty and for which there is little expertise in the institute. When this happens and the new researcher insists on continuing with the chosen subject, the risk that the research does not make a sufficiently important and novel contribution to the body of knowledge to warrant the awarding of a degree is substantially increased and frequently leads to failure.

What should be researched is further constrained by the availability of money and time. Some research topics will take much longer than others and can require a significant amount of funds. For example, a study of airline reservation systems as strategic devices would probably require the researcher to collect evidence from a number of international air carriers around the world. Such a study could require visits to American Airlines, Delta, United, British Airways, Swissair, Singapore Airlines etc., so that collecting evidence for such a research project would require a substantial budget and a great deal of time. Since masters and doctoral students frequently have limited time and money, a relatively modest project should be undertaken. This does not detract from the notion that the research should deliver material value, resulting in a new way of looking at a problem. It is important for the newcomer to research to understand that a relatively small project can lead to rich insights and thus make a substantial contribution to the body of knowledge. Even doctoral research, which clearly should be original, relevant and make a material contribution, need not be in the Nobel Prize winning category!

Business research is commonly aimed at helping to develop management understanding of how business organisations work. It is frequently suggested that the best business research should lead to the development of guidelines by which individuals in positions of responsibility can manage their business responsibilities more efficiently and effectively.

2.5   How to Research?

At the outset it is important to appreciate that the nature of the research process is often relatively unstructured and frequently unpredictable. It is sometimes described as a voyage of discovery during which the researcher learns much about research methodologies as well as about the subject being researched, and may even learn something of him or herself.

A major concern to the researcher is the ability to deliver a convincing, or at least a credible, answer or solution that will be accepted by his or her peers. It is important for the researcher to be able to convince the peer group that the approach to the research has been sound.[6] This requires an understanding of the nature of the processes required to create knowledge.

To claim that a valuable or significant addition has been made to the collection of knowledge, the researcher should comply with a *scientific method,*[7] or approach, which is an informal but strict set of rules that have evolved to ensure the integrity, reliability and reproducibility of the research work. This is not easy because there are almost as many definitions of science[8] as there are scientists[9]. In fact, according to Lee (1989),

> Scientists have not yet settled among themselves on a single model of what science is.

and Medawar (1986) expresses the view that,

> There is indeed no such thing as 'the' scientific method. A scientist uses a very great variety of exploratory stratagems.

But perhaps the most succinct and useful definition of science is offered by Einstein (1950):

> Science is the attempt to make the chaotic diversity of our sense-experience correspond to a logically uniform system of thought. In this system single experiences must be correlated with the theoretical structure in such a way that the resulting co-ordination is unique and convincing.

However Einstein does not tell us how to bring about this order in our understanding of the world, and it is as well to begin with a caution from Born (1950):

> There is no philosophical high-road in science with epistemological sign-posts. No, we are in a jungle and find our way by trial and error, building our road behind us as we proceed. We do not find sign-posts at cross-roads, but our own scouts erect them to help the rest.

To complicate matters further, the process of carrying out research is highly subjective, depending on the intuition and the inspiration of the researcher. In the words of Gould (1980b):

> Science is not an objective, truth-directed machine, but a quintessentially human activity, affected by passion, hopes, and cultural biases. Cultural traditions of thought strongly influence scientific theories.

Bearing in mind these cautions and warnings, it is nevertheless possible to develop some guidelines which those engaged in research may find useful and may wish to follow.

2.6   Research Methodologies in Perspective

Before suggesting some guidelines available to those wishing to engage in business and management research it is useful to define research methodology and to put the issue of research and its methodologies into perspective. Research methodology refers to the procedural framework within which the research is conducted. It describes an approach to a problem that can be put into practice in a research programme or process, which Leedy (1989) formally defines as 'an operational framework within which the facts are placed so that their meaning may be seen more clearly'.

2.6.1   Research into the Physical and Natural World

Research into the physical and natural world is an ancient human activity. Its roots go back before recorded time. It is reasonable to speculate that the first researchers were active perhaps 10,000 years ago. By about 7000 BC our pre-historic researchers had learnt something about agriculture and maybe animal husbandry. Some time after this date, about 2,000 years later, our ancestors had begun to work out for themselves the rudiments of architecture, and by about 3000 BC some early forms of cities began to appear. Although a substantial body of knowledge had been accumulated, at this stage of human development it is probably correct to say that the more formal process of scientific discovery and investigation really began in earnest at the time of the 'Golden Age' of ancient Greece around about 600 BC (McKeon et al. 1994).

Following the early attempts by the ancient Greeks to formalise and systematise the study of philosophy and the natural world, the history of scientific thought follows a convoluted path. While the Romans, who succeeded the Greeks as the dominant political force in the western world, developed a high level of skill in engineering, they had little time for philosophy and never developed a systematic theoretical basis for their technologies. Eventually the torch of scientific enquiry was passed to the Arabic civilisations where the philosophy of Aristotle and the other early Greeks was critically examined and debated and where many of the mathematical concepts that were being developed in India were investigated and extended. During these centuries Europe was in the 'Dark Ages' and made little if any contribution to the furtherance of science or philosophy. However, by the sixteenth century natural philosophy again took root in Europe, drawing on the writings of the Arab scholars and returning to the philosophy of the ancient Greeks.

The roots of our modern view of science in which rigorous mathematical formulations are combined with careful experimentation date from Kepler (1571–1630) and his studies of the orbits of the planets in which, for the first time, mathematical relationships were used to describe a natural phenomenon. In turn, Galileo (1564–1642) showed that the results of his experiments on falling bodies could be described using mathematical equations. But Newton (1642–1727) took the crucial step when he formulated his theory of gravity in terms of a mathematical equation relating the gravitational attraction between two bodies to their separation. He showed that from this law the relationships discovered by Kepler and by Galileo could now be predicted from a single unifying theory (Bynum et al. (eds) 1982). Thus, in the modern physical sciences, the solid tradition of experimental research and careful observation was combined with a rigorous formulation based in mathematics. Indeed, Needham (1988) has argued that 'Modern [as opposed to mediaeval or ancient] science is the mathematisation of hypotheses about nature ... combined with rigorous experimentation.'

Following several hundred years of investigation and development the methods of research into the physical and natural sciences, as well as their unifying theories, are well understood and generally agreed on. This is so much the case that now the rules of scientific experiments are seldom explicitly taught to aspirant natural scientists. Those beginning a career as a research scientist in physics, chemistry, botany or even medicine learn the scientific method by carrying out well-established experiments and by learning the well-defined and explicit theories that underpin their disciplines. For the physical or natural scientists the research methods have become internalised and can be taught by example. Research scientists and research engineers are so close to and immersed in their research methodology that they seldom discuss it as part of their post-graduate degrees. Many would argue that if a methodology has to be taught, it is, almost by definition, suspect.

Their confidence in the correctness of their approach is the result of several hundred years of work and progress during which they have refined, debated and come to agree on acceptable research methodologies. This is not the case in the social sciences.

2.6.2   Research in the Social World

Plato, Aristotle, Saint Augustine, Thomas Aquinas and many others through the ages have made important contributions to social science. None the less social science in any rigorous sense is perhaps only in the order of 200 years old and it might be argued that modern social science is a phenomenon of the twentieth century with less than 100 years of experience behind it. Research into business and management is even more recent with the Hawthorne (Parsons, 1992) experiments in the late 1920s and early 1930s probably being among the earliest structured business research studies.

Because research into business and management has developed relatively recently, much attention is given to the methods employed to justify the claim that something material and valuable has been added to the body of accumulated knowledge. As a result, research methodology is explicitly taught to those undertaking business and management studies.

Furthermore any material research in business or management, such as that undertaken for a masters or a doctoral degree, requires that the methodology used be clearly spelt out, perhaps in a chapter of its own (Remenyi, 1990b), so that the results of the research are convincing or at least credible. This care and attention to methodology is sometimes said to reflect the social scientists' lack of conviction, at least in a relative sense to the natural scientists, of the correctness of their methodologies.[10] This attention to methods is especially true when more sophisticated techniques which go beyond traditional experiments are being employed by business and management researchers. After all, little was added to the body of knowledge through simple experiments such as those carried out at Hawthorne where the intensity of the factory lighting available to the shop floor staff was altered and changes in the staff's productivity was recorded. More sophisticated methods are required if one is to increase the understanding of the complex issues in business and management.

Some physical and natural scientists maintain that social science is not 'real' or 'proper' science because the work of the social scientist seldom results in the development of general laws which are robust and applicable under a wide variety of situations. This view is generally regarded, especially by social scientists as being misinformed and this is well expressed by Habermas (1993) who observes that, 'Now we think more tolerantly about what might count as science.' Indeed, the physical sciences, with their roots in alchemy and astrology, might regard the social sciences less critically if they remembered their own antecedents. Furthermore, the laws developed by the physical and natural scientists are not as general as they sometimes claim and, in addition, a degree of generality is intrinsically built into the laws developed by the social scientist even when generalisation is not a key issue. *This occurs because once a phenomenon has been identified, even only once, the probability of it being unique is so low as to make it almost impossible.* In fact there is a growing confidence among social scientists that their work is fully scientific and that in some cases traditional physical and natural scientists are actually being left behind because of their reluctance to consider new ways of thinking about scientific methods.

Perhaps in the end the view of Marx (1844) will prevail, 'Natural science will in time incorporate into itself the science of man, just as the science of man will incorporate into itself natural science: there will be *one* science.'

2.7 Empirical versus Theoretical Research

The various approaches to research can be classified under different taxonomies. One of the most commonly used differentiates research into empirical or theoretical studies. Empirical is defined by the *Shorter Oxford English Dictionary* as: 'based on, or guided by, the results of observation or experiment only', while theoretical is defined as, 'contemplative, of the mind or intellectual faculties'. Modern empiricism is regarded as having begun with John Locke (1632–1704) with his clear attack on metaphysics in his essay 'Concerning Human Understanding', published in 1690. A large amount of academic research conducted today is based on empirical techniques.[11] This is true for the physical and natural worlds, as well as the social world. The rationale behind this bias for empiricism is a philosophical assumption that evidence, as opposed to thought or discourse, is required to be able to make a satisfactory claim to have added to the body of knowledge. Of course it is not always easy to collect usable evidence which can lead to convincing and believable results (Millar, 1994). Furthermore, every empirical investigation presupposes an understanding of the material under investigation and therefore some kind of theoretical position.

To put the philosophical argument of the need for evidence into perspective, it is necessary to appreciate that the two approaches to research, empirical and theoretical, are sometimes regarded as distinct and separate. The empiricist goes out into the world and observes through experiment or even by relatively passive observation of what is happening. By studying these observations and collecting related evidence, the empiricist will draw conclusions and make the claim that something of value has been added to the body of knowledge.

The research theorist, on the other hand, studies the subject through the writings of others and through discourse with learned or informed individuals who can comment on the subject area, usually without any direct involvement in observation of behaviour and the collection of actual evidence. The theorist reflects on these ideas and using his or her intellectual capabilities constructs a new or different view of the situation, which sometimes may be regarded as a new theory. At the end of the theorist's work conclusions are also drawn and a claim is made that the researcher has added to the body of knowledge.

Although it is clear that these two approaches to research are quite different, they are both regarded by a large number of scientists as perfectly acceptable methods for adding value to the body of knowledge. If there is any problem in focusing on these two categories of research it is because it is not particularly useful to think of them as being entirely distinct. In fact in a special sense they are intimately intertwined. It is not possible to be an empiricist without having a thorough understanding of the theoretical issues surrounding the subject which will be studied, and about which evidence will be collected. It is well accepted that what is observed is often and largely a function of the preconceptions that scientists bring to the problem. A paradigm or theory is no more than the conventional wisdom of the subject. Thus empirical research should be fundamentally rooted in theory and it is impossible to conduct such research in a meaningful way without the researcher taking a specific theoretical standpoint.

On the other hand theoretical research, although not directly based on evidence collected from observation, also relies on ideas which have at some previous time been based on specific observations or original evidence collected by means of empirical work. Theoretical research does not occur in a vacuum, it is rather the result of thinking about the findings of previous empirical research and of debating the different theoretical interpretations that others have made.

Some scientists find the relationship between theoretical and empirical work difficult to deal with and are especially concerned about how theory and data relate to one another. This dilemma is sometimes presented by asking which comes first, data[12] or theory? The proposition advanced here is that theory cannot be generated without data and data cannot be collected without a theoretical framework. This persistent dilemma, the paradox of data and theory, is not simply resolvable. In practice there is a dialectical relationship between these two aspects of research that reinforce each other. There are always theoretical assumptions associated with the collection of evidence and there is always evidence that underpins theory. Far too much is made of the distinction between empirical and theoretical research as both are central to any significant research activity and both are required to make any real scientific progress.

Empirical research is the dominant paradigm in business and management research. Theoretical research plays a lesser role today and it would be difficult, although not impossible, to obtain a senior degree from a major university on the basis of a theoretical research paradigm alone. Empirical research is frequently associated with a positivist view which has sometimes been described as a tough-minded approach to facts and figures, derived from the physical and natural sciences. This view is not actually correct, as empiricism can be either positivist or phenomenological in nature.

2.7.1 *Characteristics of a Positivist*

Being a positivist, or perhaps more correctly a logical positivist, implies that the researcher is working with an observable social reality and that the end product of such research can be the derivation of laws or law-like generalisations similar to those produced by the physical and natural scientists. Positivism came into its own with the work of Auguste Comte (1798–1857) who outlined an approach to positivism in his 'Course of Positive Philosophy', published in six volumes between 1830 and 1842.

This philosophical stance or paradigm sees the researcher as an objective analyst and interpreter of a tangible social reality. Underlying positivism is the assumption that the researcher is independent of and neither affects nor is affected by the subject of the research. It is assumed that there are independent causes that lead to the observed effects, that evidence is critical, that parsimony is important and that it should be possible to generalise or to model, especially in the mathematical sense, the observed phenomena. Positivism emphasises quantifiable observations that lend themselves to statistical analysis. In recent years positivism has come under increasing criticism. Medawar (1986) is highly critical of the positivistic approach and in support of his position quotes a discussion he had with Sir Karl Popper: 'Boswell-like,[13] I once asked Karl Popper to express in a sentence the quintessence of the teaching of positivism. He at once replied: "The world is all surface."'

Thus positivism, especially in the social sciences, is not regarded as an approach that will lead to interesting or profound insights into complex problems especially in the field of business and management studies.[14] Perhaps this is what Jung (1995) was referring to when he said, 'During my first years at the university I made the discovery that while science opened the door to enormous quantities of knowledge, it provided genuine insights sparingly, and these in the main were of a specialised nature.' Using the same sort of thinking Jung also points out that, 'Science works with concepts of averages which are far too general to do justice to the subjective variety of an individual life.'

2.7.1.1 Falsification and Revolution

One of the central tenets of positivism is the idea of falsification, which was introduced by Karl Popper. According to Popper an idea could not be regarded as scientific unless it was falsifiable. The thinking behind this was that it was not possible to prove a scientific proposition, as whatever amount of evidence was acquired one could not collect all relevant evidence. Thus scientific propositions were always contingent. However, it is possible to disprove an apparent scientific proposition, and thus to be scientific a proposition needs to be falsifiable. In its pure or naïve form falsification means that once the proposition has been falsified the theory relating to it should then be abandoned.

However, this view of scientific verification is generally thought to be naïve and the *naïveté* of the Popper position is well illustrated by Imre Lakatos (1970) in his parable about planetary misbehaviour.

> The story is about an imaginary case of planetary misbehaviour. A physicist of the pre-Einsteinian era takes Newton's mechanics and his law of gravitation, (N), the accepted initial conditions, (I), and calculates, with their help, the path of a newly discovered small planet, p. But the planet deviates from the calculated path. Does our Newtonian physicist consider that the deviation was forbidden by Newton's theory and therefore that, once established, it refutes the theory N? No. He suggests that there should be a hitherto unknown planet q which perturbs the path of p. He calculates the mass, orbit, etc. of this hypothetical planet and then asks an experimental astronomer to test his hypothesis. The planet q is so small that even the biggest available telescopes cannot possibly observe it: the experimental astronomer applies for a research grant to build a yet bigger one. In three years' time the new telescope is ready. Were the

unknown planet q to be discovered, it would be hailed as a new victory for Newtonian science. But it is not. Does our scientist abandon Newton's theory and his idea of the perturbing planet? No. He suggests that a cloud of cosmic dust hides the planet from us. He calculates the location and properties of this cloud and asks for a research grant to send up a satellite to test his calculations. Were the satellite's instruments (possibly new ones, based on a little tested theory) to record the existence of the conjectural cloud, the result would be hailed as an outstanding victory for Newtonian science. But the cloud is not found. Does our scientist abandon Newton's theory, together with the idea of the perturbing cloud and the cloud which hides it? No, he suggests that there is some magnetic field in that region of the universe which disturbed the instruments of the satellite. A new satellite is sent up. Were the magnetic field to be found, Newtonians would celebrate a sensational victory. But it is not. Is this regarded as a refutation of Newtonian science? No. Either yet another ingenious auxiliary hypothesis is proposed or the whole story is buried in the dusty volumes of periodicals and the story never mentioned again. (At least not until a new research programme supersedes Newton's programme which happens to explain this previously recalcitrant phenomenon. In this case the phenomenon will be unearthed and enthroned as a 'crucial experiment'.)

It is clear from the above that scientists have difficulty in rejecting their theories even when there is evidence that the theories are not exactly correct. The difficulty in changing scientific minds has been discussed by Thomas Kuhn (1962), who introduced the notion of paradigm shifts. Kuhn pointed out that scientific ideas shift, sometimes quite suddenly and abruptly. This may be seen as the way that falsification actually works its way through to theory or paradigm rejection.

2.7.2   Phenomenology

The positivist approach to research needs to be contrasted with the phenomenological approach. According to Cohen and Manion (1987), 'Phenomenology is a theoretical point of view that advocates the study of direct experience taken at face value; and one which sees behaviour as determined by the phenomena of experience rather than by external, objective and physically described reality.' The phenomenological school of thought started with the work of Franz Brentano (1838–1917) and was developed by Edmund Husserl (1859–1938) who set out the basic methods of phenomenology in his work *Logical Investigations*. Unlike the positivist, the phenomenologist[15] does not consider the world to consist of an objective reality but instead focuses on the primacy of subjective consciousness. Each situation is seen as unique and its meaning is a function of the circumstances and the individuals involved. To the phenomenologist[16] the researcher is not independent of what is being researched but is an intrinsic part of it. This is well described by Wheatley (1992): 'No longer, in this rational universe, can we study anything as separate from ourselves. Our acts of observations are part of the process that brings forth the manifestation of what we are observing', and this point is strongly supported by Ray (1993) when he says, 'We are beginning to realise that if we don't believe in something, it doesn't exist – no matter how much data is thrown in front of us.' The world, especially the world of business and management is not essentially deterministic, but rather stochastic, and parsimony is not a central issue. The phenomenologist believes that the world can be modelled, but not necessarily in a mathematical sense. A verbal, diagrammatic, or descriptive model could be acceptable.

To use a phenomenological approach the researcher has to look beyond the details of the situation to understand the reality or perhaps a reality working behind them. The researcher constructs a meaning in terms of the situation being studied. Furthermore the phenomenologist understands that the world is not composed of a single objective reality, but rather is composed of a series of multiple realities, each of which should be understood and taken into account. Each reality is an artefact in its own right. It is generally of little interest to the phenomenologist that his or her work will not lead to law-like generalisations in the same sense as that of the positivist. For the phenomenologist the world is socially constructed.

This research paradigm is sometimes described as the descriptive/ interpretative approach and implies that every event studied is a unique incident in its own right. In this school of thought there is nothing other than phenomena and the essence of a phenomenon is understood intuitively. It is not usually possible or desirable to spell out *a priori* the steps in a phenomenological study in the same way as one can for a positivist research programme. The approach to phenomenology unfolds as the research proceeds. Early evidence collection suggests how to proceed to the subsequent phase of evidence collection, as does the interpretation of the evidence itself. Rich descriptions are sought which are the building blocks of the argument that the researcher then develops.

Some argue that it is through phenomenological research that it is possible to cope with the complexities of business and management. Wheatley (1992) points out that, 'We inhabit a world that is always subjective and shaped by our interactions with it. Our world is impossible to pin down, constantly and infinitely, more interesting than we ever imagined.' In terms of this thinking, causal determinism and reductionism, which focus on quantifiable issues and overvalued statistics, actually obscure the essence of the objects being researched.

Again, it is important to stress that this point of view is not universally accepted. Phenomenological research is not readily conducive to generalisations, other than the type that states that as the phenomenon has been shown to exist or occur at least once, it is most probable that it will exist or occur again. However, this is a fairly popular research paradigm in social science and of growing importance in the business and management arena where it is sometimes referred to as hermeneutics (Rosenthal and Rosnow, 1991).

Once a researcher has made a choice between positivism and phenomenology it is not uncommon for there to be a fervent adherence to the approach chosen, often leading to acrimonious debate.

2.7.3   Comparison between Positivism and Phenomenology

It may be argued, as follows, that positivism and phenomenology are not totally different in their impact on research and in the generalisability[17] of their findings. One of the key tenets of positivism is that it takes a reductionist approach to exploring the relationships among the variables being studied. This is necessary in order to be able to control an experiment or an investigation and thus be able to understand how the variables concerned are behaving. This reductionist approach should by its very nature lead to simplifications of the real world environment in which the variables naturally or usually exist. This simplification means that in the results of positivist research some of the complicating factors, and possibly most interesting factors, have been stripped out.

When the research has been concluded and the findings proclaimed, they are at best an indication of how the real world will actually behave because they are based on a reduced set of variables.[18] Thus these findings would not be *per se* generalisable to the real world until the research had been replicated a number of times. It is important that the replications are made by different groups of researchers, under different conditions and at different times (Wessley, 1994). Now each replication may be seen as the researcher taking another still photograph of the situation and this process is repeated until enough evidence has been collected to make some sort of generalisation. In addition, because in reality the world is essentially not deterministic in any absolute sense, the results of repeated research will generally not produce identical results. Some sort of accommodation should be made for the presence of unexplained fluctuations in the results, usually referred to as errors. Before the positivist's work will be accepted as a valuable addition to the body of knowledge he or she should argue convincingly that the findings are valid and that the errors are random.

On the other hand, a phenomenological approach to research is not reductionist but holistic. This approach to research allows much more complicated situations to be examined. It involves itself not only in as many as possible of the variables being studied but also the context of the study. Thus part of the context of any research study is the nature of the researcher and the characteristics of the setting. These issues are included in a phenomenological study, while they would be removed from a positivist study. At the end of the research study the phenomenological researcher has also produced a still photograph of the variables being studied. Although this photograph is more sophisticated than the one obtained by the positivist it achieves approximately the same result. It is one view of a set of variables. Like positivist research, such a study needs to be replicated before any generalisations can be made.

By definition, it is more difficult to replicate such holistic studies and generalisations are much more problematical. None the less similar studies may be undertaken and if these studies produce consistent findings which support an emerging theory, it may be granted some degree of general validity. Under these circumstances there is likely to be much greater variation in the results of different studies and thus a higher degree of error. However, in exactly the same way as with the positivist, before the phenomenologist's work will be accepted as being a valuable addition to the body of knowledge, he or she should argue convincingly that the findings are valid.

Sometimes the two approaches are distinguished by arguing that the positivist's findings can be modelled, while the phenomenologist's findings cannot. This view is a misunderstanding of the concept of a model. A map of the world is no less a model than is $E=mc^2$, which is Einstein's model for the relationship between energy and mass. Admittedly the positivist's model is more likely to be expressed mathematically than the phenomenologist's, which is usually expressed either in words or in diagrams. But both are models and can be used to explore different assumptions. Ultimately, however, perhaps the only really significant difference between positivist and phenomenological research is the degree of caution with which the results will be used, which needs to be explained and thus accommodated.

Collins (1994) provides an interesting insight into this process when he says:

> It is important to note that there is always a judgement to be made. That scientific discoveries are not made at a single point in time and at single places and with single demonstrations. They are made through a process of argument and disagreement. They are made with the scientific community coming slowly toward a consensus.

This point made by Collins is similar to that asserted by Wittgenstein (1969) when he said, 'Knowledge is in the end based on acknowledgement.' Thus whether a positivist approach or a phenomenological approach is being employed the researcher can expect to have to argue strongly for his or her case as it is unlikely that it will be readily accepted without a convincing set of reasons.

The point made by Collins (1994) concerning 'argument and disagreement' is important and is based on the notion of the dialectic which is the process of arriving at a so-called truth[19] by using an analytic tool in which a thesis is stated. Then a contradictory antithesis is developed and the two are then combined or the apparent contradictions resolved to provide a coherent synthesis. The synthesis then becomes the established truth, but it now presents a new thesis that will eventually bring forth a new antithesis, which will go through another round of synthesis. In this way knowledge is created. The dialectic, originally attributed by Plato to Socrates, who called it the 'midwife of knowledge', was also used in ancient times by Aristotle. However in recent, if not quite modern times, the dialectic was further developed by Hegel[20] and eventually adopted by Karl Marx and others. In modern research methodology argument or disagreement usually replaces the term dialectic.

Seeing positivism and phenomenology as related concepts rather than as two extreme and separate approaches is useful. This view, together with the understanding that empirical and theoretical research should also not be seen as operating separately, but rather as being in a dialectical relationship, helps in seeing research methods as providing a set of tools or directions which the researcher may draw on as and when appropriate.

Approaching these difficult issues of empiricism, theoretical research, positivism and phenomenology should encourage the researcher to draw on whichever is appropriate in a particular situation, to triangulate the findings and theories and in this way to validate findings, even within one research project.

2.8   Choosing a Research Strategy

The philosophical orientation that is adopted plays an important role in business and management research and the researcher needs to establish his or her approach early on in the research process. Usually the choice between the different approaches is not difficult for researchers to make. Despite the fact that certain subjects lend themselves to certain approaches there is some scope for choice.

Most research at the masters and doctoral level will require both theoretical and empirical work. Few business and management students would attempt purely theoretical research as this would be difficult and it would be neither academically acceptable nor really possible to undertake a purely theoretical research project at this level.

Whether a positivistic or a phenomenological approach is taken will largely depend on the background of the researcher. If the first discipline of the researcher has been in the numerical sciences then he or she will probably be most comfortable with a positivistic research paradigm, but if the researcher has come from a sociological field then the phenomenological approach may be the right choice. Whatever research paradigm is chosen the ability to develop a convincing argument in support of the research findings is paramount.

2.9   Summary and Conclusion

Because of the need to convince the research audience of the fact that the researcher has made a contribution it is necessary for a researcher to be concerned with a number of philosophical questions concerning *why*, *what* and *how* to research. The researcher's audience is composed of at least a supervisor and an examiner, who require evidence that the research has been soundly based.

With a considerable range of approaches to choose from, selecting and using a philosophical stance is not a simple matter for the business and management researcher. In the first place the key issues of empiricism and theory should be understood and addressed. Then there are the issues of positivism and phenomenology that have to be understood and resolved.

The issues discussed in this chapter are not simple. They require an understanding of the nature of academic research and an ability to put these issues into a philosophical context. Some researchers find this view difficult to grasp and question why it is necessary. Where a doctor of philosophy (PhD) degree is being pursued the answer is in the title of the degree. To hold a PhD individuals should have their own philosophical stance towards their research clear in their minds. However the same is still true for other doctorate degrees and even partly true for masters degrees. Perhaps this is actually true for any level of education?

In practical terms researchers will find it worthwhile to think about research philosophy. They should make themselves familiar with the various options and they should discuss them with their supervisor or prospective supervisor. Researchers should ensure that the paradigm they choose is understood by their supervisor, and that he or she is sympathetic to the approach the student wishes to follow.

Suggested Further Reading

Collins, H. and Pinch, T. (1994) *The Golem*, Canto Cambridge University Press, New York.
Easterby-Smith, M., Thorpe, R. and Lowe, A. (1994) *Management Research: An Introduction*. Sage Publications, London.
Eastman, W. N. and Nailey, J. R. (1996) 'Epistemology, action and rhetoric: Past and present connections', *Journal of Applied Behavioural Science*, 32 (4), December: 455–61.
Gummesson, E. (1991) *Qualitative Methods in Management Research*. Sage Publications, London.
Hughes, J. (1990) *The Philosophy of Science*. Longman, London.
Marshall, C. and Rossman, G. (1995) *Designing Qualitative Research*, Sage Publications, Thousand Oaks, CA.
Raferty, J., McGeorge, D. and Walters, M. (1997) 'Breaking up methodological monopolies: A multi-paradigm approach to construction management research', *Construction Management and Economics*, 15(3), May: 291–7.
Rosenthal, R. and Rosnow, R.L. (1991) *Essentials of Behavioral Research Methods and Data Analysis*, Second Edn, McGraw-Hill, New York.
Silverman, D. (1994) *Interpreting Qualitative Data: Methods for Analysing Talk, Text and Interaction*, Sage Publications, London.

Notes

[1] Philosophical questions are regarded for the purposes of this chapter as those that help set the framework in which the research will be conducted. This framework includes the type of problem researched, where it will be researched and how it will be researched.

[2] The subject matter of the research determines what is likely to be of value. With regard to business and management research, economists distinguish between two main types of value which are described as *value in use* and *value in exchange*. In terms of research in the business and management arena value in use is the primary objective with value in exchange being a serendipitous event if it occurs. Value in use in this context means that business and management practitioners, or perhaps even other business and management academics, will be able to obtain some useful ideas from the concepts and theories generated by the research which may be helpful to them in their daily work (Storey, 1994). Value in exchange refers to the possibility of earning money from the results of the research. Thus, if a PhD dissertation is published, bringing fame and fortune to the researcher, this is an additional bonus.

[3] Prediction may be less appropriate in this context than understanding. None the less Pascale's point is quite clear.

[4] Remember how celebrated IBM was as one of the best managed business organisations in the world, if not the best, and how in recent years this view has been largely reversed.

[5] It is interesting to note that Storey (1994) suggests that government policy should be based upon historical research rather than simply the pleading of powerful stakeholders whose interests may be partisan and who may not have a long-term perspective of what is useful to society.

[6] As well as convincing his or her audience, it is of course essential that the researcher also convinces him or herself in the first place of the soundness of the research findings, and the research methodology.

[7] Many business and management researchers associate the term *scientific method* only with an empirical and positivistic approach to research. This does not have to be the case as will be explained later in this chapter.

[8] In business and management studies, undertaking a doctorate and perhaps even a masters degree is essentially embarking upon an apprenticeship as a scientist, albeit a social scientist.

[9] It is not possible to suggest a rigorous definition of science and anyone who attempts to do so is suffering from self-delusion. One of the more honest and amusing accounts of difficulty with the definition is provided by Rosenthal and Rosnow (1991: 6) when they said, 'One contemporary philosopher, Abraham Kaplan, when asked to define the *scientific method*, answered that the "scientist has no other method than doing his damnedest"' (Kaplan, 1964: 27). Not all philosophers or scientists would accept Kaplan's answer, but instead would call for a new, unified model of

scientific rationality that recognises the subjective nature of discovery and proof (e.g., Laudan, 1977).

[10] Another interpretation of the physical and natural scientists' lack of attention to spelling out their research methodologies is that they are simply arrogant. Social scientists now have an established tradition of explicitly showing concern about how claims that they have added something of value to the body of knowledge may be justified.

[11] There are a number of empirical approaches to research including, *inter alia*, realism, instrumentalism and nomothicism.

[12] The term data is regarded with suspicion by some researchers because it is a Latin word meaning 'things given'. Researchers need to ensure that they minimise their assumptions or givens and in so doing they sometimes try to avoid the word data. The word evidence is regarded as a suitable substitute.

[13] James Boswell (1740–95) was Samuel Johnson's biographer and he recorded Johnson's conversation so minutely that Johnson is better remembered today for the sayings attributed to him by Boswell, than for his own literary works. Boswell often triggered the conversations that he recorded by asking Johnson a leading question. This approach was also used by Medawar with Popper.

[14] This comment is, of course, a product of the end of the twentieth century. Writing about positivism in 1795, the French scientist Laplace took an entirely different view:

> Given for one instant an intelligence which could comprehend all the forces by which nature is animated and the respective situations of the being which compose it – an intelligence sufficiently vast to submit these data to analysis – it would embrace in the same formula the movements of the greatest bodies and those of the lightest atoms: for it, nothing would be uncertain and the future, as the past, would be present to its eyes. (Cited in Hodges, 1992.)

[15] There are a number of different approaches to phenomenology including, but not limited to, hermeneutics, interpretist and naturalist methods. Furthermore, the post-modern movement in management thinking is firmly based on the view that positivism has been over-influential in the development of management theory and needs to be balanced by a much more phenomenologically based outlook.

[16] Phenomenology is often thought of as being only relevant to the social sciences and not to the physical or natural sciences. However, in physics itself the state of sub-atomic particles is determined in part by the act of measurement so that atomic 'reality' is dependent on the measuring process. In addition, quantum mechanics has drawn physics away from its traditional empiricist position to one which comes quite close to phenomenology. Some quantum physicists go so far as to argue that the mental state of the researcher directly influences the experiment.

[17] Generalisability has been an important issue in the debate between those in favour of the positivistic approach and those who advocate a phenomenological orientation. It has traditionally been assumed that only through the rigour of positivism can business and management research make any claim for the generalisability of its findings and it has been argued that without generalisability research findings are not of much value.

[18] The idea behind the notion of there being a difference between the real world and the world studied through research processes is an old one. The first exposition of this notion was provided by Plato in *The Republic*, when he spoke of forms and the caves and the shadows. Plato makes the point by using his famous simile in which men are chained with their faces to the wall and their backs to the light, so that they see only the shadows of reality. These men shrink from what is real and permanent, believing that the shadows are the reality. In his dialogue *Theaetetus*, Plato suggests that knowledge cannot have physical reality as its object because knowledge cannot be the same as sensation or perception. Thus there will always be a gap between the reality of a situation or an object and the knowledge of it.

[19] The issue of whether research or science in general attempts to discover truth has been side-stepped in this book. Because of the obvious problems with the definition of the term 'truth', the more modern view that the objective of research is to add something of value to the body of knowledge has been followed. Thus this book is fundamentally instrumentalist in its own philosophical approach.

[20] It is dialectic type thinking which underpins the use of the opponent in the PhD examination process in the Netherlands and in Sweden. It is essentially the same thinking that requires academic papers to be subjected to peer review before publication.

3

Research Strategies and Tactics

Normal science often suppresses fundamental novelties because they are necessarily subversive of its basic commitment.

(T. Kuhn, *The Structure of Scientific Revolutions*, 1962)

3.1   Introduction

This chapter discusses the research strategies and tactics that are available to the academic researcher when considering his or her masters or doctoral degree in business and management studies.

Establishing an overall strategy and detailed tactics for a research project is an important step in the initiation of a masters or PhD project and where possible the rationale for the choices made should be clearly understood and articulated by both the researcher and his or her supervisor. The primary benefits of clearly articulating the research strategy and tactics are that:

- It facilitates communication between researchers. This allows them to share common experiences. It also makes replication of the research much easier. Replication of research is a useful safeguard against unintentional errors as well as deception or fraud.
- It ensures that an acceptable logical structure is being used. Research requires both empirical observation and valid logical reasoning. The rules of classification, definition, deduction and indirect sampling, if used, should be articulated in the methodology.
- It institutionalises conceptual frameworks for communication, rules of reasoning, procedures and methods for observation and verification. These aspects of research methodology demand conformity. However, care should be taken that methodological issues do not hinder new discoveries, and by implication, progress (Nachmias and Nachmias, 1989).

Establishing a research strategy and a research tactic are the most important issues facing the social scientist in that they provide a basis from which the researcher may assert the validity of his or her findings. Scientific knowledge should be supported by both reason and by logic[1] and observation, and the methodology should address both these issues. However, the methodology should not, regardless of all other considerations, dominate the research procedure – 'one must regard all analytical methodologies or structures ... as mere intellectual frameworks and be cautious about their overuse in detail' (Quinn, 1988a). In the final analysis, the researcher's creativity and imagination are of paramount importance and the research strategy and tactics are there to support rather than hinder the researcher's creative faculties.

3.2   Research Strategy

A research strategy may be thought of as providing the overall direction of the research including the process by which the research is conducted. At a strategic level the research process is defined in broad terms that take into account the general philosophical approach adopted by the researcher. This includes being aware of the ontological and epistemological assumptions that underpin each different research methodological strategy (Morgan, 1980).

In deciding on a research strategy the masters and doctorate students should first decide if the research is to be essentially theoretical or empirical. In some fields of study deciding which of these two approaches to choose could be a difficult decision. However, in the field of business and management studies at masters and doctoral level the vast majority of the research is traditionally empirical in nature and students should respect this precedent unless there is good reason for doing otherwise.[2] If the student undertakes to conduct a piece of theoretical research it should be pointed out that this will often mean a considerably greater amount of work in the preparation of a rigorous and well-supported argument. The final choice may well be mostly related to the personal inclination of the researcher. Theoretical research requires intensive textual investigation while empirical research in business and management studies requires extensive interaction with people.

Within the empirical approach to research there are two major options or research orientations: positivistic (which is an approach which is essentially derived from the natural sciences) and phenomenological (which is an approach which is essentially derived from the social sciences). Once a strategy has been decided, consideration can be given to the specific research methods or tactics that will be used. As a guide to making these decisions the researcher should:

1   establish a research question or problem;
2   examine the major constraints imposed by the availability of resources as described below;
3   decide on a research strategy;
4   examine the constraints imposed by the research strategy as described below;
5   choose a research tactic.

This process is illustrated in Figure 3.1. It is unlikely that the researcher will follow the steps shown in Figure 3.1 in a simple linear way. It will usually be necessary to revisit decisions in the light of developments, and therefore an open mind and a flexible approach need to be maintained throughout the research process.

3.2.1   Factors Influencing the Choice of Research Strategy

The research strategy is determined by four key issues, three of which are to do with resources and one is a direct function of the research question. These key issues are:

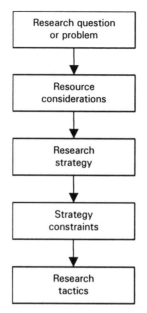

Figure 3.1   *The process from research question through research strategy to research*
tactics

1   research question;
2   costs or budget available to the researcher;[3]
3   time available and target date for completion;
4   skills of the researcher.

Of these four factors the research question is usually the most important. Figure
3.2 illustrates the starting point and shows the other important issues relating to
resources and constraints which follow and lead to the development of research
tactics. The choice of strategy adopted by the researcher will depend on each of
these four factors: the nature of the question, the costs of carrying out the work,
the skills available and the time needed.

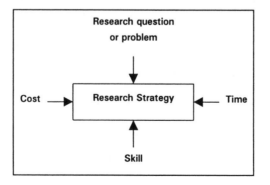

Figure 3.2   *The four issues affecting the research strategy*

3.2.2   *Research Problem or Question*

The first issue that the masters or PhD student needs to consider is the research problem or question. Some research problems require certain types of strategies and do not leave much room for flexibility. For example, research into share price performance in relation to risk profiles and return on investment of listed companies on the stock exchange would generally require a positivistic approach involving the analysis of large quantities of stock market data. On the other hand research into employee reactions to random checking in the work place for substance abuse would probably be more effectively undertaken through the use of phenomenological work with small groups of informants. Thus before any thought can be given to the strategy, the research question or problem needs to be clearly defined.

3.2.3   *Skills of the Researcher*

Hand in hand with the research question there needs to be an understanding of the research skills available and those that are needed. No matter how appropriate a particular approach may be, if the researcher does not have the appropriate skills then that particular strategy should not be pursued. Thus those educated in mathematics or natural and life sciences should be cautious if they decide to adopt a phenomenological strategy. Phenomenology and positivism are so different that few individuals can bridge the two research cultures and those who attempt to so do need to be aware of the potential problems.

The amount of money available is another important strategic or tactical consideration. Research that will be based on questionnaires administered to large samples is not only time-consuming but also expensive in terms of cash outflow because of reproduction or photocopying and postage costs. If the questionnaires are to be administered by others they will need both training and paying. Thus students often feel that they are better off using small samples requiring a more personal approach. Furthermore the question of money arises in relation to travel expenses.[4] Sometimes researchers try to overcome this obstacle by using fellow students as surrogate informants, but this may introduce biases and is generally considered suspect. In short the financial budget is always an issue as is the ability of researchers to gain access to the type of informants they require.

Time constraints should also be considered when choosing a strategy. Some masters degrees, such as the MBA, are designed so that the research element of the degree has to be completed in three to six months if the student is to receive his or her degree at the following graduation. For this reason it is likely that only a limited number of approaches will be feasible.

3.2.4   *The Place for Theoretical Research*

The above comments have largely focused on the issue of choosing between a positivistic and a phenomenological strategy. However there is also the question of choosing between a theoretical as opposed to an empirical approach, each of which can be done within either the positivistic or the phenomenological strategies. Although there are important exceptions, masters and PhD research at most business schools and many universities is conducted using an empirical strategy. It has become expected of research candidates that they can demonstrate an ability to collect and work with primary data. The most important reason for this is that empirical research is generally less intellectually demanding than theoretical research and the risk of failure with a theoretical research project is greater than with an empirical project. As most masters and PhD candidates, as well as their supervisors, are risk-averse it is not surprising that the theoretical approach is less popular. For this and other reasons, empirical research is better understood than theoretical research, making the former easier than the latter. Anyone undertaking a theoretical masters and especially a theoretical PhD will need to be extraordinarily competent.[5]

The choice of a research strategy is important and should not be made without a considerable amount of thought as to how the research question can be answered with the resources available to the researcher.

3.3 Longitudinal versus Cross-Sectional Research

An issue which arises directly out of the above considerations and is closely allied to the research strategy issue is whether the research will be longitudinal or cross-sectional.

The term longitudinal is used to describe a study that extends over a substantial period of time and involves studying changes over time. In the physical and life sciences it is not uncommon to hear of research studies which have been in progress for five, ten or even twenty years. There are a number of advantages to this type of research, including the fact that extended periods of research are usually required in order to be able to observe medium- to long-term trends.

Cross-sectional research refers to studies which take a snapshot of a situation in time. This type of research does not attempt to comment on trends or on how situations develop over a time period. Rather cross-sectional research examines how something is done at the time of the research study and will generally seek to identify and understand differences between the various members of the study population.

Thus longitudinal research requires a period of time sufficiently long for changes to have occurred and to be observed. A doctoral dissertation lasting three to five years might qualify for a longitudinal study whereas a masters degree pursued over a one to two year period would clearly not. In business and management studies longitudinal research usually offers the best opportunity to obtain useful insights into practices and policies and thus this approach is more valuable at the PhD level. This is not to imply in any way that cross-sectional research does not also deliver valuable results. Longitudinal research studies conducted over a period of several years can be used to monitor the progress of a situation and to observe how it develops as a result of a series of interventions over time (Pettigrew, 1985). This paradigm is not extensively used in business and management research at universities for the reasons of time and costs noted above. It is important to stress that both the longitudinal and the cross-sectional approaches can be carried out within a positivistic or a phenomenological research programme.

3.4   Different Tactics for Pursuing Research

Besides the empirical–theoretical and the positivistic–phenomenological classifications there are many other different ways of describing research approaches and methods. But within each of these the detailed research approaches or methods which determine the techniques which will be used to collect evidence and which influence the way in which the evidence will be analysed is referred to here as the research tactic. There is an almost limitless number of research tactics and variations in business and management studies, many of which have been borrowed from other disciplines when researchers have brought them with them from their original field of study. In fact, there are so many research tactics available to the business and management researcher that some regard research in these areas as not 'properly' scientific. However this is a gross misunderstanding of the nature of scientific enquiry which welcomes any approach or tactic that can help add something of value to the body of knowledge and that can be shown to be rigorous.[6]

Galliers (1992) provides a list of approaches or tactics, a subset of which has been reproduced in alphabetical order in Figure 3.3. Figure 3.3 also contains a number of additional tactics not included in the Galliers' list. It is not suggested that this taxonomy is exhaustive, nor that all of these approaches are necessarily suitable for all types of business and management researchers. However, it is a useful list for the purposes of pursuing the discussion on research tactics.

Research approaches
Action research
Case studies
Ethnographic
Field experiments
Focus groups
Forecasting
Futures research
Game or role playing
In-depth surveys
Laboratory experiments
Large-scale surveys
Participant–observer
Scenario discussions
Simulation

Figure 3.3   *Approaches to research as described by Galliers (1992)*

This list may be considered as a set of well-known and accepted research tactics or tools that are available to the aspirant researcher. It is therefore important for the researcher to be familiar with the characteristics of these tools, as they will determine the route to evidence collection, evidence analysis and theory generation. Some of these tactics are predominant positivistic in nature while others are basically phenomenological; some may be used with either philosophical approach.

Sometimes a researcher may use one or more of these tools on different facets of one research project in order to get closer to producing a convincing argument. However, this eclectic approach needs to be conducted with considerable skill and great care in order for it to be acceptable to the business and management studies community.[7]

3.4.1 Action Research

Action research was developed during the 1960s and has proved particularly useful in the area of managing change. French and Bell (1978) have defined it as:

> The process of systematically collecting research data about an ongoing system relative to some objective, goal or need of that system; feeding these data back into the system; taking action by altering selected variables within the system based both on the data and on hypotheses; and evaluating the results of the actions by collecting more data.

As a process, action research is dependent upon an external view of a situation and it essentially involves:

- taking a static picture of the organisational situation;
- formulating a hypotheses based on the picture;
- the manipulation of variables in control of the researcher;
- taking and evaluating a second static picture of the situation.

The action researcher is thus involved in a real manner in an organisational situation where there is not only an expectation that a 'contribution to knowledge' should be made, but also to directly produce usable knowledge that 'can be applied and validated in action' (Gummesson, 1991). In addition Gummesson points out that there is an expectation that the researcher should also develop a sensitivity to the theoretical categories which are being used so that they are transcended and transformed into better theory.

It should be clear from the above that action research provides the researcher with good quality access, but constitutes a potentially demanding process for the collection of data given the location of the researcher within a 'live' situation. The co-operation of staff or company personnel involved will be crucial to the success of this strategy. As Gummesson points out, the skill here is whether the researcher can successfully combine the role of almost a consultant and that of academic researcher.

Action research usually involves a small-scale intervention on the part of the researcher in the phenomenon being studied. In this paradigm the researcher becomes actively involved with the situation or phenomenon being studied (Aguinis, 1993; Ledford and Mohrman, 1993). Frequently action research needs a considerable amount of time for the effects of the intervention to be observed, and so it is not usually appropriate for a relatively short-term research project such as that typically required for a masters degree. An exception might be where the degree is undertaken on a part-time basis over a number of years and the researcher is involved in action research in a direct professional work setting.

Action research is participatory and specific. An important feature of action research is that it is self-evaluative. It is most important for this type of research for the researcher to be aware of the impact that his or her presence has on the situation. Depending on the circumstances, quantitative or qualitative analytical techniques may be required to analyse the evidence being collected. This approach, which is also sometimes referred to or closely related to participant observer research, is relatively new but its popularity is increasing. However, action research is frequently not seen to be sufficiently rigorous and if used at PhD level it needs to be implemented with considerable care and attention.

Action research is essentially phenomenological in nature. It would clearly not be replicable. Any attempt to use action research as though it was capable of producing positivistic type results would be an abuse of its role in business and management research.

A recent example of a dissertation based on action research involved a researcher who implemented a new activity based costing system in an organisation. This required two separate initiatives from the researcher which were the academic activities and the practical work involved in preparing the staff and the firm's systems which they used to facilitate this new management technique. The focus of the research was to understand how this new technique was being used to improve corporate financial performance. The researcher collected a variety of evidence and both qualitative and quantitative approaches were used to analyse the evidence (see Chapters 6 and 12). The researcher reported that the action research approach to the dissertation was rewarding, but at the same time demanding and exceptionally time-consuming – the main problem being how to ensure that the researcher remained sufficiently intellectually independent.

3.4.2 Case Studies

The case study[8] is a sophisticated research tactic that will be discussed in detail in Chapter 10. For the purposes of this section the case study methodology is a way of establishing valid and reliable evidence for the research process as well as presenting findings which result from the research. The case study is a research tactic for the social scientist as experiments are a research strategy for the natural scientist (Kasanen and Suomi, 1987; Smith, 1990; Jocher, 1928/29). Yin (1989) states that

> a case study from a research strategy[9] point of view may be defined as an empirical inquiry that investigates a contemporary phenomenon within its real life context, when the boundaries between phenomenon and the context are not clearly evident, and in which multiple sources of evidence are used. It is particularly valuable in answering **who, why** and **how** questions in management research.

According to Bell (1993) the case study methodology has also been used as an umbrella term for a family of research methods having in common the decision to focus on an enquiry around a specific instance or event. The philosophy behind the case study is that sometimes only by looking carefully at a practical, real-life instance can a full picture be obtained of the actual interaction of variables or events. The case study allows the investigator to concentrate on specific instances in an attempt to identify detailed interactive processes which may be crucial, but which are transparent to the large-scale survey. Thus it is the aim of the case study to provide a multi-dimensional picture of the situation. It can illustrate relationships, corporate political issues and patterns of influence in particular contexts. Case studies are an important approach for business and management researchers and some masters and much doctoral research work is conducted using this method.

Because of its flexible nature a case study may be an almost entirely positivistic or almost entirely phenomenological study or anything between these two extremes. As the case study is an umbrella term which includes a wide range of evidence capture and analysis procedures, all these different orientations and approaches may fall within its domain.

A recent example of a dissertation based on a case study approach involved the detailed examination of a large industrial conglomerate over a substantial period of time. The focus of this case study was to understand the inter-relationships between the group corporate strategy and the individual strategies of the separate and somewhat independent subsidiaries in the group. Although this case study collected a wide variety of evidence from the key members of the group, the main focus of the analytical work was on quantitative issues that employed the extensive use of statistical packages (see Chapters 11 and 12).

For another dissertation an intensive case study of a medium-sized specialist consulting practice was conducted. The objective here was to investigate the evolution of power relationships in the organisation. The researcher spent at least one or even two days a week working at a desk in the office of the consulting practice which enabled some observation of interaction between consultants during the normal course of the working day. The company also allowed the researcher access to board and weekly planning meetings. In addition, interviews were conducted with at least ten consultants and support staff. The chairperson and managing director were also interviewed as they both consulted with clients. The data collected was then analysed using the grounded theory method (see Chapters 5, 6 and 10).

3.4.3   *Ethnography*

Borrowed from social anthropologists, ethnographic research requires the researcher to become part of the 'tribe' and to fully participate in its society. A more formal definition is offered by Rosenthal and Rosnow (1991), when they say, 'Ethnography is that type of field observation in which a society's culture is studied.' It is usually necessary for the researcher to become involved with the group that is being studied for a substantial period of months or even years. Although this approach has some application in business and management studies it is not used extensively.

Ethnographic research is essentially phenomenological in nature. It would clearly not be replicable. Any attempt to use ethnographic research as though it was capable of producing positivistic type results would be an abuse of its role in business and management research.

A recent dissertation that used elements of ethnography was produced for a PhD where the student spent three years studying how the corporate culture changed as an organisation went on the acquisition trail. This dissertation was not exclusively ethnographic and it would be quite unusual for a business and management research degree only to employ a pure ethnographic approach. This is primarily because a fully ethnographic approach usually requires a long-term study over a large number of years. In a classical ethnographic situation a researcher would live with a tribe for five or more years and then return to his or her institution and write up the findings. In business and management studies, especially at the masters and even the doctoral level, this would usually not be feasible. However, ethnographic type research whereby the student would spend a long period of time, such as two days a week over three years, is sometime used. Under the heading of participant–observer in this chapter a research study is described which has many of the characteristics of an ethnographic study. The length of time taken by ethnographers is not the only dimension that distinguishes this type of research. An ethnographer will be concerned with a detailed understanding of how the society being studied works, i.e. its culture, and thus when this approach is used in business and management studies it will focus on detailed aspects of corporate relationships. Furthermore, an ethnographic approach would imply the use of multiple sources of evidence for the purposes of triangulation, in order to support the researcher as the main instrument of enquiry.

3.4.4   Field Experiments

Field experiments are more common and regarded as far more authentic than laboratory experiments in business and management research. The famous Hawthorne studies (Parsons, 1992) that signalled the beginning of formal research studies in this field of endeavour, were field experiments that provided insight into issues concerning worker productivity.

However there are definite limits to the type of question that can be addressed using field studies. For example, it is not usually possible to persuade an organisation to deploy substantial resources such as a new computer system for a field experiment so that researchers may study its impact on efficiency or effectiveness. Researchers may have to wait for an auspicious occasion to arise which makes such studies possible. Similarly, it is seldom the case that an organisation will change its marketing policy in order to understand how this policy change will affect the market. However, a field experiment probably could be conducted around a change of policy or a new investment, and the student would simply have to obtain the agreement of the organisation to participate in this event as an observer. Thus field experiments do have an important role in business and management research and this will be fully explained in Chapter 5 under the heading of 'Deliberate Intervention'. Field experiments are less positivistic as they clearly do not present the same opportunity for control and replication as the laboratory experiment. Therefore field experiments are approached from a less traditional scientific point of view. The results of a field experiment will often be interpreted in a much more phenomenological way.

Research in business and management studies is no longer largely, or even substantially, experimental in either the laboratory or in a field study setting, but rather is based on the observation of actual business and management functions as they happen or as they have happened. Experiments are frequently regarded as too artificial in the business and management world to be of any real applicability and thus many masters and PhD students tend to avoid them.

A recent example of a dissertation based on a field experiment was a study as to how a group of sales people responded to a new incentive payment in one particular part of an organisation. The researcher was able to examine the sales group performance before the introduction of the new incentive scheme and was then able to observe the differences in performance after the change. Using primarily quantitative techniques (see Chapters 5 and 12), this research confirmed that the new arrangements did in fact work and that they were suitable to be employed throughout the whole organisation. This approach to research is usually straightforward, with the main problem for the researcher being the acquisition of access to organisations undertaking changes in the field.

3.4.5 Focus Groups

This is a research approach for collecting evidence from a highly specialised group of individuals. It is usually considered necessary to have a group of more than four individuals to constitute a focus group that will debate an issue of interest to the researcher. This is a relatively easy way for a researcher to accumulate some evidence from a number of experts. Again, the way in which this evidence is processed is similar to that described above under the heading of in-depth surveys and the positivistic and phenomenological implications are similar.

There would be no point in giving one example of the use of a focus group in masters and doctoral research. Focus groups are frequently used as one of several different evidence collection techniques within a single project for business and management research at the masters and doctoral levels. Sometimes focus groups are used at the outset of the research to support the literature review in the formulation of a research question. At other times the focus group is an approach to validating the research conclusions at the end of the project. The evidence collected during a focus group is usually analysed using qualitative techniques (see Chapter 6). Focus groups are a useful way of obtaining evidence from experts in an intense or concentrated way.

3.4.6 Forecasting

Forecasting research tends to be associated with mathematical and statistical techniques of regression and time series analysis (Collopy and Armstrong, 1992; Sutrick, 1993). This type of research may also be regarded as falling under the heading of mathematical simulation. These techniques allow projections to be made on the basis of past or historic evidence. This is usually a highly quantitative approach in which mathematical models are fitted to empirical data or evidence points. This research attempts to establish relationships between different sets of historical evidence and to understand why these relationships exist.

The techniques used in forecasting are essentially positivistic in nature. However, the results of forecasting research can be interpreted in a more phenomenological way and thus be integrated into a greater business and management paradigm than simply a mathematical view of the situation.

A recent example of a dissertation based on forecasting research was work conducted to establish the viability of multiple regression analysis in supporting decisions to invest in plant and equipment in a large-scale processing industry. This was a highly quantitative and mathematical piece of work which relied on a high degree of numerical sophistication as well as the ability to interpret the results in a way which was of value to management (see Chapter 12). The result of this work showed that the forecasting approach being studied did in fact contribute to the organisation's ability to forecast their need for more investment.

3.4.7   Futures Research

Although not as mathematical or technical as, but at the same time similar in intent to, forecasting research, futures research also provides a way of considering and developing predictions. However, unlike forecasting, futures research has a forward orientation and thus looks ahead, rather than backwards, using techniques such as scenario projections and Delphi studies (McCarthy, 1992; Maital, 1993; Goldfisher, 1992–93). The work involves the summation of opinions of experts as well as attempting to draw divergent expert opinions towards a group consensus. The experts in a Delphi study are normally physically separated and are unknown to one another. The purpose of a Delphi study is to produce a relatively narrow spread of opinions.

Futures research is not extensively used, except perhaps in a number of specialised areas such as technology forecasting and business trend analysis. This research tactic would not generally be sufficient on its own as the main focus for a PhD, but it could be used to support other tactics in an attempt to triangulate and thereby validate the conclusions. The techniques used for futures research are relatively positivistic in nature but the results may be interpreted in a more phenomenological way.

A recent example of a masters dissertation that involved futures research was a study to establish what leading firms of chartered accountants thought were the main technological developments that would affect their practices or businesses over the next five years. A group of 20 partners from the larger accountancy firms agreed to undertake a Delphi study that was performed over three rounds. The findings of the Delphi study were used to suggest how to prepare for a new environment for their practices. The participants in this study, who were given access to the results, found this work useful. This was a straightforward project that produced competent results for a masters degree (see Chapters 11 and 12).

3.4.8   Game or Role Playing

This research tactic or approach involves asking individuals to participate in a business or management game by playing out a specific role. This is a popular approach to research in the field of human relations and organisational behaviour, although it may provide insights for other disciplines as well. Game or role playing can be regarded as high-level simulation of interpersonal reactions, as well as group decision making. The way in which the evidence is processed is similar to that described under the heading of in-depth surveys, and the positivistic and phenomenological implications are similar.

A recent example of a dissertation based on game or role playing considered how managers made different decisions when they were put in different competitive situations. A role-playing game was set up based on the classical proposition of the prisoners' dilemma and the results of different decisions were noted. Game or role playing activity provides the evidence in the same way as the laboratory experiment.

3.4.9   In-depth Surveys

This type of survey generally attempts to obtain detailed in-depth evidence from a relatively small number of informants through a series of interviews. In this case a questionnaire is generally not used, but rather the informant is allowed to speak freely on the subject of interest to the researcher.

Sometimes the researcher will have a prepared list of issues and even prompts to use during the interview. Such a list is usually referred to as an interview schedule. Sometimes the researcher will take copious notes during the interview, while on other occasions the interview will be recorded. After the interview it is usual for the researcher to compile a transcript of the discussion which has taken place. At the end of an in-depth survey the researcher will have a series of transcripts and the task is then to analyse these and to produce appropriate findings.

The in-depth survey may be used either in a positivistic or in a phenomenological mode. As a positivistic tool the transcript would be subjected to a technique such as content analysis whereby the number of occasions on which an issue is mentioned is counted. These counts are then used to demonstrate the importance of the issue. In the hands of a phenomenologist, the occurrences would not be counted, but rather the researcher would postulate the importance of the issues from a more interpretivist stance.

The use of in-depth surveys is well illustrated by research conducted into how innovative companies manage to maintain an environment that supports new product development. Twelve companies were identified and asked to identify three innovative products. From the project teams that had worked on these products, a marketing, a technical (R&D) and one mid-level manager were selected for interview. Interviews were semi-structured in nature and two interviewers were present at every interview to facilitate accurate data collection. Respondents were encouraged to embroider in greater detail when it became evident that they felt particularly strongly about a particular issue that was being investigated. This resulted in rich data and stories about the successes and failures that they had been involved in while working for the companies concerned. The data was analysed through the use of quantitative methods where researchers compared quantifiable data across companies. However, the primary focus of analysis was on the qualitative data in the form of stories (see Chapter 6).

3.4.10 Laboratory Experiments

Borrowed from the physical and life sciences laboratory, experiments are sometimes used in business and management research. However, they are not much used in practice, except in limited or specific circumstances, because many of the issues which are of most interest to business and management researchers cannot easily or convincingly be studied in laboratory settings. Organisations and even individual managers will not usually collaborate in such experiments. Sometimes students are used as surrogates for managers and executives in laboratory settings, but this is not often considered convincing.

Laboratory experiments are none the less sometimes employed to answer specific questions such as how certain decisions are made concerning various aspects of managerial choice. This approach is sometimes also used to explore an idea before embarking on a major survey or case study project. In business and management research for masters and PhD students, laboratory experiments are used far more frequently in the USA than in other parts of the world (Tung and Heminger, 1993).

Some degree of experimental rigour is required, although there is not the need for the same level of control design[10] that would be expected in a natural or life science experiment.

Laboratory experiments are intrinsically positivistic in nature. They appear to offer a high degree of control of the subject of the experiment. Furthermore, they generally rely on observations which will be reduced to numbers and which will be structured in such a way that they can be replicated. However, in business and management studies much of this is illusory because the same individuals are not always used when the experiment is repeated and individual people are decidedly not homogeneous. Even if the same individuals are involved in the replication they may not react in the same way when the experiment is repeated.

Laboratory experiments for the purposes of business and management research for a masters or doctoral degree are not common, especially outside of the USA. However, a recent example of a dissertation based on this approach was one in which the researcher used a group decision support system to examine how decision making differed depending upon a variety of different variables, including the number of decision makers participating in the meeting. This experiment provided an insight into how different types of questions are best handled under different circumstances. Laboratory experiments use quantitative techniques of evidence analysis to deliver answers to highly structured research questions (see Chapters 5, 11 and 12).

3.4.11 Large-scale Surveys

Surveys are a common approach to research in business and management. Surveys, which for the purpose of this chapter are concerned with the administration of questionnaires, offer an opportunity to collect large quantities of data or evidence (Oppenheim, 1966) in a quick and convenient manner. In business and management research, questionnaires are often used to collect evidence concerning management opinions.

Questionnaires allow evidence to be gathered concerning *how much* or *how long* or *when*, but are of less value when the researcher is asking about *how* or *why*. As a general rule the nature of the evidence which may be collected by means of a questionnaire is regarded as relatively superficial, especially in comparison to the evidence that it is possible to collect from other techniques such as case studies or personal interviews. Surveys are thus more often used as the sole or primary source of evidence at the masters level than at the PhD level.[11] However, some PhD dissertations might include a survey as an attempt to corroborate a theoretical conjecture. More detail will be supplied on the issue of the survey in Chapter 9.

The logic of a traditional survey is strictly positivistic. The evidence is frequently treated as though it were the result of measurements of a machine used in an entirely physical or life science environment. Standard statistical techniques used for ordinal numbers are increasingly applied with no recognition of the problems of the subjectivity of the opinions. Although surveys are still extensively used in business and management research there is an increasing feeling that they are not suitable for the collection of evidence about management issues.

A recent example of a dissertation based on a large-scale survey was an exploration into the acceptance of an organisation's computer strategy by its staff, by examining the level of user satisfaction with a management information systems based on end-user computing. Some 1,500 computer users within the organisation were asked to complete a questionnaire, and approximately 300 completed forms were returned. These were analysed using a number of statistical approaches. As a result of the evidence collected it was possible to suggest ways in which the organisation could improve the implementation of its strategy (see Chapters 5, 9, 11 and 12).

3.4.12 Participant–Observer Approach

Using the participant–observer tactic the researcher joins a team of individuals who are part of the phenomenon being studied. The researcher takes part in the phenomenon in the same way as the other participants, but at the same time focuses on observing the way in which the group operates. This research technique is essentially phenomenological in nature and is discussed in more detail in Chapter 6.

A recent example of the participant–observer approach involved research conducted into the management of design and manufacturing processes in small textile companies in central England. The student conducted research in two companies and spent some time working as an employee in these organisations. Access was negotiated with the owner-manager of the organisations and the researcher participated as a complete participant (see Chapter 6), or a normal member of the organisation, gathering information on how the design and the production process was managed by working alongside the mainly female workforce. The information collected in this manner was then written up in the evening when the researcher left work. The eventual outcome of the work was the production of two case studies.

3.4.13 Scenario Research

Similar to game or role playing and focus groups, this research tactic involves collecting evidence from a group of suitably qualified experts who are asked to discuss the implications of a particular hypothetical situation occurring. The group may be asked to comment on the result of a new competitive climate developing in a particular industry, or to consider the results of the deregulation of the telecommunications industry. Using this technique the researcher hopes to elicit useful comments about the opinions of the experts as well as observing how these opinions evolve during their deliberations. This evidence too is collected and processed in much the same way as in in-depth surveys and again the positivistic and phenomenological implications are similar.

A recent example of a dissertation using scenario discussions as part of an evidence collection strategy involved the presentation of a number of views as to how the market for a product might change over the next five years. Each scenario was fully debated by a group of informants and the researcher collected their evidence. This evidence was then analysed in the same way as it would be in the case of in-depth interviews or focus groups (see Chapter 6).

3.4.14 Simulation or Stochastic Modelling

In the context of this chapter, simulation or stochastic modelling may be defined as a domain of study in which the input variables and the manner in which they interact is generally known to an uncertain level of accuracy. In such situations, when there is some question as to the accuracy, it is considered inappropriate to use single point estimates of the variables.

Stochastic modelling is used to investigate situations that do not readily lend themselves to a strictly deterministic or analytical treatment. Sometimes simulation can be used as a substitute for a laboratory or field experiment. Simulation is particularly relevant where there is a requirement for the evaluation of formal mathematical relationships under a large variety of assumptions (Freedman, 1992; Reiman, Simon and Willie, 1992). There is not a high degree of utilisation of this research paradigm in business or management research except where mathematical modelling is a key part of the study. The techniques used for stochastic modelling are positivistic in nature but the results may be interpreted in a more phenomenological way.

A recent example of a dissertation based on simulation involved the building of a mathematical model which was used to describe how to optimise the logistics function of a large manufacturing firm. This model included a large number of variables. Some of these variables were quite difficult to estimate and as a result a stochastic rather than a deterministic approach was taken. The model was eventually computerised and a large number of simulated trials were performed in order to obtain a better understanding of the impact of different values for the variables, and thus to understand better how to optimise the logistics function. This was a highly mathematical dissertation requiring the researcher to have a strong quantitative background, as well as an ability to be able to present the findings to management in terms that were comprehensible to them (see Chapter 12).

3.5   Research Tactics and their Philosophical Bases

Table 3.1 summarises the general philosophical bases underpinning the different research tactics. It should be noted that most research tactics can be used, at least to some extent, as either positivistic or phenomenological devices. However some tactics are much more suited to one type of research than another and appropriate comments are made in the table.

The comments in Table 3.1 concerning the nature of the different types of research tactics are approximate indications because it is sometimes possible to use a tactic that is essentially positivistic in nature, in a largely phenomenological way. Similarly, the reverse is also possible whereby a phenomenologically oriented approach can be used to produce a positivistic view of the subject being studied. For example, in-depth interviews, which can provide good results if used in association with an interpretist view of evidence analysis, can also be used with content analysis, which is essentially a positivistic way of assessing evidence.

Table 3.1   *Research tactics and their philosophical bases*

Research approaches	Positivistic	Phenomenological
Action research		Strictly interpretivist
Case studies	Have scope to be either	Have scope to be either
Ethnographic		Strictly interpretivist
Field experiments	Have scope to be either	Have scope to be either
Focus groups		Mostly interpretivist
Forecasting research	Strictly positivistic with some room for interpretation	
Futures research	Have scope to be either	
Game or role playing		Strictly interpretivist
In-depth surveys		Mostly interpretivist
Laboratory experiments	Strictly positivistic with some room for interpretation	
Large-scale surveys	Strictly positivistic with some room for interpretation	
Participant–observer		Strictly interpretivist
Scenario research		Mostly interpretivist
Simulation and stochastic modelling	Strictly positivistic with some room for interpretation	

3.6   Summary and Conclusion

After identifying the research problem or question, the selection of a research strategy is one of the most important decisions made by the researcher. The research strategy dictates the major direction of the research and it narrows the range of research tactics available to the student. The issue of whether the research will be longitudinal or cross-sectional is also important and clearly has substantial impact on the work involved. The research strategy should not be decided too early in the research process unless there is a compelling reason for so doing. The choice of strategy will dictate much of the detail of the actual work that will follow. With a large number of choices available the research tactic defines the approach at a much more routine level than the research strategy. Each tactic has a greater or lesser ability to support a particular strategy and care needs to be taken to ensure that there is little or no mismatch in this respect.

However, in the final analysis the researcher will call upon his or her imagination and creative talents to pursue the research project successfully. The research strategy and research tactics are only there to assist or promote this creativity.

Suggested Further Reading

Adams, R. and Preiss, J. (eds) (1960) *Human Organisation Research: Field Relations and Techniques.* Dorsey, Homewood, IL.

Bausell, R.B. (1994) *Conducting Meaningful Experiments, 40 Steps to Becoming a Scientist.* Sage Publications, London.

Cavusgil, S.T. and Das, A. (1997) 'Methodological issues in empirical cross-cultural research: A survey of the management literature and a framework', *Management International Review*, 37 (1), First Quarter: 71–96.

Chapman, M. (1996/97) 'Social anthropology, business studies, and cultural issues', *International Studies of Management and Organization*, 26 (4), Winter: 3–29.

Cho, M. (1996) 'House price dynamics: A survey of theoretical and empirical issues', *Journal of Housing Research*, 7 (2): 145–72.

Galliers, R. (1992) *Information Systems Research. Issues, Methods and Practical Guidelines*, Alfred Waller Information Systems Series, Henley-on-Thames.

Hammersley, M. and Atkinson, P. (1983) *Ethnography: Principles in Practice*, Tavistock, London.

Katcher, B.L. (1997) 'Getting answers from a focus group', *Folio*, 25 (18): 222.

Krueger, R.A. (1994) *Focus Groups: A Practical Guide for Applied Research*, Second Edn. Sage Publications.

Lee, H. Lindquist, J. and Acito, F. (1997) 'Managers' evaluation of research design and its impact on the use of research: An experimental approach', *Journal of Business Research*, 39 (3), July: 231–40.

Maanen, J. van (ed.) (1995) *Representation in Ethnography.* Sage Publications, London.

McCall, G. J. and Simmons, J. (1969) *Issues in Participant Observation.* Addison-Wesley, London.

McLaughlin, H. and Thorpe, R. (1993) 'Action learning – a paradigm in emergence: the problems facing a challenge to traditional management education and development', *British Journal of Management*, 4 (1): 19–28.

Simonsen, J. and Kensing, F. (1997) 'Using ethnography in contextual design', *Communications of the ACM*, 40 (7), July: 82–8.

Tapio, P. (1996) 'From technocracy to participation?' *Futures*, 28 (5), June: 453–70.

Varki, S. and Rust, R.T. (1997) 'Satisfaction is relative', *Marketing Research: A Magazine of Management and Applications*, 19 (2), Summer: 14–19.

Whyte, W.F. (1985) *Participatory Action Research.* Sage Focus Editions, vol. 123.

Notes

[1] Sometimes this idea is expressed by the use of the word rhetoric, which refers to an effective and persuasive argument.

[2] The reason why the research student should respect precedent is that the further away the student strays from the dominant research paradigm the greater the need there is to justify the research in terms of validity, reliability and repeatability.

[3] Many masters and PhD students will not have a budget and thus have no funds available. In such case the main consideration is to find a strategy and tactic which involves as little cash cost as possible. On the other hand some masters and doctoral students have generous grants, bursaries and scholarships and thus have a range of strategies and tactics open to them.

[4] Although it is not often admitted, financial constraints frequently play a decisive role in the choice of research problem even before the questions of strategy and tactics are raised.

[5] Some academics would regard this view as controversial. However, it is true to say that empirical research dominates the agenda in most business and management faculties in the western world.

[6] The fact that research, or perhaps more correctly science, allows a wide range of methodological approaches is sometimes a problem for students who are more comfortable with a definite formula for research success. Unfortunately for novices this is not the case and researchers have to compile their own individual understanding of what constitutes science or sound research.

[7] Eclecticism is a controversial issue among methodologists. Some argue that eclecticism is not acceptable as it shows a lack of commitment to an ontological and/or a epistemological view. Perhaps a more practical objection is the fact that it is difficult to be fully competent in more than one research strategy and thus any one researcher is unlikely to be expert in more than one basic approach.

[8] The term case study is used in business and management studies in at least two different ways. See Chapter 10 for a full discussion of this. In this section, however, it could be argued that the term case history would be more descriptive of its function.

[9] Clearly we disagree with Yin's use of the word strategy and prefer the use of the word tactic. The word strategy is better reserved for a higher level of decision related to the approach to the research. In the instance of the case study research tactic this approach may be used either positivistically or phenomenologically.

[10] In the physical and life sciences laboratory experiments can be conducted under highly controlled conditions that make it possible to isolate the relationships among a small number of variables. The conditions of the experiment should also be carefully noted to ensure that other researchers are able to replicate the experiments with the necessary precision.

[11] Most research dissertations at both the masters and PhD levels would require both primary and secondary sources of evidence.

4

The Research Programme and Process

They seemed to me like people who knew by hearsay that elephants existed, but had never seen one, and were trying to prove by argument that on logical grounds such animals must exist and must be constituted as in fact they are.

(C. G. Jung, *Memories, Dreams, Reflections*, 1995 [Speaking about philosophers])

4.1   Introduction

Research is not a linear process, and many masters and doctoral students in business and management studies pursue their research in a recursive and reiterative way. However, researchers frequently find it useful to have a research programme or structured plan of the research process that they can, at least theoretically, think about, if not actually follow step by step. In some universities and business schools a structured research plan is considered so essential that it is an integral part of the research proposal. In other institutions the research proposal is simply a document which indicates that the proposed research candidate is familiar with the literature. In either event a formal or informal plan needs to be established.

This chapter outlines the main steps in such a research programme which the researcher could follow when getting started with his or her research for a masters or doctoral degree in the field of business and management studies. It provides a general framework which, if followed, will lead the researcher in a logical way into the research process. Once the research process is underway, it is quite likely that each individual researcher will develop a personal route from that point onwards.

In thinking about a research programme or process, it is useful to keep in mind that the objective of the masters or doctorate degree is as much the personal development of the researcher, especially in so far as the researcher is learning to conduct high quality research, as it is in the adding of something of value to the body of knowledge in business and management studies.

4.2   Where to Start

Choosing the starting point can be one of the most difficult problems facing the researcher, although in some cases it may be obvious and the decision quickly made. If the researcher has been previously involved in academic research for a degree then he or she may wish to extend their research activities in the same field of study and area of interest. In this case the research simply follows on from previous work. This is the way that most senior research degrees are initiated in the physical and life sciences.

In the field of business and management studies many masters and doctoral candidates are relatively mature students who have often not been involved in academic research as undergraduates or in any other way in recent years. For these students the starting point means establishing a novel research problem or question, as well as deciding on a research methodology, including the strategy and the tactics.

4.3   The Field of Study and the Research Problem

The first step in deciding on a research problem or question is to establish a field of study that determines the overall discipline within which the work will be done, but also focuses on a specific area within the discipline. Thus a field of study within business and management research could be consumer behaviour in supermarkets, or the way in which financial institutions are restructured to cope with competition, or how information systems can deliver competitive advantage.

Establishing a field of study is usually straightforward and most researchers will decide to study a problem either in their original discipline or in the area in which they are or have recently been working. Clearly the more competence the researcher has in the proposed field of study the easier it will be to identify a suitable research problem or question. Prospective candidates who are not familiar with the field of study they wish to pursue need to take the time to read and discuss widely in order to find a subject that is of interest to them and will continue to engage their attention for a number of years. It is essential that the candidate feels enthusiastic about the area of research at this early stage as research degrees take a considerable amount of time, and enthusiasm may decline over time.

The final decision as to the research problem or question should not be made too early on in the research process. It can be an indication that the research will not progress well when the prospective research candidate believes right at the outset that the research problem has been settled. The research problem should remain open at least until the literature review has been completed because this will reveal interesting research questions and problems that the researcher needs to consider.

Marshall and Rossman (1995) use the analogy of a funnel in the exploration process of selecting a research problem. The wide end of the funnel is where the general field of study is selected and as the researcher travels further into the funnel so different issues are considered. Some are rejected in the process, and on arriving at the point at the end of the funnel the research question has become obvious.

4.4   Eight Phases of the Research Process

It is useful to think of the research process as consisting of eight specific phases. These are:

1   reviewing the literature;
2   formalising a research question;

3 establishing the methodology;
4 collecting evidence;
5 analysing the evidence;
6 developing conclusions;
7 understanding the limitations of the research;
8 producing management guidelines or recommendations.

4.4.1   The Literature Review

The literature review is a material part of the research process, taking a significant amount of the time and the energy to be expended on the research degree. Furthermore the literature review is never completed, as the researcher has to remain abreast of the latest literature right up to the final publication of the dissertation.

As already mentioned, in the first instance the researcher should have some idea of the field of study, or the area of his or her interest in which the research is to be carried out. This will perhaps be related to earlier undergraduate academic interests, or to current working experience, or both.

It is important at the outset of the research process, not to be too specific about the subject to be researched. For example, a researcher with a background in information systems or computer science might wish to look at strategic information systems, and defining the field of study in such broad terms would be specific enough at the early stage of the research project.

The next step is to review the literature in this general area in some detail. This means reading as much of the published material on the subject area as possible. Initially the researcher needs to review all possible references available, including textbooks, academic papers, professional magazines and newspapers. In addition television broadcasts and video recordings are also acceptable sources during this stage of the literature review. Emphasis should be placed on the most recent material

However, as the researchers' interests begin to focus on a possible research topic, the literature emphasis should be increasingly placed on papers published in academically reviewed journals. The popular press and even textbooks should be given relatively low emphasis at this stage. Of course, it is sometimes the case that the topic is so new or novel that the popular press or videos have be used as a primary source of reference material. In such cases it is important that support for views expressed in these media be sought from experts in the field.

The literature review should indicate a suitable problem to research as well as give the researcher some idea of the research methods or approaches that have been traditionally used in this field (Creswell, 1994).

In reviewing the literature it is useful to look for contradictions or paradoxes. These usually suggest that there is an interesting research question which could be addressed for a masters or doctoral degree.

It is important to note that in the dissertation the literature should be critically evaluated and not just accepted on face value. It is this critical evaluation of the thoughts of other academics which usually leads to the formulation of a suitable research question.

Traditionally researchers used paper reference indexes available in the university or business school library as the way of initiating a literature search. These references lead researchers to seminal papers in the field of interest and these papers in turn contained references to other important papers. However, increasingly this type of paper-based literature search is being replaced by electronic searchers. Many libraries now supply their students with access to electronic databases, either over telecommunications networks or on CD-ROM. In addition, there are extensive literature search facilities on the Internet, which is currently available to researchers at a low cost.

By the end of the literature review the researcher should have a vision of what he or she wishes to achieve in his or her research

4.4.2   Choosing the Methodology

There are many factors to be considered when choosing an appropriate research methodology. In the first place the literature review should reveal not only a suitable problem to be researched but also a suitable methodology which has been applied to this type of research question in previous research projects. This implies that the researcher is familiar with the range of methodologies, research strategies and tactics available, and knows something about their individual strengths and weaknesses.

The topic to be researched and the specific research question is one of the primary drivers in the choice of methodology. As a general rule, precedent should be followed, although this may be abandoned if a suitable case can be made for a new methodological approach. The research culture in the university, business school or the institute where the work will be conducted is also an important determining factor, as is the skill and interest of the researcher's supervisor. Other stakeholders, such as the sponsors of the research, may also be influential.

Some business and management researchers adopt a pluralistic approach using multiple methodologies. For example case studies may be used to establish a grounded theory (Glaser and Strauss, 1967), a survey may be used to confirm a theoretical conjecture and a longitudinal study may be employed to see if the effect of some action research is sustained.

The choice of methodology can change during the research project. It can be seen as a journey in which the researcher may develop from one research methodology or paradigm to another as his or her understanding of the research problem changes.

In choosing the research paradigm researchers should be cognisant of the weakness of their preferred approach. They should be aware of the reaction of their stakeholders. But perhaps most of all they need to be able to satisfy their own ideological or ontological and epistemological preferences.

Finally, it is worth pointing out again that the choice of methodology is sometimes influenced by the issue of time and money which can become of critical importance, especially when there is little or no budget for the masters and doctoral research student. Compromises will regularly have to be made between what would be ideal and what is practical.

4.4.3 Formalising a Research Question

Research questions usually mature and develop throughout the early part of the research project. They are artefacts that help direct and focus the researcher's thinking in the creation of new knowledge. As research questions develop they should become more focused on the subject area and more specific in terms of the problem which they will try to answer.

Although working experience is a good starting point for establishing the research question, it is the literature review that should reveal problems or areas of incomplete knowledge in the field of interest. Establishing a research question without appropriate evidence from the literature is a risky approach and should not be undertaken lightly. There are several reasons for this, but the most important is that the proposed research question may have already been answered by researchers elsewhere, and this can sometimes be established by reference to the literature.

The research problem areas will usually first manifest themselves as general research considerations which will need to be reduced to a formal set of specific and detailed research questions. These detailed research questions need to be stated in such a way that they are testable. This usually means developing a theoretical conjecture and deriving from this statement a set of hypotheses or empirical generalisations. This is discussed in full in Chapter 5.

Research questions should always be seen as contingent and thus the researcher should at any stage be prepared to modify the questions if they do not prove to be as useful as they were first envisaged.

It is important that there should only be a small number of research questions in any one study, in the order of three to five. A larger number may lead to the research losing its focus and consequently being of less value. In fact some researchers suggest that there should really only be one main or over-arching question with a number of sub-questions leading directly from the major one.

4.4.4 Evidence Collection

The essence of the research process is to answer the research questions, by producing suitable evidence supported by appropriate arguments. Thus a suitable tactic for the collection of evidence is required and the researcher may choose from those listed in Chapter 3.

In general, business and management researchers at the masters and doctoral level ask questions related to *how* and *why*. To answer these types of questions it is necessary to use evidence collection techniques that focus on these sorts of questions. These tend to be phenomenological approaches that are generally of more value in the academic environment than those concerned with questions of *how much* or *when*. On the other hand, some research questions such as those involving the financial and international currency markets, do actually lend themselves to qualitative evidence as opposed to the more quantitative evidence. This is discussed in full in Chapter 6.

4.4.5   *Analysis of Evidence*

Once the evidence has been collected it is necessary to analyse it. Approaches to evidence analysis vary enormously. It depends on whether quantitative or qualitative evidence has been acquired. The analysis of quantitative evidence is discussed in Chapter 9 and the analysis of qualitative evidence is discussed in Chapter 10.

The amount of quantitative analysis undertaken is dependent upon the mathematical sophistication of the researcher as well as the information technology facilities, especially the software products available, but a great deal of analysis may be still be done with relatively little mathematical or statistical background.

Interpretative analysis which is employed by the phenomenologist relies on an entirely different skill set which is at least as demanding as the mathematical skills required for quantitative analysis. This skill set consists of the ability to conceptualise on the basis of the evidence available and the patterns emerging from it. This type of analysis may be referred to as hermeneutics.

4.4.6   *Conclusions of the Research*

Drawing conclusions from the evidence and presenting it as a convincing argument can be the most creative part of a research project. The conclusions should convince the reader that something of value has been added to the body of knowledge. As Collins (1994) points out, the conclusions deduced from the research need to be carefully argued in such a way that they will convince the research community, which in the case of masters or doctoral research will be the supervisor, the external examiners and perhaps the research sponsor.

The conclusions in business and management research should offer advice to practising managers as to how to conduct their business and management practices more efficiently and more effectively. Good research results are those that are put to use and which remain in use for some time. Bad or poor research results are either not used at all or are only used for a short period. The conclusions section of a dissertation will usually suggest ideas for further research.

It is important to understand that the conclusion of a masters or doctorate degree may be to reject the theoretical conjecture from which the research questions have been derived. This is sometimes seen as a problem by the researcher, but in fact it is not. The refutation of a conjecture is generally regarded as just as important a contribution to the body of knowledge as the confirmation of a conjecture. Of course in such a case the reasons why the original conjecture are rejected will have to be carefully argued.

4.4.7   *Understanding the Limitations of the Research*

As the research proceeds the researcher develops a greater understanding of the research question, the research process and the research findings. This means that the final dissertation will be a piece of work that could be improved upon if the researcher were to start the research project again. An understanding of the limitations of the dissertation is a key part of the development of the researcher and this self-discovery needs to be demonstrated in the final chapter of the dissertation. This is sometimes referred to as reflectivity because it represents the main opportunity the researcher has to reflect on his or her work and to be self-critical of the approach taken as well as of the findings produced. This is a critical part of a research degree, especially at the doctoral level.

4.4.8   Producing Management Guidelines or Recommendations

As business and management research is essentially a field of applied studies it is appropriate that a masters or doctoral degree should conclude by converting its findings into a series of practical management guidelines. These management guidelines will simply offer advice to managers on how they may improve the performance of the operation either in terms of increased efficiency or enhanced effectiveness. This is a useful way to conclude the research for a masters or doctoral degree especially if the researcher is able to offer these guidelines or suggestions to managers and see if they agree with the proposals.

4.5   Summary and Conclusion

It is necessary for a researcher to be concerned with a number of methodological questions concerning how research is carried out both in relation to the research programme and the research process. This is because a researcher has to be able to convince an audience that by his or her research efforts something of value has been added to the body of knowledge. The researcher's audience can be highly critical, being composed of examiners, sponsors or colleagues.

Selecting and developing a research programme or a research process is not a simple matter for the business and management researcher. There is a considerable amount of flexibility and a research programme or a structured research process should not in any way interfere with the creative elements of masters and doctoral research. The choice of topic is certainly a function of the subject being researched as well as the education of the researcher and the culture and skills available in the institute. Compromises always have to be made and these may follow from restrictions on time and limitations on money.

The issues discussed in this chapter require an understanding of the nature of academic research and an ability to put these issues into practice, without impairing the imagination and creative impulses of the researcher.

Suggested Further Reading

Easterby-Smith, M., Thorpe, R. and Lowe, A. (1994) *Management Research: An Introduction*. Sage Publications, London.
Gill, J. and Johnson, P. (1991) *Research Methods for Managers*. Paul Chapman Publishing Limited, London.
Jurek, R. J. (1997) 'Tools of the trade', *Marketing Research*, 9 (2) Summer: 31–3.
Marshall, C. and Rossman, G. (1995) *Designing Qualitative Research*. Sage Publications, Thousand Oaks, CA.

Rudestein, K. E. and Newton, R. R. (1992) *Surviving your Dissertation: A Comprehensive Guide to Content and Process*. Sage, Newbury Park, CA.

Walker, D. H. T. (1997) 'Choosing an appropriate research methodology', *Construction Management and Economics*, 15 (2) March: 149–59.

Wax. R. (1971) *Doing Fieldwork: Warnings and Advice*. University of Chicago.

II APPROACH, METHOD AND DATA

5

The Positivist Approach to Empirical Research

Here is Edward Bear, coming downstairs now, bump, bump, bump, on the
back of his head, behind Christopher Robin. It is, as far as he knows, the only
way of coming downstairs, but sometimes he feels that there is another way,
if only he could stop bumping for a moment and think of it.

(A. A. Milne, *Winnie-the-Pooh*, 1926)

5.1   Introduction

This chapter addresses some of the issues that need to be thought through when
pursuing a positivistic strategy to research in the field of business and
management studies for masters and doctoral degrees. Three different
approaches to the research process are offered together with some guidelines for
selecting between these methodological options.

5.2   The Central Role of Observation

The essence of modern[1] knowledge is that it is derived from observations made
on the world. All our research derives from, and ultimately refers back, directly
or indirectly to our observations, our experiences and our measurements. Things
that cannot be observed either directly or indirectly through their effects or
consequences are generally regarded as being outside the domain of science and
thus not amenable to research.

There are several ways in which observations can be made of the world
around us, including passive observations, observations of the consequences of
uncontrolled interventions, or observations of the results of deliberate
interventions. These three types of observation are not mutually exclusive and a
single research project could include any or all of these approaches.

1 *Passive Observation*[2] is the method most frequently used in business and
management research when the researcher is unable to conduct an experiment
and has to rely on evidence that already exists. The researcher collects evidence
in the form of interviews, written reports, questionnaires, artefacts and so on.
The researcher may be investigating one or many phenomena, but in all cases it
is essential to realise that many different influences or variables in the
environment will be active and will be reflected in the evidence being collected.
Using passive observation, it is sometimes difficult to determine which variables
or influences are causes, and which are effects of the factors being observed. For
example, in the study of information systems, research into the reasons why
computer aided systems engineering (CASE) tools do not always produce the
anticipated benefits would be conducted, at least in part, by passive observation.
The archetypal example of passive observation is astronomy from which all

modern, natural philosophy[3] is ultimately derived. Later in this chapter research on passive observation will be referred to as category one research.

2 *Uncontrolled Intervention* involves observing the effect of a major change in a driving variable on one or more dependent variables. The change in the driving variable will have occurred when something in the environment has changed, entirely beyond the control of the researcher. In this type of research the relationship between cause and effect is usually much clearer than in the case of passive observation, although noise in the environment may obscure the effects of the primary cause and there may be secondary driving variables which complicate the interpretation of the evidence. For example, in the study of manufacturing, research into whether an organisation purchases more equipment after a major devaluation of the pound would be typical of research based on observation of an uncontrolled intervention. A modern archetype in natural or physical science for this kind of research might be the observations of the consequences of increased carbon dioxide emission over this century on global temperature. More recently, biologists have learned much about the way biological systems respond to dramatic changes in the environment by following the way in which organisms have recolonised the area around Mount St Helen's after the recent and dramatic explosion of that volcano. Later in this chapter research on uncontrolled intervention will be referred to as category two research.

3 *Observation of Deliberate Intervention* also involves observing the effect of a major change in a driving variable on one or more dependent variables, but in this case the researcher deliberately brings about the change in the driving variable. Here the researcher has more control over what is being changed as well as what is being observed, and the relationships between cause and effect are therefore relatively easier to interpret. It is not easy to find circumstances in business and management research, or for that matter in most aspects of social science research, where it is possible to conduct such controlled experimental research. In fact it may be argued that because each situation in information systems is so different from any other, controlled research in this field would often not be appropriate, even if it were possible.[4] None the less, an example of the use of deliberate intervention in information systems research could be a firm deciding to introduce a graphical user interface into a department first, in order to determine the costs and the increase in productivity, before deciding to expand the use of the new system across the whole firm. The archetype for this approach in the physical sciences was Galileo's[5] observations of the effects of the acceleration of bodies rolling down inclined planes of varying slopes. Later in this chapter research on deliberate intervention will be referred to as category three research.

5.3   Combinations of Approaches

In a research project it is possible to employ more than one of the above three approaches. This is especially true in business and management studies at the doctoral level where the researcher might begin with a study based on passive observation, follow this by studying the effects of an uncontrolled intervention, and then try a deliberate intervention to see if it confirms the deductions made from the earlier studies.

5.4 Passive Observation

This section describes the main steps involved if one chooses to carry out passive observation within a positivistic strategy for a research programme in business and management studies for a master or doctoral degree.

5.4.1 Literature Review

As discussed in Chapter 4 an extensive literature review is an essential prerequisite for research in all three categories listed above. The literature review will reveal the established and generally accepted facts of the situation and these need to be fully understood by the researcher. In addition the review should enable the researcher to identify and understand the theories or models which have been used by previous researchers in the field. Finally the literature review should assist the researcher in identifying an unsolved problem in the field being studied that will become the focus of the research project (Leedy, 1989).

In order to review the literature adequately it is essential that the researcher examines the published work critically; not all that is published should be taken at face value for, as von Clausewitz (1832) observed, 'it is a maxim in all books that we should trust only certain information and that we be always suspicious'. Once the literature has been fully and critically reviewed the researcher should be able to provide a narrative description of the current understanding in the field of study, including at least one area where there is incomplete knowledge which could be further investigated.

5.4.2 Assessment of the Established Theory

It is important to decide early on if the problem identified in the literature is sufficiently explicit and generally accepted by people working in the field as a relevant problem for the researcher to be able to develop a theoretical framework and to derive workable and testable hypotheses. In a relatively mature field of study, such as psychology, sociology or economics, there are agreed facts and established (if sometimes conflicting) theories, and the researcher may have deduced a new theory by analysing and then synthesising ideas and concepts already present in the literature of the discipline. The emphasis in this type of research will be on the deduction of ideas or facts from the new theory in the hope that it provides a better or more coherent framework than the theories that preceded it. Darwin's theory of natural selection, arising in the context of detailed and extensive biological observations, and many competing theories concerning the process of evolution, illustrates this process well.

In business and management studies established and accepted theories are unlikely to be available. There is little grand theory and few, if any, authors who have developed seminal theories of the kind offered by Freud, Marx or Keynes. As a result the business and management researcher needs to generate a *grounded theory*, a concept developed by Glaser and Strauss (1967), which they define as: 'an inductive, theory discovery methodology that allows the researcher to develop a theoretical account of the general features of a topic while simultaneously grounding the account in empirical observations or evidence'.

In attempting to develop a grounded theory the researcher will approach the enquiry with a reasonably open mind as to the kind of theory that will emerge from the study. Of course, preconceptions derived from the literature survey and owing much to the researchers' own knowledge, experience and intellectual background cannot be avoided, but where possible they should be identified and recognised. The grounded theory methodology normally relies heavily on the use of in-depth interviews with experts in the field of study for the collection of evidence that will be used in an inductive way to assist in the theory generation. Where interviews are used to collect evidence an interview schedule can be prepared to remind the interviewer of the topics being investigated.

5.4.3   Theoretical Conjecture

The primary aim of the researcher developing a grounded theory is to describe the phenomena of interest accurately. Once this is achieved the researcher will begin to develop theoretical conjectures and hypotheses about the nature of the relationships between the observed variables. The grounded theory emerges through the process of *concept discovery*, within which the researcher develops abstract concepts and categories from the evidence. This is achieved by identifying, describing, defining and specifying relationships. The result is that the researcher moves to a level of abstraction in which the concepts generated by this process develop into a theoretical framework (Martin and Turner, 1986). It is important to note that in this approach to research, concepts and theories are regarded simply as more or less useful and not as more or less true or valid (Cohen and Nagel, 1984).

Once the grounded theory has been developed, the researcher in business and management studies is in a position to make a theoretical conjecture or thesis,[6] but there is no structured methodology for doing this. Rather, this aspect of research or scientific study can be regarded as an art that relies almost entirely on the imagination and creative abilities of the researcher. It is precisely here that science and thus research becomes truly creative.

As there are no rules for developing a theoretical conjecture students can find this one of the most difficult parts of their masters or doctoral degree. The only guidelines that can be given are that there should be a degree of resonance between the literature, the evidence collected and the theoretical conjecture developed. Sometimes using an analogy to systems, or law or ideas from other fields of study may be helpful in creating a useful theoretical conjecture. The research of Gersick (1992) illustrates this as she borrowed the concept of punctuated equilibrium from Stephen Jay Gould and used it to understand how teams operate when they reach the mid-point of their existence.

It is not acceptable for the researcher completely to invent a theoretical conjecture, and he or she needs to be able to defend how the concepts and ideas which exist in the literature and which arose from the evidence lead to the theoretical conjecture.

The following is an example of a theoretical conjecture developed through the use of the grounded theory approach for a doctoral dissertation in information systems management (Remenyi, 1990a).

> Strategic Information Systems (SIS) occur as a result of pressure or opportunities directly related to industry drivers. The firm's response to this pressure or opportunity is influenced by its strategy and by its critical success factors (CSF), and these issues determine the formulation of the SIS. The decision to attempt to take advantage of SIS is made with little attention to detail concerning cost-justification and vendor selection, but with more attention to communicating with the staff, training appropriate people and setting up support facilities.

An important change occurs at this stage of the research. Whereas the formulation of the research problem began as a description of the known facts from which a narrative theory was developed, this narrative will now be used paradigmatically. That is to say, it will provide a set of logical conjectures as the basis on which to predict and explain observations.

Whereas in the physical sciences the theoretical conjecture will frequently be expressed as a formula or as a series of simple propositions, in business and management research the theory or thesis will often be reduced to a diagram for the purpose of clarification (Miles and Huberman, 1984). Figure 5.1 is an example of how the theoretical conjecture can be reduced to a diagram.

The presentation of the theoretical conjecture in the form of a diagram is important because it requires the researcher to once again think through and identify all the variables involved, as well as to describe the possible relationships between them. In fact some researchers will actually produce the diagrammatic or graphical representation of the theoretical conjecture before reducing it to words as most people find it easier to conceptualise variables and relationships through pictures rather than through words.

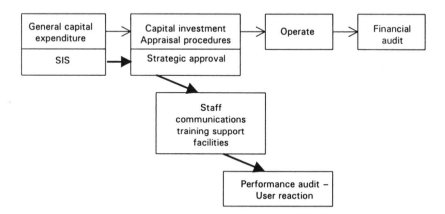

Figure 5.1   *Graphical representation of the theoretical conjecture*

5.4.4   Hypotheses or Empirical Generalisations

When the new theoretical conjecture or paradigm has been developed the next step is to use it to derive hypotheses or empirical generalisations. If the theory or thesis has been derived from a review of the literature without recourse to grounded theory then the term hypothesis[7] is more generally used, while if the grounded theory approach was employed then the term empirical generalisation[8] is usually more appropriate. In either event a series of clear statements will be produced which will be testable against further evidence.

The following set of empirical generalisations have been developed from the above example of a theoretical conjecture from the doctoral dissertation in information systems management (Remenyi, 1990a):

Strategic Information Systems occur as a result of pressure or opportunities directly related to industry drivers.

The firm's response to this pressure or opportunity is influenced by its strategy and by its CSFs and these issues determine the formulation of the SIS.

The decision to attempt to take advantage of SIS is made with little attention to detail concerning cost-justification and supplier selection.

More attention is given to communicating with the staff, training appropriate people and setting up support facilities.

Note that from the theoretical conjecture provided on the previous page, four hypotheses or empirical generalisations were developed. This is regarded as a reasonable number of empirical generalisations with which to work at a doctoral level.

Some research studies stop at the stage of theoretical conjecture, perhaps having developed some hypotheses or empirical generalisations. It is argued that at this stage a contribution has already been made to knowledge and this may well be so. Certainly achieving a theoretical conjecture and producing empirical generalisation would normally be more than adequate for a masters degree and depending on the subject area it might even be enough for a doctorate. However, if the newly discovered knowledge is to be more widely useful, then it is usually necessary to progress to a further stage in the research in which the new thesis is tested against a larger sample population. In most circumstances this additional step would be required for a doctorate degree.

5.4.5 *Measuring Instrument*

In business and management studies the collection of evidence for the purposes of testing empirical generalisations frequently, although not by any means always, requires the preparation of a questionnaire which is sometimes referred to as a measuring instrument (Oppenheim, 1966). A full discussion of questionnaires is provided in Chapter 9.

The preparation of questionnaires is an art in its own right and the researcher needs to be familiar with the guidelines for good practice in this field. However, it is absolutely essential that a pilot study be conducted to establish that the proposed questionnaire is intelligible and clear to members of the target population. The researcher needs to ensure that the questionnaire is unambiguous, reliable and valid for the purpose for which it is to be used.

5.4.6   Sampling

As it is rarely possible to test the empirical generalisations against all the members of the target population it is necessary to select a sample of the overall population on which to conduct the test. In the traditional positivistic approach to research, selecting a sample to ensure that it is both representative and unbiased is important. It requires considerable attention and is discussed more fully in Chapter 11. Suffice to say in the current context that if statistical inference is to be used then it is necessary to ensure that the sample has been randomly selected from the whole population or from stratified subsamples of the population[9] (Remenyi et al. 1991). In any event the evidence collected in this way will be used to test the thesis. A full discussion on sampling is provided in Chapter 11.

5.4.7   Testing and Analysis

A variety of statistical techniques may be used to test the hypotheses or the empirical generalisations. Univariate[10] methods such as regression analysis or analysis of variance may be used to investigate the effects of the independent variables on the variable of interest. Various types of multivariate analysis may also be used to look for relationships between variables that are not otherwise apparent, or to establish super-variables that simplify the interpretation of the evidence. Multivariate techniques may be used to produce perceptual maps that are valuable for the understanding of relationships between variables. A full discussion of quantitative analysis is provided in Chapter 12.

5.4.8   Confirmation and Refined Theory

Testing and analysing the evidence may lead the researcher to confirm or reject the theoretical conjecture or to develop a fuller or more refined theory. This expanding and refining of the theory should help to bring the original theoretical conjecture more closely into line with the evidence of the findings of the empirical research. In addition, provided that the sample was representative of the broader population and the measuring instrument was valid and reliable, it should be possible, at least to some extent, to generalise the theory.

The above steps in the methodology can be illustrated by means of the flowchart shown in Figure 5.2.

It is important to mention here that the above model of research, which could be referred to as a 'waterfall' model, in which the research process is essentially sequential and linear, seldom works out in practice in such a simple or straightforward way. Frequently the researcher finds him or herself retracing one or more of these steps in a recursive or reiterative manner. Research is almost always too complex for each step to follow from the previous step in the planned or desired way the first time it is attempted, and sometimes a problem that arises in one step will only become apparent when a later step is in progress. Thus the researcher may have to retrace his or her steps several time during a major project such as a doctorate degree.[11]

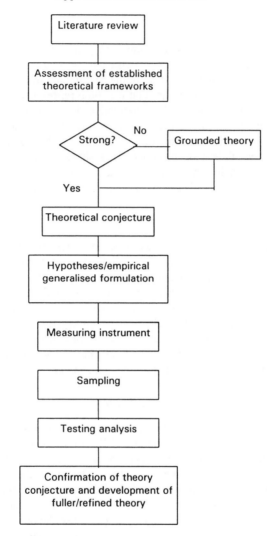

Figure 5.2   *Steps in the research process – category one*

5.5   Uncontrolled Interventions

The second research category or approach referred to as uncontrolled intervention arises as a result of a change that has been brought about by an agency external to and independent of the researcher. This approach to research comes close to what could be regarded as a field experiment.

5.5.1 Literature Review

Again it is necessary to start by reviewing the literature carefully and in detail. In this case however, the literature review might be used to identify and consider likely events which could be regarded as uncontrolled interventions and which thus could provide the focus for the research.

It is unusual, although sometimes necessary for the researcher to need to develop a grounded theory in this second category of research and the methodology usually passes on to the next stage of theoretical conjecture.[12] In this category of research the problems being studied will probably be well defined and will relate to some aspect of a previously established theory that is now being tested.

5.5.2 Theoretical Conjectures and Hypotheses Formulation

Making theoretical conjectures and formulating hypotheses are central to research based on an uncontrolled intervention approach and require close attention. The way the theory is stated and the way the hypotheses are formulated will be important in determining how and why the evidence is collected.

Issues such as what evidence is relevant and available, and what evidence should not be collected may be raised at this stage. The intention here is to focus the collection of evidence on the variables and issues that are most likely to be related to the cause and to explain the impact of the uncontrolled intervention.

5.5.3 Evidence Collection Design

Evidence needs to be collected relating to the situation both before and after the uncontrolled intervention and, where possible, for a control group that is unaffected by the intervention. For example, if the research problem is to determine how purchases of computer equipment in the UK were affected by the major devaluation of the pound sterling in October 1992, then it would be necessary to collect evidence on computer purchases both before and after that date. Referring back to the example of global warming, interpreting recent temperature trends requires knowledge of how temperatures have changed in past times.

5.5.4 Primary and Control Evidence

The evidence reflecting the purchases of computer equipment in the UK might be considered to be the primary source of evidence and the findings of the research would be based on tests and analysis conducted on this evidence. At the same time, evidence reflecting the same processes in a control group should be collected wherever possible. In the case of the devaluation of the pound sterling described above, a control source of evidence might be the purchases of computer equipment in France or Germany before and after October 1992 as there was no devaluation in the French franc or the German mark. However, for the evidence from France or Germany to be useful for control purposes, convincing arguments would be needed to show that the French or German economy was similar to the economy of the UK, and that French organisations would react to a devaluation in a similar manner, at least in so far as this issue is concerned. The use of control evidence is typical of an experimental design that will be discussed below under research based on deliberate interventions.

5.5.5   Testing and Analysis

As mentioned above for research based on passive observations, a variety of statistical techniques may be used to test the hypotheses or the empirical generalisations, and the various techniques of univariate and multivariate analysis are equally applicable here. However univariate statistical analysis is more likely to be the central analytical tool in the case of this category of research.

5.5.6   Confirmation and Refined Theory

In the first category of research, in which passive observations are made, many uncontrolled events will bring about changes in a variety of possible response variables. Multivariate statistical techniques will play a central role in the analysis, and deciding on the critical inter-relationships will be difficult. In the second category, the consequences of a major change in a single driving variable are studied in the hope that this will enable many other extraneous factors to be excluded, leading to a deeper understanding of a more specific aspect of a problem. Thus this approach is much more focused in the type of research problem or question than research based on passive observation. The relevant steps in this methodology are outlined using a flowchart as shown in Figure 5.3.

5.6   Deliberate Intervention

The most powerful experimental methodology involves imposing a controlled and deliberate change on a system and observing the effects that it has on other variables. In this case the researcher has much more control over what is happening to the driving variables and what is being observed in the behaviour of the dependent variables. It is important to emphasise that it is not easy to find circumstances in business and management research, or for that matter in most aspects of social science research, where it is possible to conduct such controlled experiments. People, and generally with good cause, do not like to participate in experiments, except of the most bland type, and for this reason psychologists are frequently reduced to observing rats rather than people. Commercial and even public sector organisations rarely choose to be involved with such experiments. Commercial firms believe that experiments, and especially academic experiments, can adversely affect their profits, and public sector organisations are concerned that experiments could disturb their routine. None the less there are circumstances where some degree of experimentation in an organisation is possible and the controlled introduction of a computer system to a part of the firm on a trial basis might be just such an example.

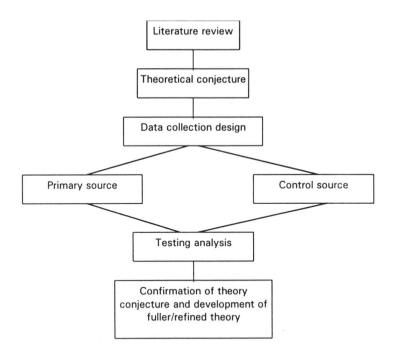

Figure 5.3   *Typical steps in the research process - category two*

5.6.1   Literature Review

Once again a thorough review of the literature is of paramount importance. As before, at the conclusion of the literature review the researcher should be able to create a narrative model of the current state of knowledge in the field of study, including at least one area where the knowledge is incomplete, and suggests a problem that should be researched. Research problems in the natural or physical sciences are often well defined and researchers sometimes begin their experiments before the literature review has been completed. This of course carries a degree of risk because it may only later come to light that someone else, in another part of the world, has already conducted the experiment. This risk becomes unacceptably high in the physical and life sciences.[13]

5.6.2   Theoretical Conjecture

The development of a theoretical conjecture together with formulation of hypotheses is again central to research based on deliberate interventions and in fact the intervention that is chosen will usually follow directly from the theoretical conjecture. Here the theoretical conjecture will generally arise out of an established theory, which it is intended will be explored in more depth and be tested empirically. Because the theoretical conjecture and the hypothesis will usually be deduced from a more general theory, the way the thesis is stated and the way the hypotheses are formulated will be important in determining the next stage, which is experimental design.

5.6.3   Experimental Design

The design of experiments is an extensive and involved topic of considerable importance to the researcher. The key issues involved are:

1   the form that the intervention will take;
2   what evidence will be collected before, during and after the intervention;
3   what sort of control group(s) is required;
4   how a sample may be chosen to represent the whole population;
5   who will make up the experimental team;
6   who in the organisation will provide the interface for the purposes of evidence collection.

The essence of good experimental design is that it will minimise the effect of extraneous influences and variables on the evidence being collected, and elicit the effects arising directly from the intervention. Noise from the economy or from other aspects of the organisation can seriously affect the experimental evidence in business and management studies and where this cannot be altogether avoided by the design of the experiment, these influences need to be investigated in the testing phase.

The timing of the intervention is a central aspect of the experimental design. It is important to decide when the evidence collection will begin, when the intervention will be initiated, when the ex-post evidence collection will commence and for how long the evidence will be recorded. The answers to these questions will in turn depend on whether there are any cycles in the operations of the target organisation that could substantially affect the evidence.

5.6.4   Measuring the Variables Ex-Ante

If an organisation is to be studied by way of an experiment, the first stage is to collect evidence concerning the performance of the organisation before the deliberate intervention occurs. This evidence might be based on accounting or statistical data or on opinion surveys. This is the base evidence that will be compared to the corresponding evidence after the intervention has been completed. If, as is desirable, there is a separate control group to which the intervention is not applied, the evidence for the control group should clearly be collected at the same time as the evidence for the intervention group. The importance of a control group, which should match the intervention group in all of the relevant parameters, is that if the change is not in fact due to the intervention, it should be observed in the control group. Conversely, if it is due to the intervention it should not be observed in the control group.

5.6.5   Deliberate Intervention

At the agreed time the intervention is initiated. This could be the introduction of a new system in the southern regional office of an organisation, for example. The intervention period could take place over a matter of hours or it could take days, weeks or months. The deliberate intervention needs to be controlled as carefully as possible in order to ensure that it complies with the plan laid down in the experimental design. Where the intervention deviates from the plan, detailed notes need to be made of how the experiment differed from the original plan.

5.6.6 Measuring the Variables Ex-Post

It is usually necessary to allow a period to elapse between the deliberate intervention and the collection of the ex-post evidence. This is because it can take a while for the results of the intervention to produce a material effect on the observable evidence. This response time can take from days to months. However, the situation in the organisation participating in the experiment does not affect the collection of evidence in the control organisation which will continue uninterrupted. An important issue here is when to stop the collection of the evidence as it is possible to continue to observe beyond a useful period.

5.6.7 Testing and Analysis

Once the evidence has been collected it needs to be processed to see if it supports or contradicts the hypotheses. However, in addition to hypotheses testing there is frequently scope for modelling of the evidence to see if new patterns emerge. The subject of modelling was dealt with in Chapter 4 and some of the mathematical techniques required are discussed in Chapter 12 under the heading of statistical analysis. It is worth pointing out that in this context modelling refers to the creation of simplified abstractions of reality which capture the critical or key features of the situation. The use of models to consider various scenarios is a powerful approach and is perhaps the most creative aspect of this category of research.

5.6.8 Confirmation and Refined Theory

As in the first two categories of research, passive observation and the study of uncontrolled interventions, the testing and analysis allows for the theory to be confirmed or rejected, or a fuller or more refined theory may be postulated offering a greater degree of generalisability.[14] This methodology is illustrated in the flowchart in Figure 5.4

5.7 Relationship Between the Three Categories

Although in this chapter research methodologies have been divided into three distinct categories, these different approaches to research overlap and have many points in common. It may therefore be instructive to consider their inter-relationships as demonstrated in Figure 5.5.

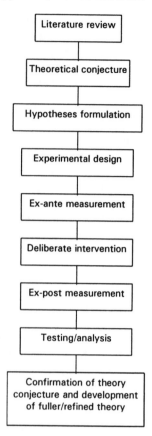

Figure 5.4   *Steps in the research process – category three*

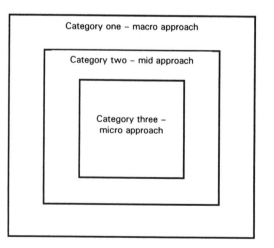

Figure 5.5   *Relationships between the three categories*

Category one, passive observation, is generally concerned with events that happen on a macro scale; category two, uncontrolled interventions, with events that happen on a somewhat smaller scale; and category three, deliberate interventions on a micro scale.

Passive observation is the most general category. Here there may not be a prior theory and therefore the researcher may have to develop a grounded theory by induction from *a priori* observations. The development of theories of gravitation, from Keppler through to Newton and eventually Einstein represents the most important example of this in the natural sciences. Now research of this kind is often undertaken in the newer aspects of business and management studies such as information systems (Mintzberg, 1973).

Studying the consequences of uncontrolled interventions provides more detailed information about a smaller part of the system under investigation. Normally such studies do not start from an attempt to derive inductively a new theoretical framework, but rather begin with an already established theory that will be tested by observing the effects of the uncontrolled intervention.

The third category in which one intervenes deliberately, focuses even more closely on a particular aspect of the problem and should provide, at least from a positivist's point of view, the most detailed information. This research relies on having an established theory as the basis from which the hypotheses may be deduced and which will determine the nature of the intervention. This research is the most specific and the most directed, with the most structured methodology. This approach is clearly aligned with the so-called scientific method of the physical and life sciences, although it is important to note that this is now possible only because natural philosophy has, over the last 400 years, gone though stages not unlike those now experienced in the social sciences in general, and business and management studies in particular.

In fact all three of these categories are essentially positivistic in nature in that they assume a world in which research questions may be reduced to relatively simple ones and in which it is possible to theorise about research findings in deterministic terms. These approaches are attempts to create knowledge in such a way that theory may be developed with some sort of predictive power. However, the three approaches differ on the issue of reductionism. Category one research actually has holistic undertones, while categories two and three are clearly reductionistic.[15]

It may be argued that category one research is suited for macro problems in the social sciences while category three research is more appropriate for micro problems, especially in the physical sciences. Category two research clearly lies between these two extremes. Any given research problem may be considered as consisting of macro as well as micro issues. The relationship between the different categories of research may alternatively be described as shown in Figure 5.6 where it can be seen that one problem may require a number of different category two and category three research projects.

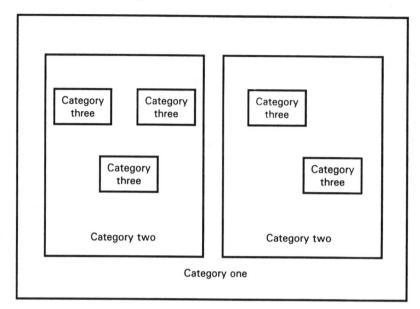

Figure 5.6   *Micro and macro relationships between the three categories*

5.8   Summary and Conclusion

There is no uniquely best approach to research, either in the natural or in the social sciences, and the best that can be done is to describe the ways in which research is carried out in a variety of situations. Nevertheless, there are general lessons that can be learned and some of these are discussed in this chapter.

The central issue in the positivistic approach to modern science concerns the relationship between that part of the world which is the object of a particular study and the theoretical framework which is constructed in order to explain the observations that are made on the world. However, experiments and observations made on the world do not immediately suggest the nature of the theory that will explain them and the particular observations that are made will be constrained by the currently held theory. The best research will often owe as much to the imagination, the intuition and inspiration associated with art as to the logic and reason normally attributed to traditional academic science. This is especially the case in business and management studies. Einstein (1931) says that,

> The most beautiful experience we can have is the mysterious. It is the fundamental emotion which stands at the cradle of true art and true science. Whoever does not know it and can no longer wonder, no longer marvel, is as good as dead, and his eyes are dimmed.

The way in which information about the object of study is gathered may usefully be divided into three categories and most research projects can be fitted into one of these. Sometimes, as in astronomy, it is not possible to intervene directly or indirectly and this has been called passive observation (category one). In business and management studies this may also be the case and the best that can be done is to observe the evolution of the system under investigation and then to construct theories to explain the observations. It is then essential to have a firm grasp of the currently accepted theories in order to decide if they provide an adequate account of the observed phenomena.

It is generally true that within the positivist's strategy to research one builds a broad understanding of the nature of a system by first investigating small parts of the overall system and trying to understand these. For this reason important insights can be gained by studying the response of the system of interest to an abrupt change in a single factor or perhaps a few factors. In this chapter this has been called uncontrolled intervention (category two). The hope is that other things being constant, it is possible to relate the effect of this single change to the effects that it produces.

From a positivist's point of view an even more powerful approach involves perturbing the system directly in a controlled manner. This has been called controlled intervention (category three). By choosing the nature of the intervention it is hoped that specific aspects of the system can be explored, but this cannot always be done for ethical or economic reasons. When such interventions can be made, the design of the experimental intervention is crucial in order to ensure that the observed changes in the system are indeed the result of the intervention and are not due to other, uncontrolled factors. The interventions that are ultimately chosen will depend on the theoretical framework that in turn will cause certain factors to be important.

Clearly there is overlap between these three categories of research and thus one research project may involve elements from all three approaches.

Scientific theories may be regarded as the free invention of the human mind with the constraint that good or powerful theories are those that give insight into the nature of the system under investigation. Paradigmatic theories of great power nearly always begin as narrative descriptions that allow us to grope our way closer to an understanding of the essence of the world around us. Success depends not on the discovery of final truth but on the discovery of useful knowledge that leads to a better understanding of the environment, which may be people and their ways, organisms and their interactions, or physical objects and the forces between them.

This chapter reviews various approaches to empirical based research in the social sciences in general and in business and management studies in particular. It is not a definitive discussion of research paradigms in this field. Purely theoretical research has not been specifically addressed because empirically based research is the dominant approach in social science today.

To phenomenologists this chapter could be seen as a manifesto for positivism. Although the interest in phenomenology is rapidly growing in business and management studies there is still a strong positivistic tradition in this field in many universities and business schools.

Furthermore, non-empirical or theoretical research is also highly relevant in business and management studies. Scientists who construct general theories may make important contributions, and such theories should ultimately be grounded on empirical observations. The complexity and diversity of business and management studies means that theories of generality and power, such as exist in the natural sciences are not available, and the best research is likely to be that which is firmly based on empirical studies. Some of this research will be positivistic while some will be phenomenological.

Suggested Further Reading

Boland, R. and Hirschheim, R. (1987) *Critical Issues in Information Systems Research*. Wiley Series in Information Systems, Chichester.

Feyerabend, P. (1983) *Science in a Free Society*. Verso Edition, London.

Galliers, R. and Land, F. (1987) 'Choosing appropriate information systems research methodologies', *Communications of the ACM*, 30 (11): 900–2.

Glaser, B. and Strauss, A. (1967) *The Discovery of Grounded Theory: Strategies for Qualitative Research*. Aldine, New York.

Gould, S.J. (1988) *The Mismeasure of Man*. Fourth Edn, Penguin Books, London.

Kazdin, A. E. (1980) *Behaviour Modification in Applied Settings*. The Dorsey Press, Irwin-Dorsey Ltd, Ontario.

Medawar, P. (1986) *The Limits of Science*. Oxford University Press, Oxford.

Notes

[1] The term modern is used here in a fairly general manner and it is not suggested that it be directly contrasted with the concepts of post-modernism which will be addressed later in Chapter 6.

[2] In the context of positivistic research, the idea of passive observation describes activities ranging from pure observation, during which the act of observation appears to in no way affect the situation being observed (counting the number of cigarettes a person smokes for example), to observations based for example on questionnaires (asking people how many cigarettes they smoke), in which the act of asking and the relationship between observer and observed may influence the reply that is given. Passive observation, like the other categories, covers a range of activities and the division between them is made, at least partly, for conceptual convenience. Of course there are some phenomenologists who would argue that passive observation does not exist in any of the social sciences and especially in the field of business and management studies, as the observer is an intrinsic part of the process of observation and cannot by definition be passive. There are other phenomenologists who believe that it is possible to disengage from the environment and thus be a passive observer.

[3] Modern natural philosophy starts from the work of Keppler, Galileo and Newton. Keppler discovered that simple algebraic expressions could be used to describe natural phenomena such as the relationship between the period of the planets around the sun and their distance from the sun. Galileo carried out careful and extensive experiments concerning the acceleration of bodies falling under the force of gravity. But perhaps the most important step was taken by Newton who showed, for the first time, that simple mathematical laws could be used to relate the forces of nature, in particular the force of gravity, to the acceleration of bodies, and therefore to the way in which gravitational systems would evolve over time. All of modern natural philosophy has been an extension and development of the approach pioneered by Newton.

[4] One important exception to this is the use of experiments in business and management studies in American universities where doctoral students are routinely allowed to perform experiments as the main approach to their research in business and management studies. Of course in a field of study which is sometimes closely allied to business and management studies, such as psychology, experiments are pretty well the norm.

[5] Galileo's observation of the moons of Jupiter is a classical example of passive observation in astronomy and one of the oldest examples of the modern physical sciences.

[6] This is the correct use of the term thesis, but commonly the word is used interchangeably with the word dissertation which can lead to some confusion. According to *The Shorter Oxford English Dictionary*, the word thesis means 'a proposition laid down or stated especially as a theme to be discussed and proved or to be maintained against attack'.

[7]The term hypothesis is generally used to mean a tentative explanation or subset of a theory that is taken to be true for the purpose of argument or a study or investigation. In the context of research methodology a hypothesis should be expressed in such a way that it directly follows from a theoretical conjecture found in the literature and potentially can be falsified.

[8]The term empirical generalisation has much the same concept as the hypothesis, except it would typically not be derived directly from a theoretical conjecture found in the literature, but from empirically determined evidence in an inductive manner.

[9] In an ideal world one would study every member of the population of interest. Since this is neither necessary nor feasible one will generally study a smaller sample which adequately represents the total population. The danger always is that one chooses the sub sample in a way that ensures that the conjecture one hopes to confirm will be true. In other words one chooses the subsample in a biased fashion. Assuming that the research is not deliberately fraudulent this may nevertheless happen as a result of unconscious biases. One way to avoid this is to list the members of the parent population and then choose a random number generator to generate a random subset that forms the study population. While this will ensure that there are no deliberate biases in the choice of the study population, the nature of random sampling means that there is always a chance that certain important subgroups will be left out. For example if one chooses a random sample from a parent population of firms of varying size, and assuming that there are many more small firms than there are large firms, one might choose a sample in which large firms are not represented. If large firms behave or respond differently from small firms this would give a misleading impression. In such a case, all of the variables that the researcher thinks are likely to be important are stratified. This would include the size of firm, annual turnover, nature of the business and so on. Then within each of these strata the individual firms that will be included in the study are randomly chosen. In such a stratified random sample the stratification ensures that all of the factors that are believed to be important are represented in the sample and the randomisation avoids unconscious biases on the part of the researcher.

[10]There is considerable overlap between univariate and multivariate methods of analysis. Univariate analysis is usually regarded as covering situations in which one or more independent variables are used to explain changes in a dependent variable. Multivariate analysis is usually regarded as covering situations in which several independent variables are used to explain changes in more than one dependent variable. Multivariate analysis can also be used for situations in which a number of variables are analysed on an equal footing in order to identify groups or combinations of variables that enable the evidence to be separated or classified into useful categories.

[11] A question which sometimes arises is 'Can a research degree be done backwards?' This is clearly not a simple issue. A tentative answer is that the overall direction should be forwards but that there may be a lot of to-ing and fro-ing in between. It may be that when major conceptual shifts are made it is actually necessary to go back before one can branch off in a new direction. The book *Newton for Beginners* essentially argues that Descartes' book *Principia Philosophiae* was a triumph of fantastic imagination which, unfortunately, never once hits on a correct explanation. However, by offering an alternative to Aristotle it frees Newton to take a new path and find the correct way forward. Thus research can be done backwards but perhaps this approach is more appropriate for the Descartes and the Newtons of the world.

[12]This is because the category two approach, i.e. the uncontrolled intervention, will usually be applied in circumstances where there is already some well-established theory and therefore there should not be the need to start off at the grounded theory level.

[13] The tight and well-defined nature of research in the natural sciences means that someone may have done exactly your experiment quite independently.

[14] Generalisability is essentially an issue of positivism and would not be of much concern to the researcher engaged in a phenomenological research study.

[15] When conducting research into a broad issue in business and management studies such as that implied by category one research it is quite difficult to use a deductionist approach due to the large number of variables which are active in the environment. However masters and doctoral students sometimes do attempt to achieve this and it may lead to their research not being as credible as it could otherwise have been.

6

Phenomenology: The Non-Positivist Approach

The wheel of learning consists of question, theory, test and reflection.

(C. Handy, *The Age of Unreason*, Arrow, London, 1989)

Insight, untested and unsupported, is an insufficient guarantee of truth, in spite of the fact that much of the most important truth is first suggested by its means.

(B. Russell, *Mysticism and Logic*, Unwin Books, London, 1970)

6.1   Introduction

This chapter further explores the philosophical origins of phenomenology or non-positivism and considers some of the practical aspects of the research tactics and methods that flow from this approach to research in business and management studies at the masters and doctoral degree level. The chapter also addresses the issue of validity and reliability in so far as they apply to phenomenological research work.

6.2   Phenomenology and Non-Positivism

Much, although not all, of business and management studies focuses on people and organisations.[1] Many scholars believe that the traditional approach to research in the physical and life sciences, sometimes called the scientific method,[2] is not entirely appropriate to the study of human beings or to the organisations they have created. This is clearly illustrated by Carr (1967):

> I do not wish to suggest that the inferences of the social scientist or of the historian can match that of the physical scientist in precision, or that their inferiority in this respect is due merely to the greater backwardness of the social sciences. The human being is on any view the most complex entity known to us, and the study of his behaviour may well involve differences in kind from those confronting the physical scientists.

Many would argue that phenomenology, sometimes called the non-positivistic approach, is the appropriate strategy for research into people and their organisations. In general those who propose a phenomenological or non-positivistic approach to research do not deny the value of the positivist approach to research in the physical and life sciences.[3] Positivism has, after all, led to the creation of our twentieth-century material reality including space travel, heart transplants, beef mountains, the Empire State Building and a life expectancy of 100 years or more for girls born in the western world in the 1990s.

But positivism has trouble[4] in explaining why so many people hate their jobs, why customer service is so frequently poor, why some staff are achievement oriented and others are not, why some corporate cultures are highly centralised while others need high degrees of autonomy. When it comes to answering these questions, positivism provides few insights or even convincing and useful explanations. To cope with the problems of people and organisations it is necessary to go beyond positivism and use a phenomenological approach to research. Although non-positivistic approaches are increasingly used in research in business and management and in social science in general, the more traditional natural and life scientists sometimes regard such approaches as inferior or even as non-science. However the view that only positivism can deliver valid research results and so add something of value to the body of knowledge is generally on the decline. It is increasingly accepted among business and management scholars that phenomenology is better suited to this type of research where the central issues concern people and their behaviour.

6.2.1 *Different Meaning to Different Researchers*

The term phenomenology means different things to different people. Many different names or words used to describe similar research strategies and tactics are used loosely which may confuse researchers, especially at the masters and doctorate level in business and management studies. As previously stated in Chapter 2, Cohen and Manion (1987) provide the following definition of phenomenology: 'Phenomenology is a theoretical point of view that advocates the study of direct experience taken at face value; and one which sees behaviour as determined by the phenomena of experience rather than by external, objective and physically described reality'. On the other hand Rudestein and Newton (1992) suggest that phenomenology 'attempts to describe and elucidate the meanings of human experience', while according to Camus (O'Brien, 1965), 'phenomenology declines to explain the world, it wants to be merely a description of actual experience'. Perhaps the essence of the subject was captured by Boland (1985), when he said that phenomenology is 'a term that carries a great deal of ambiguity along with its sometimes confused and faddish use'.

Thus although none of the first definitions cited here is contradictory, each has a slightly different emphasis and thus considerable care needs to be taken when the masters or doctoral student enters the world of phenomenology. However, if this research strategy is employed successfully it may deliver an opportunity to produce a high-quality contribution to the body of knowledge and thus it is certainly worthwhile for the masters or doctoral student to employ the phenomenological approach to research.

6.2.2 *Phenomenology – What? Why? and How?*

There is a painting by Renoir[5] of the Pont Neuf bridge in Paris in 1872 that provides an analogy for the different approaches to research. The immediate impression of the painting is of people and horse-drawn carriages crossing the bridge. On both sides of the bridge the Seine is visible and the sky and the buildings along the bank of the river provide the backdrop. However, when viewed with a searching mind, one begins to see the outline of a man's face embedded in the picture. Thus two levels of communication are enacted through

Renoir's painting: the general Parisian scene and the personal feeling expressed in the face of the man.

In a similar way, the non-positivist searches for the embedded face in the picture rather than remaining content with a description of the patterns, figures and outlines which define and describe the larger scale objects in the picture. Medawar attributes to Popper the observation that positivism suggests that the world is all surface. Thus the essence of phenomenology is an attempt to delve below the surface to understand the essence of what is happening.

The central premise of non-positivist research is that the researcher should be concerned to understand phenomena in depth and that this understanding should result from attempting to find tentative answers to questions such as 'What?' 'Why?' and 'How?' Phenomenology contends that such an understanding can result from using methods other than measurement, unlike the assumption of positivism which is ultimately concerned with answering the questions of 'How many?' or 'How much?'

The above example indicates that different methods are appropriate for research into different types of problems and the nature of the research problem suggests the most appropriate method. For instance, Bernstein (1996: 202) writing about probability and risk management points out that 'Where information is lacking, we have to fall back on inductive reasoning and try to guess the odds.' And Bernstein reinforces this by quoting Keynes (1921: 3) on the limitations of measurement by saying, 'There is a relation between the evidence and the event considered, but it is not necessarily measurable.' The spirit underlying this way of thinking, that has moved beyond traditional measurement, can also be seen in a different context when one considers Stephen Jay Gould's (1995: 17) attitude on discovering that he was suffering from mesothelioma (an incurable cancer with a median mortality of only eight months after diagnosis). He drew comfort from the realisation that 'attitude clearly matters in fighting cancer' and this was confirmed when speaking to Peter Medawar (Nobel laureate in immunology) who suggested that 'a sanguine personality', and not how much chemotherapy, or how many drugs, or how much exposure to radiotherapy, was the best recipe for success against cancer.

This theme of the limitations of quantitative evidence and research also recurs in the *Mismeasure of Man*, where Gould (1988: 239) suggests that the mere fact of measuring something does not lead to understanding, as was clearly demonstrated in the misuse of intelligence testing by many who believed in eugenics.

6.3   The Context of the Research

In business and management studies it is essential to understand the context within which the research is being conducted by considering social or cultural factors that impinge on the research problem. Henry Mintzberg (1996), in his work on organisational context, relates how he had always been a *lumper* rather than a *splitter* when it came to researching organisations. In other words, he liked to categorise and achieve consistency in evidence. Thus, 'strategies are generic, structures are types, managers have a style'. In contrast, splitters analyse and distinguish and question, and thus 'strategies, structures and styles all vary infinitely'. Business and management research requires both lumping and splitting, but often in management research the former predominates and not enough 'splitting' is done. Mintzberg's own realisation of his lack of splitting, or consideration of the organisational context, occurred when one of his students questioned his well-known attempts to describe the configurations of organisations. He suggested that 'fit' was always essential and the result of his thinking was a prescription on structure, power and processes.

In reality it is almost impossible to engineer neatly such a fit between organisational processes. The overview of the organisation implied in Mintzberg's 'lumping' approach would not enable one to make any sense of the 'messiness' of organisational life, whereas splitting enables a way of thinking and a way of seeing beyond the prescription.

6.3.1 Some Philosophical Underpinnings

Philosophically the non-positivist position derives from phenomenology, which emphasises the primacy of unique experience without attempting to label or categorise these experiences. In other words, people construct their own worlds and give meaning to their own realities (Easterby-Smith et al., 1994). It is important to distinguish between phenomenology itself and the range of different research methods that have developed out of this particular world view.

The term phenomenology essentially describes the philosophical approach that what is directly perceived and felt is considered more reliable than explanations or interpretations in communication. It is a search for understanding based on what is apparent in the individual environment rather than on interpretations made by the observer.

The approach is often confused with the qualitative approach to research. However, phenomenology is merely a philosophical stance or orientation to research and not all qualitative researchers necessarily subscribe to it.

6.3.2 The Primacy of Context

To understand phenomenology, it is useful to trace its origins in the social science literature, and in particular in the area of psychology where it has developed into a recognised branch of the discipline. The essence of the approach is that, 'People cannot be understood outside of the context of their ongoing relationships with other people or separate from their interconnectedness with the world' (Clarkson, 1989: 14). Thus, the context within which social action or behaviour occurs is of the utmost importance in understanding actions or behaviours. Further, phenomenology assumes that knowledge can be gained by concentrating on phenomena as experienced by people.

At the heart of phenomenology is the relationship between self and society, as expressed in the work of Mead (1934), the originator of phenomenological psychology. Mead accorded primacy to the process from which the 'organism creates its environment' (Clegg and Dunkerley, 1980: 267) which leads to the distinction between act and content, with the stress on the act and what that means to the actor (Yontef, 1993).

To appreciate this, consider the outcomes of the Hawthorne studies (Clegg and Dunkerley, 1980: 127). The research project investigated the effect of different types of working conditions on productivity. The results of the research were inconclusive, as it appeared that any manipulation of the independent variables produced increases in productivity. However, the learning that emerged from the studies was, as Clegg and Dunkerley (1980) suggest, the variables being manipulated could not be treated as independent of the 'meaning which individuals assigned to them'. Today this is one of the fundamental assumptions of phenomenological researchers (Collins and Young, 1988).

6.4   Phenomenology and Qualitative Methods

However, as already mentioned, not all researchers who regard themselves as adopting a non-positivist orientation towards management research regard themselves as subscribing to a phenomenological approach to research.[6] For instance, it is possible to distinguish between phenomenological interviewing and other non-positivist interviews used to gather qualitative evidence (Marshall and Rossman, 1995). Researchers adopting phenomenology deliberately group their evidence-gathering technique in the theoretical tradition of phenomenology. This results in a very specific method which guides evidence collection during which the researcher must first attempt to remove all traces of personal involvement in the phenomena being researched. Similarly the researcher has to limit any other influences from impinging on the evidence-collection exercise before finally gathering data around specific themes. This process is clearly very different from the interviewing process that a feminist or a hermeneutic researcher would adopt. In essence, the latter two traditions place less stress on the primacy of the respondent experience.

However, having noted the differences that exist among researchers coming from different schools of thought, we see that there are clearly some common beliefs which enable us to bracket such researchers together as non-positivists. These beliefs include their assumptions made about human nature and the extent to which it is possible to control research. Non-positivist research assumes that objects of enquiry in the social sciences are social issues – a key concern is that research should acknowledge and treat people as essentially human rather than as mere objects. There is clearly an ethical dimension to this question, which is explored in greater depth in Chapter 13.

Central to this argument is the fact that people have the ability to think, argue, and experience the world or events in idiosyncratic ways and that positivistic research strategies are unable to deliver an understanding of these human dimensions. Clear evidence of the failure of the positivist approach was provided during the UK general election in 1992 when the polls, including the exit polls, predicted a Labour victory, but the actual result was a Conservative victory instead. It seems that people were simply unwilling to tell the truth as to how they had actually voted. It is therefore important to acknowledge this uncertainty and take account of it when research is conducted.[7]

6.4.1   Control and the Research Process

In designing a research project the assumption is made that one can control for extraneous variables so that causal relationships between pairs of variables can be established. This is often done by working with a control group which is matched to the intervention group as regards factors that might affect the outcome but are not of immediate interest.

However, these assumptions about the use of controls are seldom relevant in non-positivist research, due to the difficulty of controlling variables in social settings. Indeed, how does one control the effect of the researcher involved in the research? In the experiments at Hawthorn mentioned above, Mayo confronted exactly this problem when investigating increases in productivity (Clegg and Dunkerley, 1980). This has become the classic example of the difficulty in adhering to the dictates of the stimulus–response model, which, according to Gill and Johnson (1991: 33), explain past and predict future observations through causal analysis and hypothesis testing.

How does one control for the effect of culture? As discussed earlier, our cultural backgrounds fundamentally determine our frames of reference – even for 'scientific' theories (Gould, 1980a). Gummesson (1991) quotes Harold Geneen, the former Chief Executive Officer (CEO) of the conglomerate ITT, on the difficulty in gaining access to Japanese companies such that they could truly evaluate where management decisions were made. He argues that Japanese respondents would find it difficult to verbalise subtle decision-making procedures and merely interviewing such respondents would not be illuminating. The type of access required to conduct research that would be illuminating might not always be possible (Kazdin, 1980).

6.5   Evidence Collection in a Natural Setting

Non-positivist research essentially relies on collecting evidence in as natural and non-controlled a setting as possible, rejecting the formalism imposed on research activity by a positivist approach. Furthermore, it assumes that human beings should be treated as people rather than objects. This calls into question the extent to which the research process can be governed by objectivity on the part of the researcher. Today it is accepted that instead of this being a purely negative feature of non-positivist research, it can be a strength, provided that it is recognised in the interpretation of the research results.

Thus, for instance, Ann Oakley (1981) argued that her research on motherhood would have suffered if she had applied the traditionally prescribed rules on evidence gathering. In particular she argued that the ideal of the non-involved, depersonalised researcher deliberately mystifies the role of researcher and respondent during the interview process and further personal involvement is consequently seen as biasing the evidence. She suggests that this perspective does not fit with her experience as a feminist interviewer where her primary interest is in the 'validation of women's subjective experiences as women and as people' (Oakley, 1981: 30). Her research clearly relies upon such involvement. At this point, however, it is necessary to point out that the above assumptions are not the only ones regarded as common to non-positivist methods as there is no 'agreed-upon set that everyone understands' (Marshall and Rossman, 1995: 2).

Researchers who wish to conduct non-positivist research have to contend with many variations on the use of different methods, the degree of involvement of the researcher, how evidence should be analysed and whether it is appropriate to take account of the respondent's world view (Marshall and Rossman, 1995).

6.6   Using Non-Positivist Methods

The many varieties of non-positivist approaches follow from the perspective adopted by the researcher, as is clear from the feminist research of Oakley (1981). Marshall and Rossman (1995) discuss several distinct research traditions based on the researcher's perspective on issues such as the interaction of people and the environment, views on culture, a commitment to radical ways of schooling children, etc. This serves to remind us that researchers are subject to prejudices, cultural beliefs and values that they bring into the research process with them. These help to shape what Morgan (1980) calls the researcher's 'frame of reference' or 'mode of engagement' which include socialisation, the nature of the object being investigated, the outcomes sought from research and who is funding the research.

6.6.1   Socialisation

Gill and Johnson (1991) discuss the Kolb learning cycle shown in Figure 6.1 and explain how people all start out at different parts of the cycle when doing research. The cycle describes individual learning experiences and how individual socialisation will influence where on the cycle the research process is started. The disciplines from which the researcher comes, as well as his or her work experiences, will have a strong influence upon the research strategy that is favoured. For instance, one of the authors used as inspiration for PhD research the experience of working with small firms. The starting point here was therefore concrete experience, leading eventually around the cycle as the research process progressed. Thus, the researcher brings into the research process a ready state of knowledge which is drawn upon and which non-positivist researchers accept as valid. Indeed, Gummesson (1991) refers to such knowledge as 'pre-knowledge'. This essentially refers to the tacit knowledge that a person might have developed through exposure to phenomena, existing knowledge and/or being given information by colleagues or contacts. Gummesson regards this as vital if the researcher is to be adequately equipped to understand and explain processes within the research setting.

A more critical look at the Kolb cycle reveals further influences that can be categorised under socialisation. The Kolb cycle assumes that learning is an inherent part of the process. It assumes that the loop is closed and the cycle is self-contained. It seems to us that this is not necessarily the case and that additional influences come to bear on the process in the form of the learning/research institution in which the student is located.

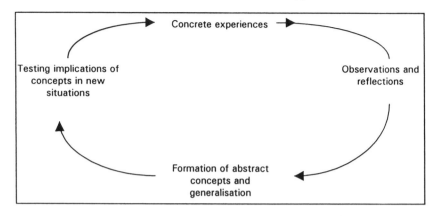

Figure 6.1   *Kolb's experimental learning cycle*

Jankowski and Webster (1991) for instance note how up to the 1930s the work conducted by researchers at the Chicago school was primarily qualitative in nature. A change occurred around the 1930s when there was a resurgence of positivism when social scientists turned to natural sciences and copied their methods. This resulted in researchers in Chicago, especially junior researchers, having to adopt a positivistic approach as this had become the research culture of the institution. Hence, the wider environment also influences what are regarded as acceptable methods for conducting research.

6.6.2   The Nature of the Object Being Investigated

From our experience, the tangibility of the phenomenon being investigated is also important in helping to decide the form in which evidence can be collected. For example, the research object is often defined in such a manner that it is immediately clear that quantitative evidence is the best way in which one can learn more about that object. This would be the case, for instance, if the researcher was required to estimate the size of a target market, or the number of UK based retailing companies that now provide childcare facilities as part of their overall service to customers. Essentially, here one is attempting to answer the question 'What?'

At other times, by way of contrast, the object might be less discrete and therefore would not easily lend itself to evidence collection through objective measurement. This would primarily be where the researcher is concerned to understand 'Why?' Consider for example the issue of the growth of female entrepreneurship in the UK during recent decades. In order to answer questions about the growth of entrepreneurship, the researcher would have to engage in estimating the number of women who are self-employed or run small firms. However, in order to understand why they occupy the positions that they do, it is vital to engage with representatives from the population and listen to the reasons offered to explain this.

6.6.3   Outcomes Sought from the Research

Cultural heritage is important in shaping the perspective within which objects of investigation are regarded, and informs the value placed upon particular outcomes.

Reference was made earlier to the value in exchange which research output might have. This again can influence the decision with regards to the research strategy to be adopted as it is often well known that certain journals favour only traditional scientific research designs, which usually translates into a quantitative, positivist approach to research. MacNaughton (1996) for instance argues that the medical community, and medical journals in particular, rates scientific, quantitative methods more highly than qualitative. The result is that qualitative researchers find it much more difficult to get their work published and it is only recently that the outcomes of such research have started to appear in medical journals.

Access to research settings also has an important influence as in most cases researchers are required to work with research respondents in organisations. Here the research may be conducted both for academic purposes and for the host organisation. In this sense the host organisation becomes the research laboratory and the nature and quality of the access which is negotiated determines the understanding of the research setting which results from the research.

6.6.4   Funding the Research

The agency or organisation that is funding the research often determines the nature of the object to be investigated and the methods that are to be used in undertaking that task. As Remenyi and Williams (1995) argue in relation to research into artificial intelligence: 'Who is funding the research and what are their public and private agendas which will directly affect control over the results of the research?' These influences are inescapable and it is important that the researcher is aware of this from the outset, throughout the process of investigation, and, crucially, when evidence is interpreted, conclusions drawn and recommendations are made.

6.7   Developing a Research Strategy

Before researchers undertake any research activity it is essential that they consider carefully an overall research strategy and that this be clearly stated in the research proposal. By research strategy is meant consideration by students as to which research community they feel they belong to, and that the researchers know the epistemological, ethical and ontological assumptions of their research. This is illustrated in Figure 6.2.

It is also important that the researcher should be clear about the research process though which the work will progress. In addition, this will help define the field of research and consequently the tactics or approaches which are logical corollaries. Clearly such a research strategy will not be set in stone and it will change as the student's understanding of the research area develops.

Ontology	Whether the object of investigation is the product of consciousness (nominalism) or whether it exists independently (realism).
Epistemology	What our grounds of knowledge are.
Human nature	Whether humans interact creatively with the environment (voluntarism) or whether they are passive objects (determinism).
Methodology	Nomothetic or ideographic approaches to evidence collection.

Figure 6.2 *Assumptions made by researchers*

In Chapter 2 the difference between positivism and non-positivism was discussed. These strategies are discussed in some detail by Burrell and Morgan (1979) and Gill and Johnson (1991) who argue that the deductive approach to research has become synonymous with positivism. The characteristics that define these different strategies are well illustrated by Burrell and Morgan (1979) who identify some of the assumptions which researchers make about the factors shown in Figure 6.2. These polarities can be represented along a subjective–objective continuum that mirrors the positivist–non-positivist divide. This is not to imply that these 'pure' positions in relation to the factors discussed in Figure 6.2 are the predominant ones. Researchers may clearly occupy a position towards the centre of the continuum or between the centre and the left or right polarities. The purpose of the continuum is to enable basic assumptions about research activity to be distinguished. This is shown in Figure 6.3.

Nominalism	**ontology**	Realism
Anti-positivism	**epistemology**	Positivism
Voluntarism	**human nature**	Determinism
Ideographic	**methodology**	Nomothetic

Figure 6.3 *Factors represented as polarities across a continuum*

Burrell and Morgan (1979) argue that the four dimensions outlined in Figure 6.3 inform radically different frames of reference or paradigms. A paradigm denotes a common perspective which underpins the work of a group of theorists in such a manner that identifies them as analysing social issues in the same way (Morgan, 1980). The Burrell and Morgan (1979) model indicates that there are discernible differences among research approaches based upon different permutations of the four factors. Easterby-Smith et al. (1994: 27) used the above analysis of philosophical positions to generate a useful classification of the key features of positivist and phenomenological paradigms. This is shown in Table 6.1, which, together with the continuum, can be used to explore the orientation of the researcher in order that strategies and tactics can be consciously selected. It is important that the researcher feels comfortable with the choice of research strategy and the methods of collecting evidence. This is discussed further in section 6.8.6.

Table 6.1   *Key features of positivist and phenomenological paradigms*

	Positivist Paradigm	Phenomenological Paradigm
Basic beliefs:	world is external and objective	world is socially constructed and subjective
	observer is independent	observer is part of what is observed
	science is value-free	science is driven by human interest
Researchers should:	focus on facts	focus on meanings
	look for causality and fundamental laws	try to understand what is happening
	reduce phenomena to simplest elements	look at totality of each situation
	formulate and test hypotheses	develop ideas through induction from evidence
Preferred methods:	operationalise concepts so they can be measured	small samples investigated in depth or over time
	take large samples	
	use multiple methods to establish different views of phenomena	

It is important that the researcher is clear about the above issues, particularly the area where the researcher feels comfortable as this will to a large extent determine the research design which he or she will adopt.

6.8   Beginning the Research

Howard and Sharp (1983) outline a process model that is useful in identifying the phases that form part of the research process. They distinguish between the 'planning' and 'effectuation' stages and these in turn can be broken down into the activities set out below:

> **Planning:**
> Identify a broad area of study
> Select the research topic
> Decide the approach
> Formulate a plan of action
> **Effectuation:**
> Collect the evidence
> Analyse or interpret the evidence
> Present the findings

These stages are not regarded as linear and the researcher will have to revisit these time and again during the planning and effectuation stages. This does not mean that there is not a method, but rather than pretend that research designs can ever be set out in a predictive way and controlled, invoking a logic that is not real, we should recognise honestly that plans have to be flexible to cope with changes in funding, access and the state of knowledge about a particular phenomenon (Jones, 1992).

The planning stage is fundamental to formulating any research strategy, but it is particularly so in non-positivist research as the use of ideographic methods to collect evidence is potentially more fraught with pitfalls. This is because the researcher has to rely on methods which are less well defined and perhaps more controversial than those used in positivist research. The absence of controlled conditions in non-positivist research means that the researcher has to be aware that the research community is likely to use different standards by which to judge the outcomes and value of the research. For example, Gummesson (1991) argues the case for good quality access being an important standard by which to judge qualitative research, and this needs to be planned if the outcomes of the research are to be regarded as valid.

As Marshall and Rossman (1995) argue, the planning stage is fundamental to the consideration of issues such as developing an argument that is convincing, showing how the particular case being investigated fits with the bigger picture, and that the design of the research is sound. It is through this planning that the competence of the researcher is demonstrated.

6.8.1   Area of Study and Topic

The selection of the area to be investigated and the research topic is the responsibility of the student in interaction with the supervisor who can often be most helpful by asking questions rather than being directive and shaping the research too closely. In this respect, creativity and immersion in a topic area are therefore important ingredients. Creativity often flows from having an open mind and being able to make connections across different disciplines. For instance, the explanation by Stephen Jay Gould of how natural systems develop (a process called punctuated equilibrium) was useful as an analogy on team development in the research done by Gersick (1992). At the stage where it became necessary to theorise, the concept was used to provide a theoretical explanation of how her observed teams operated.

6.8.1.1   Induction
As a rule it is best to start from a broad perspective and then to narrow the topic down to a specific instance. However, within a non-positivist paradigm, it is acceptable for the generation of a research topic or question to come from experience rather than reflection on theory and concepts. In other words, an inductive process to generate the research question is entirely acceptable. Intuitive notions about phenomena often form part of the practice of researchers, as Gould (1988: 22) argues: 'Science, since people must do it, is a socially embedded activity. It progresses by hunch, vision and intuition .... The most creative theories are often imaginative visions imposed upon facts.'

The previously cited work of Gersick (1992) on teams is an excellent example of the researcher having been involved in observational work of teams and using an inductive approach to generate a research question.

6.8.1.2   Deduction

Alternatively the student might well start from a deductive position and then seek to use the methods suggested by Howard and Sharp (1983) to generate research topics. These range from looking for ideas in texts (theses, journal articles, books and reviews, the media) to communication with others (experts in the field, colleagues, potential users of the research outputs).

Whether a deductive or inductive approach is used, it is important to have a good idea of the conceptual framework within which the research will be developed. By this is meant that the researcher has to be able to see how the specific instance fits into the wider whole. For instance, Gersick (1992: 58) describes how her supervisor throughout the course of her doctoral research had pushed her to become 'conceptual' and to transcend mere specific descriptions of events. For her this meant moving from an initial interest in team processes and how they operated during the course of a particular project. Gersick (ibid: 49) started out with an initial question, which was, 'What does a group in an organisation do, from the moment it convenes to the end of its life-span, to create the specific product that exists at the conclusion of its last meeting?' Becoming conceptual meant that she placed the specific instances within a wider context of team development and, through contrasting her model of mid-point transition with traditional theory, she went on to say:

> An intriguing finding may be interesting to take out and examine now and then, but without a theoretical context, there isn't much way to use it; it cannot join the circulating currency of ideas in a field. Beyond that, no one would be able to understand that I was proposing a different paradigm of group development unless I made the basic assumptions of the traditional paradigm explicit and showed exactly how and why my ideas differed. (Gersick, ibid.: 63)

6.8.2   Importance of the Literature

Non-positivist researchers will use real-life problems that emerge from experience as the inspiration for research (Marshall and Rossman, 1995: 17). It is important that this is done in tandem with at least an emerging understanding of the literature.

Formulating the research problem is the next important step in which intuitive notions should be more fully investigated and narrowed down into a researchable, informal hypothesis or statement such as the example given from the work of Gersick. This process occurs through speaking to supervisors, other researchers and practitioners. The latter are particularly useful in helping to frame the question by pointing out constraints and problems that help to redefine the problem. Linked to this, the student should also investigate theoretical or conceptual frames in order to relate the specific to the general again.

6.8.3   Feasibility of the Research

Once the research problem has been formulated, it is important to think about the feasibility of the research and to be satisfied that there is sufficient material (published literature, secondary and primary evidence) to work with. If an area is completely new or relatively unexplored, there is a case for advising against being the pioneer. The amount of research already done will be confirmed by the literature review and this should give an indication as to whether there is an opportunity to increase, or confirm knowledge (Howard and Sharp, 1983). However, the obverse also applies in that if an area is well researched, it becomes relatively difficult to add anything new and the criteria against which the work is judged are bound to be much more stringent.

6.8.4   Plan the Research

The main challenge in planning the research is for the student to consider, and explicitly state, the overall design of the study. The research design will flow from the personal inclination of the researcher, through the philosophical assumptions discussed in Section 6.7, to the nature of the research problem (Yin, 1981). Thus, a feminist researcher will specifically set out to exploit personal involvement, whereas phenomenological interviewing might stress the removal of 'all traces of personal involvement in the phenomena being studied', such that all preconceptions are removed and do not interfere with the research process (Marshall and Rossman, 1995: 82). On the other hand, a researcher wishing to undertake hermeneutical research will attempt to generate high-quality textual material for examination. Such a research design will clearly differ from feminist research, for instance, as the emphasis will be on capturing 'the words and behaviour of those studied ... without the early filtering out by the researcher of what is considered irrelevant' (Collins and Young, 1988: 195). The influence of the researcher on the respondent is considered important, but not particularly as a vehicle to facilitate the research as in feminist research.

6.8.5   Questions and Strategies

Marshall and Rossman (1995: 41) have developed a table matching research questions with strategies. The table, which is shown as Table 6.2, uses the purpose of the study and the research question as the starting point for determining specific research strategy and evidence-collection techniques.

Clearly a particular research strategy such as the use of case studies does not necessarily mean that the evidence-collection methods used should be qualitative, as Yin (1981) has pointed out. The researcher still has to decide an overall approach and choose appropriate methods best suited to the research question and only then decide on the methods to collect evidence. The latter then have to be justified. The best way to do this is through contrasting the superiority of qualitative methods in generating a rich picture to explain or understand behaviour. It is sometimes clear that the nature of the problem demands qualitative evidence. For example, the investigation of the decision-making process employed by consumers during the purchase of consumer products demanded the use of qualitative evidence to enable the researchers to frame questions before a quantitative study was conducted to test hypotheses (Philips, et al., 1997: 79–89). Another example relates to gathering evidence on potentially sensitive topics such as voting intentions and discrimination where the quality of research depends upon a relationship with the respondent rather than the research being conducted at a distance through survey evidence.

Table 6.2   *Matching research questions with strategy*

Purpose of study	Research question	Research strategy	Evidence collection
Exploratory:			
To investigate little understood phenomena; identify important variables and generate hypotheses for further research	What is happening in this social programme? What are the salient themes, patterns, categories in participants' meaning structures? How are patterns linked with one another?	Case study Field study	Participant observation In-depth interviewing Elite interviewing
Explanatory:			
To explain the forces causing the phenomenon in question; identify plausible causal networks shaping the phenomenon	What events, beliefs, attitudes, policies are shaping this phenomenon? How do these interact to result in the phenomenon?	Multi-site case study History Field study Ethnography	Participant observation In-depth interviewing Survey questionnaire Document analysis
Descriptive:			
To document the phenomenon of interest	What are the salient behaviours, events, beliefs, attitudes, structures, processes occurring in this phenomenon?	Field study Case study Ethnography	Participant observation In-depth interviewing Survey questionnaire Document analysis
Predictive:			
To predict the outcomes of the phenomenon; to forecast the events and behaviours resulting from the phenomenon	What will occur as a result of this phenomenon Who will be affected and in what ways?	Experiment Quasi-experiment	Survey questionnaire (large sample) Kinesics/proxemics Content analysis

Source: Marshall and Rossman, 1995

Marshall and Rossman (1995) argue that justification of qualitative methods should draw on the strength of qualitative methods when doing descriptive or exploratory research or where the importance of context and the respondent frame of reference is important. However, the example of research into team development conducted by Gersick shows that qualitative research can be used for theory building rather than being merely a preliminary stage to quantitative research. Silverman (1994) would support the theory-building potentiality of qualitative research and suggests that qualitative researchers need to be bolder in the horizons that they envisage for non-positivist research.

6.8.6   Research Proposal

The final outcome of the above process will be a research proposal covering the following:

What: outline of research problem, tracing historical roots and linking specific to general; conceptual framework and literature review; purpose of study and specific research questions

How: description of research strategy and design which will yield specific evidence required to answer questions; methods justified and linked back to research question and research site

Where: where the research will be conducted

When: ideally a timeline to spell out major phases of research process

6.8.7   Gaining Access

Gummesson (1991: 21) describes access (the ability to get close to the object of study, to really be able to find out what is happening) as the researcher's biggest problem. This is particularly true when researchers are conducting research in a one-off study for academic purposes and there is a short time-frame within which to do so.

The nature of the research question and the research strategy chosen will determine the type of research site to which access will be required in order for evidence to be collected. Hence the importance of deciding in broad terms these issues in as systematic a manner as possible before approaches are made to collaborating organisations. For instance, Marshall and Rossman (1995) point out that some research will require the selection of a specific site (i.e. investigating the nature of employment relationships in small firms in the UK). Alternatively, the same question can be posed without specifying the size of the firm and the choice of research sites may be increased. The choice of site should be clearly justified and a good research site will have the following properties:

1   entry should be possible;
2   the site will present the possibility of collecting pertinent evidence;
3   trust can be established with respondents;
4   evidence quality and credibility of the research can be assured.

The researcher can best ensure that conditions 1 and 3 are met by developing good relationships with gatekeepers and/or informants (Gummesson, 1991). The large numbers of students approaching companies to participate in research make the use of gatekeepers particularly important. Indeed, in many cases, gatekeepers are the only way in which a researcher can gain access.

The above approach to gaining access makes the entire process seem rational and ordered. In fact it is often difficult. Buchanan et al. (1988: 53–4) advocate the use of multiple strategies when trying to get into organisations as there are numerous ways in which the most carefully laid plans can be subverted:

> It is desirable to ensure representativeness in the sample, uniformity of interview procedures, adequate data collection across the range of topics to be explored, and so on. But the members of organisations block access to information, constrain the time allowed for interviews, lose your

questionnaires, go on holiday and join other organisations in the middle of your unfinished study.

Hence, what is possible always wins over what is desirable. Buchanan et al. (1988) recount how, when they were presented with opportunities to conduct research in a company installing a new computer system, they had no time at all to do preliminary work for the interviews. Rather, the interview opportunity was immediate and based on relevant people being available then – these opportunities had to be grasped.

6.8.8   Collecting Evidence

Once the research strategy has been decided, it is necessary to decide upon the manner in which evidence will be collected and analysed. It is now well accepted that where a non-positivist approach is adopted, it is difficult to separate evidence collection from hypothesis construction and theory building (Silverman, 1994).

Several authors use a funnel or funnelling process as an analogy to describe the relationship between evidence collection, hypothesis construction and theory building (see Marshall and Rossman, 1995; Silverman, 1994; and even Morgan, 1980). Silverman points out how research starts out on a broad front, becoming progressively more focused over time (through hypothesis generation and theory building) and out of this emerges the research question. The latter will frequently be different from the initial research question which provides the focus of the research.

Evidence collection can usefully be divided into three types: observation, interviews, textual analysis.

6.8.8.1   Observation

The main aim of observation in research is to gain an understanding of other cultures by sharing the space of the research site at least for some part of the duration of the research. This tradition developed from the anthropological influence on sociology and has latterly become established as the ethnographic tradition in business and management studies (Jankowski and Webster, 1991). The argument for adopting observation as an evidence-collection strategy is that real understanding will come about through extended observation as this enables an understanding of both the context and process of behaviour.

There is a variety of roles the researcher may adopt, depending upon the degree of involvement of the researcher in the research site, and these are shown in Table 6.3. Table 6.3 outlines the types of role which researchers may choose and the associated problems that attend the role. Thus, in choosing to become a complete participant, the researcher will first have to gain access to the organisation to be studied and this in itself might present some difficulty. Once access has been gained, it might also be difficult to know how to behave so as not to arouse the suspicions of those with whom the researcher is supposed to have a 'normal' working relationship.

Table 6.3 *Summary of Participant Observation Roles*

Role of researcher	Degree of involvement	Potential problems
Type 1	complete participant as normal member of organisation, e.g., factory, school, etc.	pretence problem – how 'normal' is behaviour to the setting?
Type 2	participant as observer–researcher and organisation members aware of researcher's status	researcher 'going native'
Type 3	observer as participant	limited involvement of researcher
Type 4	complete observer	limited usefulness – mainly for reconnaissance

Where the researcher gains access as a 'participant as observer' the attendant problem is that of the researcher developing friendships with members of the organisation. Alternatively one or more of the informants might also start to identify closely with the researcher. The third role the researcher may adopt is that of observer as participant where the researcher will usually conduct one-visit interviews with respondents. With this role potential problems with validity might arise due to the limited nature of the contact which is established with those in the research setting.

Finally, the researcher as a complete observer is recommended only where the researcher is investigating the usefulness of a particular research setting rather than proper evidence collection. The adoption of any one of the above roles should be clearly linked to the research strategy the researcher selects as outlined in Table 6.2.

6.8.8.2 Interviews
This is a method commonly used in non-positivist research. Interviews constitute an effective means of collecting large amounts of evidence in one or across several research sites. Types of interview differ depending on the amount of structure imposed by the researcher. This in turn will determine the freedom of the respondent in replying to or elaborating on questions. There are two types of interview: open-ended interviews and semi-structured interviews. In the latter the researcher will use an interview guide or questionnaire to provide some structure to the interview. Where research is being conducted across sites it is particularly important that such an instrument be used to systematise the collection of evidence and to enable comparisons to be made during the analysis phase. Otherwise there is the risk of collecting 'a wealth of evidence from a set of individually valuable interviews that collectively are difficult to generalise from' (Howard and Sharp, 1983: 140).

It is vital that any interview schedules be pre-tested in some way to ensure reliability. The schedule could for example be sent to academic and practitioner referees who can provide feedback on how they understood and responded to questions. This provides a powerful way to check that the evidence the researcher intends to gather will be produced by the use of the interview schedule. Where the interview is more open-ended, the researcher should check the consistency in coding of evidence between two researchers after the collection of evidence.

There can be many difficulties with this method of evidence collection. Interviews clearly rely on getting co-operation from the respondent. Here the interpersonal skills of the researcher become important. Buchanan et al. (1988: 59) advise that the key to getting on with evidence collection is that the researcher should really (and appear to) 'have a sincere curiosity about the lives and experiences of others'. Respondents are sensitive to such attitudes on the part of the researcher and it is important that the researcher considers how he or she can establish a relationship where trust is established early during contact. In our experience the best way to break the ice is to discuss informally an issue (mutual friends or interests, important recent news which relate to the company, etc.) unrelated to the research *per se*, which will allow both the researcher and the respondent to relax.

A second potential problem can arise from covering everything on the interview schedule or guide. This is particularly so where group interviews are being conducted or the respondent is a senior member of the organisation. It is best to conduct such interviews once the researcher has conducted interviews with respondents where the relationship is better established, and has thus gained confidence. Such confidence is vital if the researcher is to establish control over the interview. If there is an interview schedule to cover the researcher should be able to use questions as prompts to steer conversation in the desired direction or, indeed, to use these to probe particular issues.

Researchers may supply informants with a copy of the interview transcripts. This is done to ensure that the transcription is an accurate portrayal of the proceeding, which is an essential check on the validity of the evidence, but also to sustain the relationship with respondents.

6.8.9   Analysis of Texts

This is the most demanding aspect of non-positivist research. The central problem is that the researcher will have collected rich material and, particularly where he or she is working independently, can feel swamped. Most researchers also feel unable to make the tough decision to ditch any of the collected evidence as they have usually worked hard to collect it. Indeed if a hermeneutical approach is adopted, it is important that such richness be preserved. At the heart of the dilemma is the issue of imposing a framework or structure on to the evidence and deciding what is useful and what is not. It is difficult to know when to do this. Clearly one will have to take into account one's estimation of the importance of particular pieces of evidence. The only guideline here is that the researcher will be best placed to consider the research questions and the tentative theoretical framework that guided these and to consider the most significant pieces of evidence. These will then have to be compressed to adhere around manageable themes or concepts. In practice this means that the evidence has to be read, re-read, and such themes or concepts have to be catalogued. It is vital that this process is based on the evidence itself and that these themes emerge from the bottom up, rather than being the result of selecting a theory by convenience and then dipping into fragments that support such a theory. Such practice is known as circularity and is to be avoided. Instead, Collins and Young (1988) argue, categories and models must emerge from evidence collected, until saturation occurs. They further regard the respondent as having a key role to play in this process and in ordering such categories in terms of importance.

The idea of sequential analysis has been suggested in which evidence is continually checked against interpretation until one has grasped its meaning (Becker, 1970). Here the analysis of the evidence is carried out sequentially in that analysis begins while evidence collection is being undertaken, but in the interstices between observations the researcher steps back from the evidence and reflects upon possible meanings. Further evidence gathering is then undertaken in particular areas in which the researcher has become interested because of provisional analysis. Further observation or evidence collection might lead to the researcher abandoning a particular hypothesis about an organisational process to explore another more consistent with the research setting. Thus, the hypotheses about the functioning of processes are gradually refined. This is similar to the process described by Silverman (1994) as accepting that evidence collection, hypothesis construction and theory building are ongoing, iterative processes, progressively becoming more focused over time. In the secondary analysis phase, the researcher will return to the literature and attempt to work with concepts from such theory as does exist, in relation to the categories that have emerged from the evidence collected. During this process the skill is to develop existing concepts and produce new categories or concepts to explain emerging phenomena (Glaser and Strauss, 1967).

6.9   Evidence Analysis Software

Most qualitative researchers do not make use of computers in analysis, except for producing and keeping a record of interview transcripts. At most the researcher would use such computer-based files for search/find purposes but not for analysis of the content of such files. This is partly because computer-based analysis software for qualitative evidence is a recent innovation. Weitzman and Miles (1995) claim that even ten years ago researchers were handwriting field notes and then manually sorting, filing and coding written or typed notes. Today, however, the situation is different and for those researchers who feel comfortable with using a computer-based approach to analysis there is a wide choice of software available – from simple text retrievers through to conceptual network builders (Weitzman and Miles, 1995).

The advantage of using computer software to aid analysis is clearly that the most tedious aspects of analysis can be automated, leaving the researcher free to pursue theory-generating and problem-resolution. The researcher who does not adopt a purist attitude to 'closeness' to evidence (Weitzman and Miles, 1995) is therefore aided in taming the vast pool of evidence which qualitative methods usually generate. This sounds attractive, especially to lone researchers who have experienced the problem of nearly becoming lost amid evidence (Easterby-Smith et al. 1994). For instance, Silverman (1994) advocates the use of such analysis software to assist with analysis of field notes such that the researcher can more easily file and index text into several different categories (The Ethnograph).

Alternatively, NUD·IST might be used to facilitate searching by indexes and to generate new categories and relationships.

However, there is a fundamental contradiction between adopting a non-positivist position and selecting appropriate research methods, but then opting to use an analysis method that relies on placing a distance or remoteness between the researcher and the evidence. A non-positivist stance assumes involvement with the research process through all stages, and particularly the analysis, as one person's interpretation will be different from that of another or that assisted by software.

Further, given that computers essentially reduce evidence to its simplest form, how can the researcher be sure that the resultant analysis is not substantially different in a qualitative sense of meaning from a manual analysis of that evidence? Indeed, the final outcome of the process might be that what started out as non-positivist and qualitative in nature ends up as empirical–positivist.

Finally, there is the danger of ending up with an analysis that is only as good as the mechanistic rule-based software being used. Indeed, Weitzman and Miles (1995) discuss the shortcomings of the new generation of software at length and suggest a multitude of ways in which the software might be improved. All of this suggests that such software still leaves much to be desired in terms of ease of use, intuitive capability and interfacing. In fact, some might agree with the quote by Pfaffenberger (1988: 20) used in Weitzman and Miles (1995: 212): 'A technology is like a colonial power – it tells you that it is working in your best interests and, all the while, it is functioning insidiously to dim your critical perception of the world around you. You will remain its victim so along as you fail to conceptualise adequately what it's up to.' It is not at all clear that computer analysed evidence is of value to the non-positivist researcher.[8]

6.10 Validity, Reliability and Generalisability

These issues should be considered at the design stage of the research. The fact that the criteria for evaluating validity, reliability and generalisability were developed for positivist research designs does not mean that they are not valid quality checks to impose on non-positivist research. The primary reason for considering these issues is that they are the most important criteria used to evaluate research and should indicate how well the research will be accepted by a critical audience of peers and assessors or examiners.

However, given the nature of non-positivist approaches to research, the yardsticks differ from those used in positivist research. They are softer than the hard measures such as statistical validity and refer to issues such as whether there has been consistency and integrity in the design of the study. This means that the researcher should honestly represent the understanding of respondents rather than fall guilty of circularity or twist evidence to fit his or her own theories. Indeed, it has been suggested that the criteria used to evaluate positivist research (internal validity, external validity, reliability and objectivity) are all inappropriate and should not be directly transposed on to non-positivist research (Marshall and Rossman, 1995). In this section alternative constructs are presented which are more in line with the assumptions of the non-positivist approach.

6.10.1 Validity

In non-positivist research validity concerns whether the researcher has gained full access to knowledge and meanings of respondents. Hence the importance of good-quality access to enable such contact to be made within the research site. There is also the need to feed research field notes or interview transcripts back to respondents for verification to ensure that it reflects their understanding of the phenomenon (Collins and Young, 1988). Access therefore becomes one of the criteria against which the research will be evaluated.

Gummesson (1991) refers to validity as representing a 'good fit' between theory and reality in the sense that when a description of a process is evaluated, there are occasions when 'intuitively' there is an aspect which does not fit with reality. The researcher can triangulate a study in such a way as to draw upon multiple evidence-collection methods and use multiple informants and cases in order to demonstrate such a 'fit' between theory and reality. Collins and Young (1988) further contribute ideas regarding validity in hermeneutical research and these are shown in Table 6.4.

Table 6.4   *Indicative questions regarding validity*

	Concerns of the hermeneutical researcher	Indicative questions
1	Quality of researcher as a sensing instrument	How sensitively and effectively has evidence been collected?
2	Transparency of research process	Is it clear how evidence was collected and interpretations made?
3	Quality of relationship with respondent	Was the relationship sterile or has there been participation and empathy?
4.	Quality of argument in the interpretation	Is it plausible? Is it reasonable and useful? Has it been negotiated with those involved? Is there a goodness of fit with the situation? Can it be used as the basis for action?

The authors argue that a positive response to the questions in Table 6.4, together with an internally consistent argument, would place a particular research account in line to have validity conferred by readers and users of that research.

6.10.2 Reliability

The distinguishing characteristic here is that similar observations should be made by researchers on different occasions (Easterby-Smith et al., 1994) and the concern is therefore with how replicable the study is. It is important to point out that since with non-positivist research the concern is to investigate the manifestation of a particular issue in a particular setting, the conditions under which a study has been conducted would be difficult to reproduce. Hence, Marshall and Rossman (1995) advocate that, rather than pretend that research conditions can be replicable, it is much better to accept the particularist nature of the research and to follow good practice guidelines such as establishing an audit trail. This can be achieved by keeping the evidence collected in an easily retrievable form to enable others to investigate it should doubts regarding the research ever be raised. Second, the researcher should keep a log or journal cataloguing research design decisions and justifications for these. In this way the methods used become transparent and the parameters regarding the research questions, setting, assumptions and theoretical frameworks are open to scrutiny.

6.10.3 Generalisability

Here the researcher is essentially concerned with the applicability of theories that were generated in one setting to other settings. The accepted meaning of generalisable derives from hypothesis-testing research and the conventions are well established as was made clear in Chapters 2, 3 and 4. These are not appropriate to non-positivist research. Gummesson (1991: 79) argues that qualitative research is less concerned with making statements about the commonality of particular findings than with the fact that good qualitative research should enable one to attain an understanding of organisational processes. He argues that generalisation can be understood in two ways:

> quantitative studies based on a large number of observations are required in order to determine how much, how often and how many. The other ... involves the use of in-depth studies based on exhaustive investigations and analyses to identify certain phenomena, for example the effects of change in corporate strategy, and lay bare mechanisms that one suspects will also exist in other companies.

Based on such exhaustive investigation the understanding gained of a process in one setting can form the basis on which such processes are understood in other, similar companies.

In conclusion, a list of alternative constructs has been compiled which are regarded as being in line with the assumptions of the non-positivist approach. These attempt to consider evaluation criteria from a perspective that does not treat positivist research practice as 'best practice'. There is no one best way to demonstrate or evaluate the quality of research. The discussion here recognises that there is an alternative philosophical tradition and that good practice here will be different. The list was constructed by drawing on the work of Lincoln and Guba (1995), quoted in Marshall and Rossman (1995) and Gummesson (1991).

6.10.4 Credibility

The issue of credibility refers to being able to demonstrate that the research was designed in a manner that accurately identified and described the phenomenon to be investigated. Here the credibility (rather than internal validity) will derive from an in-depth description of the complexities of the research setting, drawing on empirical evidence. Such a representation of the phenomenon will therefore be valid for that particular study. This does mean that the research should explicitly state the parameters of the study in terms of the population, setting and theoretical framework used.

6.10.5 Transferability

This refers to external validity and is dependent upon the researcher stating the theoretical parameters of the research explicitly. Here it would be important to specify how the specific phenomenon or research setting being investigated ties into a broader case, making clear the specific organisational processes about which generalisations will be made.

6.10.6 Dependability

The positivist construct of reliability assumes unchanging conditions that enable replication of the study. This assumption does not hold for non-positivist research and it is more appropriate for the researcher to account for changes in the conditions of the phenomenon being investigated, as well as research design changes which are made because of a better understanding of the research setting.

6.10.7 Confirmability

With phenomenological research the concept of confirmability is used instead of objectivity. The question to pose is: does the research confirm general findings or not? The test is whether the findings of the research can be confirmed by another similar study. Those researchers interested in exploring practical ways in which the above issues can be considered when designing the research should consult Marshall and Rossman (1995) and Marshall (1990).

6.11 Summary and Conclusion

In this chapter the development of phenomenology is considered and influences on the decision to use non-positivist methods are discussed. It has been argued that a non-positivist approach recognises that research can never be value-free and objective. The management researcher has continually to confront the implications which flow from this and will have to come to terms with the values and assumptions which, as the following quote by Gunnar Myrdal, quoted in Gould (1988: 23), makes clear, will inform research activity, from the questions which are posed, to the conclusions which are drawn:

> Cultural influences have set up the assumptions about the mind, the body, and the universe with which we begin; pose the questions we ask; influence the facts we seek; determine the interpretations we give these facts; and direct our reaction to these interpretations and conclusions.

The process for conducting non-positivist research was presented and alternative methods for dealing with the issues of the validity, generalisability and the overall quality of such research were considered. It is important that researchers recognise that non-positivist or phenomenological research represents a challenging and different way to conduct management research. It is less structured and prescriptive than positivist research, and because of this potentially more difficult, particularly in analysis of such soft, rich data.

However, potentially it also offers us a more complete and rich understanding of the behaviour of that being studied.

Suggested Further Reading

Berstell, G. and Nitterhouse, D. (1997) 'Looking "outside the box"', *Marketing Research*, 9 (2) Summer: 4–13.

Coffrey, A. and Atkinson, P. (1996) *Making Sense of Qualitative Data: Complementary Research Strategies*, Sage Publications, Thousand Oaks, CA.

Devault, M. (1990), 'Talking and listening from women's standpoint: feminist strategies for interviewing and analysis', *Social Problems*, 37 (1).

Kirk, J. (1986), *Reliability and Validity in Qualitative Research*, Sage Publications, Newbury Park, CA.

Mason, J. (1996) *Qualitative Researching*, Sage Publications, London.

Masberg, B. A. and Silverman, L. H. (1996) 'Visitor experiences at heritage sites: A phenomenological approach', *Journal of Travel Research*, 34 (4) Spring: 20–5.

Moustakas, C. (1990) *Heuristic Research: Design, Methodology and Applications*, Sage Publications, Newbury Park, CA.

Myers, M. (1997) 'Qualitative research in information systems', *MIS Quarterly*, 21 (2) June: 241–2.

Rubin, H. and Rubin, I. (1995) *Qualitative Interviewing: The Art of Hearing Data*, Sage Publications, Thousand Oaks, CA.

Sapsford, R. and Jupp, V. (1996) *Data Collection and Analysis*, Sage Publications, London.

Silverman, D. (1994) *Interpreting Qualitative Data: Methods for Analysing Talk, Text and Interaction*, Sage Publications, London.

Weitzman, E. (1995) *Computer Programs for Qualitative Data Analysis: A Software Sourcebook*, Sage Publications, Thousand Oaks, CA.

Wolcott, H. F. (1994) *Transforming Qualitative Data: Description, Analysis and Interpretation*, Sage Publications, Thousand Oaks, CA.

Zald, M. N. (1996) 'More fragmentation? Unfinished business in linking the social sciences and the humanities', *Administrative Science Quarterly*, 41 (2) June: 251–61.

Notes

[1] Some research topics deal with movements on stock markets or foreign currency exchange rate markets or investment yields, to mention only a few such issues that do not or at least may not deal directly with the concerns of people as individuals.

[2] Social scientists sometimes seem to be haunted by the term scientific method and this concern goes back a long time. Medawar (1986) claimed that 'There is indeed no such thing as "the" scientific method. A scientist uses a very great variety of exploratory stratagems.' There is also the interesting remark of T. S. Eliot's (1920) which is said to have been based on a comment originally made by Aristotle in ancient times: 'There is no method but to be very intelligent.'

[3] However, positivists are sometimes very unkind about phenomenologists who can at time feel very defensive about their approach to research.

[4] The issue here is, of course, to do with delivering a convincing argument. Positivistic research techniques when applied to issues concerning people as individuals or to organisations are frequently unable to produce convincing arguments. Questionnaires and their resulting averages just cannot reach the depth of understanding required.

[5] Pierre Auguste Renoir, 1841–1919.

[6] It is most important to keep Boland's comment in mind as the term phenomenology is often used capriciously and inaccurately.

[7] It is not clear whether the polls failed to predict the result of the 1992 election in the UK because they were not able to detect the fact that a large number of people misrepresented themselves to the pollsters or whether the mathematics behind the analysis failed.

[8] Positivist researchers sometimes use qualitative data which is analysed by such methods as content analysis which requires that the manifest content categories be counted.

7

The Research Process

It is an extraordinary era in which we live. It is altogether new. The world has seen nothing like it before. I will not pretend, nobody can pretend, to discern the end. But everyone knows that the age is remarkable for scientific research … The ancients saw nothing like it. The moderns have seen nothing like it till the present generation.

(Daniel Webster, 1847, cited in J. Davidson and W. Rees-Mogg, *The Great Reckoning,* 1993)

Science works with concepts of averages which are far too general to do justice to the subjective variety of an individual life.

(C. G. Jung, *Memories, Dreams, Reflections,* 1995)

7.1 Introduction

As already stated in an earlier chapter, one of the most important aspects of research in business and management studies, is to decide on an appropriate starting point for the research and on the conceptual framework or research strategy within which the evidence will be collected and analysed. It is also important, especially in business and management studies, to decide if the evidence that is collected will be of an essentially qualitative or quantitative nature and whether a positivistic or a phenomenological approach will be taken.

Once these decisions have been made, carrying out the actual research project can then be fairly routine work[1] using well-established methods for analysing and interpreting the evidence that is collected (Remenyi and Williams, 1993). However, deciding on where to start, and establishing the basic framework for the research, is frequently challenging and can present considerable difficulties (Boland and Hirschheim, 1987; Galliers and Land, 1987; Galliers, 1992; Gable, 1994). This is particularly the case for novice researchers, not because these issues represent great intellectual challenges, but rather because these methodological issues are not always well understood and have frequently been poorly articulated by academics in business and management studies.[2]

But what is the nature of this system or framework of knowledge development and how is it derived? In this chapter some of the basic issues involved in the early stages of constructing a research project are discussed, and, in particular the relationship between the collection of evidence and the formulation of a theoretical framework or model within which to interpret the results of the study are examined. Although this chapter retains a positivistic outlook, some of the ideas presented also have a direct bearing on the phenomenological approach to research.

7.2 Kinds of Evidence, Ways of Thinking

It is especially important to understand and to contrast two kinds of evidence that may be collected in business and management studies – *qualitative* and *quantitative* – and it is useful to consider two kinds of thinking[3] which are referred to here as *narrative* and *paradigmatic*.[4] Qualitative evidence uses words to describe situations, individuals, or circumstances surrounding a phenomenon, while quantitative evidence uses numbers usually in the form of counts or measurements to attempt to give precision to a set of observations. Narrative thinking involves the construction of a consistent and convincing description of the processes or subject matter under investigation, paradigmatic thinking involves the construction of laws, rules or conjectures from which it is hoped deductions can be made that can be tested against the evidence or observations. The construction of a narrative will depend largely, but not exclusively, on the qualitative information that is available, while the construction of paradigms will generally depend on both qualitative and quantitative evidence. Of course the construction of a narrative is an art and not a science, and thus sometimes the researcher will find him or herself drawing on quantitative evidence for a narrative. Paradigmatic thinking, on the other hand, which will be illustrated below with an example from Einstein, can sometimes be based on qualitative evidence.

7.2.1 A Fine Dividing Line

Many authors would define paradigmatic thinking (Kuhn, 1962; Baker, 1993) in a way that would include much of what is referred to as narrative thinking. The notion of paradigmatic thinking is used here in a more specific, and therefore more limited way than that sometimes held by others (Baker, 1993). None the less it is difficult to trace the dividing line between these two ideas. According to Czarniawska (1997):

> Any attempt to trace the dividing line between narrative and scientific knowledge[5] in texts regarded as representing one of the two kinds of knowledge, soon reveals that 'science' is closer to 'narrative' than one might think. There is an abundance of stories and metaphors in scientific texts, while folk tales and fiction build on facts and sometimes even play with formal logic. Thus many works in the humanities and social sciences suggest a rapprochement between the two kinds of knowledge and consequently between the two types of text.

None the less, the distinction is both useful and important. Indeed the narrative form of thought is, if not essential, then of the utmost importance in facilitating the shifts described by Kuhn (1962) from one paradigm to another.

It is possible to regard narrative thought and paradigmatic thought as two poles of a continuum along which ideas are refined from descriptive generalisations to quite specific statements of relationships.[6] However, it could be argued that these two types of thinking are fundamentally different and distinct so there is a discontinuity between the two polarities. For example, Newton's theory of gravity, couched in formal mathematical terms, provides the paradigm. But this was derived from a narrative process which, in simple terms, followed from the realisation that the falling of an apple from a tree is governed by the same processes whereby the moon constantly falls towards the earth. The equivalence of these two, apparently different phenomena, represents the narrative which led to the development of the paradigm.

7.3   From Primary Narrative to Paradigm

The transition from narrative to paradigm can be described in five distinct steps, each of which requires a different type of approach. The first three steps are predominantly narrative, while the last two steps are essentially paradigmatic. These steps are displayed diagrammatically in Figure 7.1.

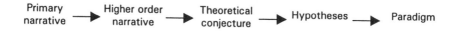

Figure 7.1   *The progression from narrative thinking to paradigmatic thinking*

The process illustrated in Figure 7.1 lies at the heart of any academic research activity for a masters or doctorate degree. It is through this process that already known and understood knowledge, derived from the literature and from other sources such as empirical evidence, is developed creatively and converted into new ideas, concepts and relationships which may in turn be developed into new theories.

Each of these ideas, concepts, relationships and theories should be tested in some way before the research can be recognised as a new contribution of value to the body of knowledge.

7.3.1   Narrative analysis

The most difficult part of the transition process from primary narrative to paradigm or scientific statement often lies in the first two steps in Figure 7.1 leading to the theoretical conjecture. In Figure 7.2 the types of procedures required are described in more detail. Of course, this is one of the more creative aspects of a research degree and researchers should not limit their thinking by adhering too strictly to any given method but should rather be open to a high degree of flexibility and creativity in their approach.

Figure 7.2 indicates that the primary narrative should be closely examined or 'trawled' for relevant concepts. In this context a concept may be defined as an idea or notion derived from one or more specific instances. A concept is formed in the mind through the creative process of imagination. Having established the underlying concepts the higher order narrative referred to in Figure 7.1 is developed. In turn this document is closely examined to understand the relationships between the concepts and in particular the way in which the concepts relate to or influence each other.

Some researchers will be able to develop the concepts and the relationships at the same time, while other researchers will require two or even more passes over

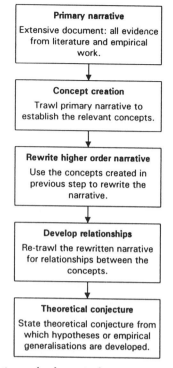

Figure 7.2 *From the narrative to the theoretical conjecture*

the material. However, the development of the theoretical conjecture is of critical importance to the research, and therefore its formulation should not be rushed. If necessary the researcher should go over the primary narrative again and again in order to come to grips with the concepts and relationships. In this regard the advice of Jung (1995) is worthy of attention: 'In general one must guard against theoretical assumptions. Today they may be valid, to-morrow it may be the turn of other assumptions.' While progress in research requires and depends on the formulation of theoretical conjectures they should always be regarded as provisional and should not prevent the researcher from changing or further developing his or her ideas.

But also as pointed out by Czarniawska (1997) narrative knowledge and paradigmatic knowledge, which lead to the formulation of the theoretical conjecture, are closely related irrespective of whether the research is based on a qualitative or a quantitative approach. In some cases an appropriate theoretical conjecture will be obvious but on other occasions this will not be the case.

Creativity in research lies primarily in the narrative mode of thinking which dominates the five steps which are described in Figure 7.2, and it is mostly here that new discoveries are made and new ideas are developed. But of course establishing a theoretical conjecture is not the same as adding to the body of knowledge. By reformulating narrative accounts of the world in terms of paradigmatic laws and theories, however, one is then able to do several important things.

First of all, the relatively loose[7] narrative description is developed into a tighter paradigmatic framework that enables the consistency of the ideas expressed in the narrative to be more rigorously tested. Secondly, by a process of measuring and quantifying observations made on the environment and suggested by the theory, it is possible to begin to make predictions that can then be tested. Finally, the paradigms so developed may be used to make predictions about what will happen in other situations, making it possible to discover both the extent to which the paradigmatic theory is of general applicability and the areas in which it breaks down and requires further elaboration. Of course this is a positivistic view which would not always be shared by a phenomenologist, who might not be interested in generalisation in this sense.

7.4   The Point of Departure

Frequently the researcher will be working in a field of study within which there are clear, unambiguous and agreed observations, concepts and theories that can be identified by reference to the published literature. The first step is therefore to review the published literature. However, as mentioned in Chapter 5, it is possible that a researcher might wish to investigate an entirely new aspect of a subject on which little has been published, perhaps based on ideas or thoughts that arise from the research worker's own experiences in organisations. In such cases various empirical techniques such as grounded theory (Glaser and Strauss, 1967), or concept discovery (Martin and Turner, 1986) can be used to establish the point of departure. Whichever technique is used, the information generated in this way will form what is referred to as the *primary narrative*. This was done in a dissertation on *Strategic Information Systems: Current Practice and Guidelines* (Remenyi, 1990a) where a grounded theory approach was applied to 55 interviews in order to develop a primary narrative.

7.4.1   Definition of a Primary Narrative

A primary narrative may be defined as a detailed textual description of the phenomenon being studied, based either on the literature or on a combination of the literature and other evidence collected through a grounded theory approach. Typically a primary narrative will be a lengthy document that tells the story of the phenomenon being researched in a comprehensive way. It is from this story that the theory will ultimately be distilled.

In the dissertation mentioned above (Remenyi, 1990a) the primary narrative was some 200 pages long. The research problem in this instance was how to establish a set of viable guidelines for the formulation and implementation of strategic information systems. Research in this field, where there is little established theory, required the use of an induction-based, grounded theory approach, in which evidence was collected from practitioners, in order to supplement the literature review as the first step in establishing the primary narrative. In keeping with the methods described above, the evidence collected in this way was used to discover useful ideas, concepts and relationships as part of the process of developing a theoretical conjecture. An example of this process is discussed later in this chapter.

7.5 Qualitative versus Quantitative Evidence

Once the starting point has been established and the general research questions to be addressed have been identified, it is necessary to decide on the kind of evidence to be collected and how it should be analysed. The evidence can be essentially qualitative, for example verbal testimony, written reports, and audio or visual images which may be collected in the form of loosely structured interviews. Alternatively the evidence can be essentially quantitative, for example in the form of measurements of the physical properties or performance of the subject of interest. Clearly these two approaches are not mutually exclusive and research scientists will often work with both, so that qualitative and quantitative research techniques are sometimes viewed as the ends of a continuum (Gable, 1994). Researchers should be ready to draw on both kinds of evidence in order to address different aspects of a research problem.

Irrespective of whether the emphasis of the research is quantitative or qualitative it is necessary to produce a primary narrative if a theoretical conjecture is to be competently developed. Figure 7.3 shows how both these types of evidence may be used to develop the primary narrative.

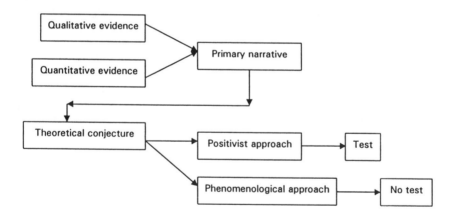

Figure 7.3 *The importance of the primary narrative and the theoretical conjecture*

Figure 7.3 also shows how a positivistic approach to research leads to an analytical test of hypotheses or empirical generalisations, whereas a phenomenological approach may, or most probably will not lead to a formal test of the hypothesis. A phenomenological approach will generally be judged by the extent to which it provides a convincing synthesis of the available information.

In the dissertation referred to above (Remenyi, 1990a) both qualitative and quantitative evidence was collected and approximately equal effort was expended on the collection and analysis of qualitative evidence through structured interviews and quantitative evidence collected through the use of self-completion, postal questionnaires.

7.6   Evidence Collection

The collection of qualitative evidence usually involves interviews, which may be structured to a greater or lesser degree, in order to collect complex information about a particular aspect of the subject, for example about how firms formulate and implement a strategy. Because research into strategic issues requires the collection of complex evidence concerning 'Why?', 'How?', and 'Who?', simple survey techniques are not appropriate and the researcher has to engage in a more sophisticated research strategy. One of the most frequently used strategies to examine complex research questions in business and management research is the case study approach.

Of course case study research is a broad concept and evidence may be collected in a variety of ways, ranging from structured interviews to active participation with the subjects being studied. However in the context of business and management research, structured interviews frequently constitute a major part of the case study research protocol (Bell, 1993; Kasanen and Suomi, 1987; Yin, 1989, 1993). During such an interview the informants will typically provide a large amount of information that will be recorded. In such circumstances, care should taken to recognise and acknowledge bias. Bias, deriving from cultural preconceptions and conventional wisdom, is always present both in the researcher (Vitalari, 1985) and the researched and thus permeates the whole research process. Bias may be in the form of perceptual distortions or deceptions (Brittain-White, 1985). Although it cannot be totally eradicated, bias may be minimised by the use of such techniques as triangulation. The issue of bias is especially important if the research is based on a single case study and any attempt to generalise from such a study should be treated cautiously. As Gould observes (1980b: 225):

> Science is not an objective, truth-directed machine, but a quintessentially human activity, affected by passions, hopes, and cultural biases. Cultural traditions of thought strongly influence scientific theories, often directing lines of speculation, especially ... when virtually no data exist to constrain either imagination or prejudice.

During the course of a research project a large amount of information may be collected and incorporated into the primary narrative. The problem now is how to use this to construct a *higher order narrative*. A high order narrative may be defined as a description which both captures the essential aspects of the information represented in the primary narrative but provides a more parsimonious conceptual framework in which the ideas, concepts and relationships have been defined. The high order narrative will form the basis of the theoretical conjecture that will eventually be presented, reduced to hypotheses or empirical generalisations, and rigorously tested.

Collecting quantitative evidence either involves the gathering of statistics using secondary sources of evidence such as published financial reports, or primary sources of evidence such as measurements or data collected directly about organisations in order to establish facts. The facts might be the size of the information systems or the amount of money invested in information technology, for example. Especially to a positivist, quantitative evidence appears to be both precise and hard because it deals with numbers. However, it is important to remember that the value of the numbers depends both upon the assumptions under which they were produced or calculated and on the way in which they are interpreted.

7.7   Narrative Thinking

The social sciences have often attempted to develop methodologies that take the natural sciences as their role model. Since the natural sciences have, over many centuries, developed precise, quantitative, well-defined paradigmatic laws and theories, the role of the narrative is played down in the attempt to formulate equivalent paradigmatic theories based on quantitative evidence.

Unfortunately the importance of narrative thinking, the construction of a consistent story[8] that describes the essential features of the problem under investigation, is frequently not recognised or at least not openly acknowledged in academic research. However, the relationship between narrative thinking and paradigmatic thinking lies at the heart of modern research into business and management and social science in general and it will be useful to examine these in relation to other sciences.

7.7.1   *Language and the Free Invention of the Mind*

When the grand theories that have been developed in the natural sciences over the last few hundred years are examined – such as Newton's theory of gravity; Maxwell's theory of electromagnetism; Einstein's theory of space and time (special relativity) and his theory of gravity (general relativity); the atomic theory of quantum mechanics; and Darwin's theory of evolution in its modern formulation – one is presented with theories that, provided one grants their premise, enable precise and testable deductions to be made as to the way in which the world behaves. Once the theories have been developed and tested they can be applied to the environment. The difficulty, however, lies in the reverse process. Starting from observations made on the environment, how can the laws be discovered or inferred, from which by a process of deduction, observations can be explained? Einstein (1954) states the problem quite explicitly: 'I am convinced that ... the concepts which arise in our thought and in our linguistic expression are all, when viewed logically, the free creations of thought which cannot inductively be gained from sense experiences.' Nevertheless, he acknowledges that such freely invented theories should be constrained in some way if one is not to be swamped in a multitude of competing theories, and argues: 'The justification (truth content) of the system rests in the proof of usefulness of the resulting theorems on the basis of the sense experiences, where the relations of the latter to the former can only be comprehended intuitively' (Einstein, 1936). The challenge to modern science, according to Einstein, is that there is no strict, well-defined inductive method that can lead to the formulation of laws and theories, i.e. the creation of knowledge, but rather that these are 'the free invention of the human mind' (Einstein, 1936). The issue then is how to go about inventing theories and discovering paradigms.

7.7.2 Mental Models

The distinctive feature of *Homo sapiens* lies in our ability to develop, change, and, where necessary, discard, mental models of the way in which the world functions. Indeed, given this flexibility and power, it is almost inevitable that one has, perhaps in the genes, not only the ability to construct such models but a compulsion to do so. This is seen directly and clearly not only in *Genesis*, for example, but in the myths and fables of all pre-literate societies. Young children delight in stories (some would say narrative models) and in imaginative play that enables them to construct their own models of the world. An extreme example of this sort of behaviour is reported by Sachs (1986) who discusses the case of a woman in whom the ability to think paradigmatically was wholly lacking while she was still able fully to comprehend the world when presented in the form of narratives. He describes her condition as follows:

> Rebecca made clear, by concrete illustrations, by her own self, the two wholly different, wholly separate forms of thought and mind, 'paradigmatic' and 'narrative' ... And though equally natural and native to the expanding human mind, the narrative comes first, has spiritual priority. Very young children love and demand stories, and can understand complex matters presented as stories, when their powers of comprehending general concepts, paradigms, are almost non-existent. It is this narrative or symbolic power which gives a sense of the world – a concrete reality in the imaginative form of symbol or story – when abstract thought can provide nothing at all. A child follows the Bible before he follows Euclid. Not because the Bible is simpler (the reverse might be said), but because it is cast in a symbolic and narrative mode.

From the above it appears that there are at least two different thought processes involved, one of which facilitates narrative thinking and the other paradigmatic thinking. It is interesting to note how Einstein as quoted by Holton (1978) makes reference to different types of thinking when he describes the drive to understand the world:

> Man seeks to form for himself in whatever manner is suitable for him, a simplified and lucid image of the world, and so to overcome the world of experience by striving to replace it to some extent by this image. This is what the painter does, and the poet, the speculative philosopher, the natural scientist, each in his own way. Into this image and its formation, he places the centre of gravity of his emotional life, in order to attain the peace and serenity that he cannot find within the narrow confines of swirling personal experience.

Popper, too (1975), is quite explicit about the importance of narrative thinking in the development of scientific theories:

> It is one of the novelties of human language that it encourages story telling and thus creative imagination. Scientific discovery is akin to explanatory story telling, to myth making and to poetic imagination.

Moszkowski (1970) quotes Einstein as describing the process of scientific discovery:

> In every true searcher of Nature there is a kind of religious reverence; for he finds it impossible to imagine that he is the first to have thought out the exceedingly delicate threads that connect

his perceptions. The aspect of knowledge which has not yet been laid bare gives the investigator a feeling akin to that experienced by a child who seeks to grasp the masterly way in which elders manipulate things.

7.7.3   Imagination and Models

When one attempts to develop models of the world, these start as narrative descriptions within which the imagination is allowed to range freely and widely over many possibilities. This can be illustrated more precisely with reference to Darwin's theory of evolution. When Darwin sailed on the *Beagle* the idea that the natural world had evolved was not widely accepted (Gould, 1980a). The problem was to provide a theory to explain this process of evolution. In the tropical world the fauna and flora were quite different from those in the temperate regions and this impressed itself greatly on Darwin, reinforcing in his mind the extraordinary diversity and flexibility of the natural world. On visiting the Galapagos Islands he discovered many new species of finches, now named after him. Believing, correctly, that in spite of their diversity in form and function they had all originally evolved from a single species that colonised the island in remote times, he began to develop a narrative theory to account for the process by which they had evolved. After many years he arrived at his now celebrated theory in which a combination of random variation and survival of the individuals best adapted to their environment leads to selection for particular traits and eventually the appearance of new species.

Darwin developed his theory entirely narratively without the use of any formal paradigms. Although Darwin's theory can be thought of as presenting a new paradigm for evolution, its essentially narrative casting left it open to criticism. His fellow positivistic scientists claimed that the theory was not falsifiable, and it was argued that a sufficiently imaginative person could always find a Darwinian explanation for any observed trait. During his lifetime Darwin's theory remained firmly rooted in its narrative structure.

As a second example one might consider Einstein's general theory of relativity. The theory seeks to explain the nature of the force of gravity whose mathematical formulation, in the hands of Newton, was one of the cornerstones of nineteenth-century physics. The problem was that Newton's theory, while providing a set of mathematical laws which could be used to describe the motion of planets around the sun, or the speed at which an apple falls to the ground, gave no hint as to the essential nature of the gravitational force. It did describe this 'thing' which bound the earth to the sun, the apple to the earth. The key to the development of Einstein's theory lay in the realisation that gravitational forces and the forces produced when a body is accelerated are in a specific, but rather profound, sense, equivalent. For the present discussion, however, it is sufficient to note how Einstein, as described by Ishiwara (1977), came to this realisation: 'I was sitting in a chair in the patent office at Bern when all of a sudden a thought occurred to me: "If a person falls freely he will not feel his own weight." I was startled. This simple thought made a deep impression on me. It impelled me toward a theory of gravitation.' The theory was born not out of the solution to complex mathematical equations, but simply out of a reflection of what would happen if one had been falling freely in space.

The strength then of narrative thinking is that it encourages the free play of the imagination. The narratives are of course constrained by currently accepted knowledge and theories. When Einstein imagined what would happen to him if he were falling in free space he was assuming the validity of Galileo's observation that bodies of different weights fall at the same speeds. Nevertheless, he might equally have wondered what would happen if Galileo had been wrong and this would have led him to develop an alternative narrative.

7.7.4   The Researcher's Natural Aptitude

It is interesting to note that some individuals have much greater skill at narrative thinking than others and it is perhaps this skill which attracts them to qualitative rather than to quantitative research. For others, narrative thinking on its own may be too difficult or there may not be sufficient structure to allow them to proceed with confidence. Various quantitative techniques, such as content analysis (Berelson, 1980) and correspondence analysis (Greenacre, 1984), may be used to help develop a higher order narrative based on the primary narrative before this is in turn developed into theoretical conjectures.

However, content analysis is quintessentially quantitative in character, as it counts the number of occurrences of different concepts which have been mentioned during the evidence-collection process. Some researchers argue that a purely narrative description is just as good a groundwork for a theoretical conjecture. In the dissertation referred to above (Remenyi, 1990a) content analysis was used as an aid to establishing the critical variables which were needed to formulate the theoretical conjecture, and correspondence analysis was used subsequently to corroborate the basic theoretical framework.

Correspondence analysis is a statistical technique using multivariate analysis that produces a perceptual map, indicating the association between different notions or concepts. Table 7.1 shows the results of the content analysis prepared for the dissertation on strategic information systems. The importance of the list in Table 7.1 is that it suggests that there are 16 key concepts which arise out of the primary narrative which need to be incorporated in the higher order narrative and perhaps ultimately in the theoretical conjecture.

In the research referred to above, only the nine top-scoring concepts were eventually incorporated into the theoretical conjecture. This is because it was felt that these were the most important issues that had been brought to the researcher's attention, and also that more than nine issues might make the theoretical conjecture unwieldy and difficult to understand.

7.8   Honing a Paradigm

According to the positivistic tradition, narrative thinking on its own does not generally yield sufficient rigour for what one now regards as modern science and it is usually necessary to progress beyond the purely narrative presentation. Darwin's theory illustrates this well. Although his *Origin of Species* may be

Table 7.1   *Content analysis used to assist in the development of the higher order narrative into a theoretical conjecture*

	Concepts	Abbrev.	Total	%	Accum. %
1	Industry drivers	ID	72	18	18
2	Corporate strategy	CS	47	12	30
3	Critical success factors	CF	43	11	41
4	Training	T	41	10	51
5	Staff communications	SC	38	9	60
6	Support facilities	SF	33	8	68
7	Cost justification	CJ	27	7	75
8	User reaction	UR	26	5	80
9	Vendor selection	VS	20	4	84
10	I s management	IS	11	4	88
11	Risk	R	9	3	91
12	Planning procedures	PP	8	3	94
13	Cash flow	CA	8	3	97
14	Case tools	CT	6	1	98
15	Central/decentralisation	CD	6	1	99
16	Organisational structure	OS	6	1	100
	Total scores		**401**		

regarded as having led to the formulation of a paradigm to describe the process of evolution, it was still firmly rooted in its essentially narrative structure. Following the rediscovery of Mendel's work and the development of modern genetics, one is now able to quantify in measurable terms, the various features of Darwin's theory such as fitness, inheritability, rates of mutation and population growth rates. It can now be said that if a certain trait in an individual has a certain inheritability and produces individuals with a certain degree of fitness relative to others, it will in a predictable period of time become the dominant trait in that population. In other words, one can subject Darwin's theory to much more stringent tests than were previously possible. One can now do more than simply argue (as Darwin did) that the validity of his theory follows from its consistent explanation of a large class of facts, but can make precise and testable predictions based on quantitative analysis of the theory.

It is equally true that many years elapsed between Einstein's reflections in the patent office and the development of his field equations and eventually the general theory of relativity which explains the nature of gravity in terms of the curvature of space–time brought about by the presence of massive bodies. However, in both cases, the narrative description can be seen as a necessary prelude to the formulation of the fully paradigmatic quantitative theory.

Medawar (1984) expresses this connection between the two modes of thought as follows:

> Scientific theories ... begin as imaginative constructions. They begin, if you like, as stories, and the purpose of the critical or rectifying episode in scientific reasoning is precisely to find out whether or not these stories are stories about real life.

The role then of paradigms in the positivist world is to take the diverse narratives and to identify the common features that run through them, to synthesise the many thoughts into a few more powerful explanations.[9] This is expressed by Whitehead (1928):

> To see what is general in what is particular and what is permanent in what is transitory is the aim of scientific thought. In the eye of science, the fall of an apple, the motion of a planet round a sun, and the clinging of the atmosphere to the earth are all seen as examples of the law of gravity. This possibility of disentangling the most complex evanescent circumstances into various examples of permanent laws is the controlling idea of modern thought.

The next step in the research process is to use the higher order narrative to develop a theoretical conjecture. If the narrative has been constructed with this in mind then the theoretical conjecture can simply be the formalisation of the conclusions of the higher order narrative in such a way that it will be relatively easy to produce empirical generalisations or hypotheses for the purposes of further testing.

At this stage a substantial amount of research has been done and it is clearly the case that if this has been conducted well, a major contribution could have been added to the body of knowledge and, in some cases, may be sufficient for a research degree.

However a theoretical conjecture alone will usually not be enough to allow the theory to be applied in a practical and useful way which is sufficient for a masters or doctorate degree. For this to happen paradigmatic thinking is needed which requires that the theoretical conjecture be developed into one or more hypotheses or empirical generalisations. Once this has been done quantitative evidence is required that can allow the hypotheses to be rigorously tested using appropriate statistical techniques.

7.9   A Model of the Qualitative Research Process

Figure 7.4 shows the different steps in the qualitative research process from literature review to hypothesis development.

7.10   The Range of Evidence

In the process of conducting a research project it is important to decide on the range of evidence that will be collected; for example, it is necessary to decide on the number of case studies or structured interviews that are required to ensure that the findings are valid and significant. Research workers who espouse the

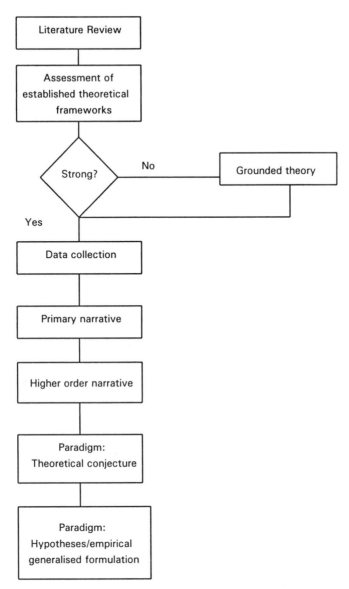

Figure 7.4 *The steps involved in qualitative research*

qualitative or narrative approach to research sometimes argue that a single case study is enough to enable the researcher to add to the body of knowledge. This single case study approach has interesting implications. Clearly the discovery of a phenomenon as a result of a single case study may add significantly to the body of knowledge simply because it is established that this phenomenon exists. But in most cases the objective of the research is, *inter alia*, to be able to comment on what one expects to find under a variety of different circumstances. If the single case study was comprehensive enough, and especially if it had a longitudinal dimension, then it could satisfy all the requirements. However, in most instances the findings of a single case study are usually only regarded as suggestive and thus only as a lead to investigate further a new phenomenon under a variety of conditions. A broader exercise, including multiple case studies or evidence from a variety of sources, is more likely to lead to interesting generalisations about the phenomenon under investigation. Nevertheless, it may be that in certain cases the construction of a significant narrative from a single case study source is as much as can be done and the development of a rigorous generalisable paradigm is either unimportant or irrelevant.

7.11 Quantitative Research and Paradigms

The qualitative approach to research and especially the construction of narrative descriptions of the problem under investigation needs to be contrasted with quantitative evidence collection and analysis techniques, which will generally be treated paradigmatically. In the latter case one is often working within a well-defined theoretical framework, derived from the literature or from previous research, and one starts with a clear underlying expectation of how a particular phenomenon is likely to behave. This understanding will have been formalised into a model or paradigm. If the model has been obtained from previous research then it is likely to have been developed by the qualitative research process described above and labelled narrative thinking.

For quantitative research it is usually obvious what evidence is required and this evidence may usually be collected within a tight structure. Thus in the social sciences in general and information systems research in particular, evidence collection often involves the use of a questionnaire. Evidence so collected may sometimes be far less 'hard' (that is less precise or less certain as a measure of what the researcher is actually seeking) than it appears and may thus undermine the validity and reliability of the quantitative research approach being used. Information systems research, especially information systems management research that relies exclusively on evidence obtained from techniques such as questionnaires, should be regarded with particular circumspection.

Quantitative research is so well established in the psyche of the research community that many researchers do not accept the validity of any other kind of research. It is then claimed that qualitative research is 'soft' research, and therefore can only add little to the real body of knowledge except in so far as it suggests new directions for quantitative or hard research. This view is no longer acceptable. It is important to remember, as Darwin shows, that qualitative research and the construction of narratives that embrace the essential features of the problem can contribute substantially to the body of knowledge even if one hopes eventually to go beyond this with the use of quantitative techniques.

It is also important to understand the part played by models in paradigmatic research. Baran and Sweezy (1970) describe the role of models as follows:

> Scientific understanding proceeds by way of constructing and analysing 'models' of the segments or aspects of reality under study. The purpose of these models is not to give a mirror image of reality, not to include all its elements in their exact sizes and proportions, but rather to single out and make available for intensive investigation those elements which are decisive. We

abstract from non-essentials, we blot out the unimportant to get an unobstructed view of the important, we magnify in order to improve the range and accuracy of our observation. A model is, and must be, unrealistic in the sense in which the word is most commonly used. Nevertheless, and in a sense paradoxically, if it is a good model it provides the key to understanding reality.

This is an excellent description of the nature and role of models in helping to understand the world. What it perhaps omits to say is exactly what is the process of deciding what to include and what to exclude, which aspects of the situation being modelled are important and which are not.

7.11.1 A Model of the Quantitative Research Process

Figure 7.5 shows the steps required in quantitative research. Note that it follows a similar pattern to qualitative research except that it omits the development of the primary and the higher order narratives as these techniques are not necessary, given that the researcher will already have a model or paradigm with which to work.

It is essential to understand that the model or the paradigm with which the quantitative researcher is working is constructed by reference to the narrative account of what are regarded as the essential features of the process under investigation. Thus even in quantitative research the narrative is an indispensable part of the formulation of the model or paradigm, as well as the development of any hypotheses from which conclusions may be drawn. If the tests conducted on the model by means of the hypotheses fail, the researcher will refer back to the narrative that has been retained and a new model and hypotheses can be created for further testing. Alternatively if the tests have failed catastrophically the researcher may discard the higher order narrative and re-use the primary narrative to try to reconstruct a new higher order narrative.

In the research referred to above (Remenyi, 1990a), the evidence collected as a result of the questionnaire was used to test and validate the empirical generalisations. A variety of standard statistical techniques was used, and as a result of these tests minor modifications were made to the empirical generalisations and the underlying theoretical conjecture. These modifications brought the theory closer into line with the evidence supplied by the questionnaires distributed to the larger sample. Consequently the changes made as a result of these tests made a contribution to generalising the theoretical conjecture.

7.12 Summary and Conclusion

Although this chapter has argued strongly that the non-paradigmatic aspect of research encourages creativity and is indeed important, and that ultimately it underpins all research, it is not the intention to minimise the power or critical importance of quantitative research. Especially in so far as models need to be generalised to cover many situations or individuals, the role of quantitative[10] research is paramount. This is the case even when qualitative techniques for

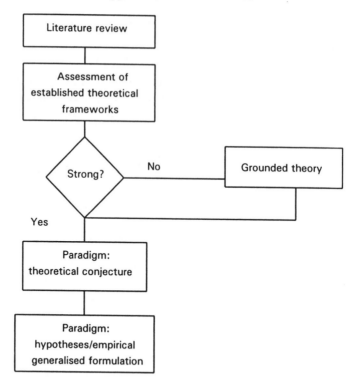

Figure 7.5   *Steps required in quantitative research*

evidence collection are being used. Thus even if a case study approach has been used to collect evidence, if the researcher wishes to claim that the results have a degree of generality then quantitative techniques for hypothesis testing will be essential.

A great deal has been written concerning various aspects of quantitative research (Snee, 1995; Whalen, 1994; Miller, 1994), including testing and validation of paradigmatic models and theories. This aspect of research is well understood and extensively utilised in business and management studies as well as the social sciences in general. Issues such as the design of experiments, the use of statistical techniques, both univariate and multivariate, can ensure that observations can be made and measures can be attributed to what are believed to be the causes. Much of the work associated with the quantitative research process and paradigmatic thinking is well established and can be relatively routinely applied. Although this requires considerable skill and expertise it does not rely on any great degree of creativity. In short, because the academic research community has employed quantitative research for hundreds of years, it is well understood and enjoys a high degree of acceptance and status.

On the other hand qualitative research has often been regarded as of secondary importance and of relatively less value (Gable, 1994). The purpose of this chapter is to suggest that both approaches to research are necessary and that each depends upon the other if significant and generalisable additions are to be made to the body of knowledge. It is hoped that this chapter will help to clarify the debate concerning these issues.

Finally the importance of qualitative evidence in the construction of narratives has been stressed. It has been suggested that in some respects qualitative research is more creative than quantitative research. Perhaps this is so because the latter is well established and its techniques and procedures are better understood and have been developed and refined to the extent that they may be relatively simply applied. However this view should not be seen as an attempt to minimise the importance of paradigmatic thinking, of quantitative evidence collection and of hypothesis testing in science. Without quantitative research smallpox would not have been eradicated, food production would have required the direct labour of an enormous percentage of the population and a man would not have walked on the moon. Indeed, the distinguishing feature of modern science is the formulation of laws, often mathematical, that capture essential features of a problem and allow predictions to be made into the future. Joseph Needham (1988) goes so far as to say that, 'Modern [as opposed to mediaeval or ancient] science is the mathematization of hypotheses about nature ... combined with rigorous experimentation.'

It is not always clear which research approach is the most appropriate. The above discussion suggests that multiple approaches to a research problem may lead to satisfactory results. In fact it is essential that the business and management studies community fully embraces the traditions of both quantitative and qualitative research and encourages their use in creative ways to answer the many interesting questions generated by the discipline.

Suggested Further Reading

Baker, J. (1993) *Paradigm – The Business of Discovering the Future*. Harper Business, New York.

Czarniawska, B. (1997) 'A four times told tale: combining narrative and scientific knowledge', *Organisation Studies*, 4 (1): 7–31.

Jacques, R. (1997) 'Classic review: the empire strikes out: Lyotard's postmodern condition and the need for a "necrology of knowledge"', *Organisation Studies*, 4 (1): 130–43.

Jung, C. G. (1995) *Memories, Dreams, Reflections*. Fontana Press, London.

Kallinikos, J. (1997) 'Classic review: science, knowledge and society: The postmodern condition revisited', *Organisation Studies*, 4 (1): 114–30.

Lee, B., Barua, A. and Whinston, A. B. (1997) 'Discovery and representation of casual relationships in MIS research: a methodological framework', *MIS Quarterly*, 21 (1) March: 109–36.

Runeson, G. (1997) 'The role of theory in construction management research: comment', *Construction Management and Economics*, 15 (3) May: 299–302.

Notes

[1] The research process itself should never be regarded as entirely routine as it always relies on the imagination and the creativity of the researcher. None the less the actual steps which are followed and the order in which they occur may often be done in a routine manner following well-established lines. This is the same idea as that expressed by Kuhn (1962) when he writes about 'puzzle solving' in normal science.

[2] It is sometimes thought surprising that there are still universities and business schools that do not devote resources to teaching research methodologies, and that, where the subject is taught, it is

generally oriented towards positivistic procedures, or concentrates on statistical methods largely borrowed from engineering and the physical sciences.

[3] The existence of the two different kinds of thinking is clear to anyone who reflects on the fact that some people have considerable difficulty with numbers, arithmetic and mathematics but are good at languages and vice versa. This is especially obvious when considering the development of children during their early schooldays. Some take to mathematics naturally while other struggle with the subject. Some children seem to be able to spell with no difficulty while others have extreme problems.

[4] Although there is no difficulty with the word paradigm in general usage, there is some controversy about the use of the word among researchers.

> Kuhn himself used the paradigm concept in no less than 21 different ways consistent with three broad senses of the term: (1) as a complete view of reality, or a way of seeing; (2) as relating to the social organisation of science in terms of schools of thought connected with particular kinds of scientific achievements, and (3) as relating to the concrete use of different kinds of tools and texts for the process of scientific puzzle solving. (Morgan, 1980)

[5] Czarniawska's (1997) expression 'scientific knowledge' is a direct equivalent to the way the term paradigm is used in this chapter. It is also interesting that she uses the term 'stories'. The issue of the role of stories in the creation of knowledge is addressed at some length in Chapter 9.

[6] The relationships between the variables in the paradigm could be expressed in mathematical symbols or they could be expressed pictorially or graphically as was demonstrated in Figure 5.2 in Chapter 5.

[7] The term loose is used here to contrast how the narrative may appear relative to the formal presentation of mathematics or traditional positivistic science. Of course, from the perspective of a phenomenologist a description may be written in rigorous terms. However the results of such phenomenological research may well not be reducible to what Czarniawska (1997) calls scientific knowledge or what is called a paradigm in this chapter.

[8] Story telling is an essential part of any research effort but it plays a particularly important role in business and management studies. This issue will be elaborated upon in Chapter 10 on Case Study Research.

[9] In this context the authors are using the term paradigm in an especially idiosyncratic way, to refer specifically to a quantifiable or near quantifiable model of the phenomenon being studied. If we take a broader view of the word paradigm, then these comments would of course also apply to a phenomenologist.

[10] In this specific context the terms quantitative research and positivistic research are synonymous.

8

Collecting Empirical Data

Get your facts first, and then you can distort them as much as you please.

(Mark Twain, cited in Rudyard Kipling, *From Sea to Sea*, 1899)

8.1   Introduction

This chapter discusses various approaches to the acquisition of appropriate evidence which will be used to support or refute the theory or hypothesis developed by the researcher. Attention is also given to the way in which a researcher should approach the collection of evidence for a masters or doctorate degree in business and management studies. The chapter further considers the role of evidence in formulating a theory, as happens when using a grounded theory approach.

8.2   Why Collect Empirical Evidence?

The essence of empirical research is that it relies on the production and accumulation of evidence to support its findings, and the collection of evidence is the corner-stone of this research strategy. However, evidence is never collected in a theoretical vacuum and it is important to see the collection of evidence in relation to the underlying concepts and paradigms which will shape and determine the evidence that is collected. Sometimes empirical research projects fail because the researcher has been unable to obtain the kind of evidence that is required in order to develop a theory or to test an already established one. A common reason for this is that the researcher cannot gain access to the appropriate organisations or people, or because the evidence required does not exist.

8.2.1   Refuting or Accepting a Theory

In order to decide if a hypothesis or empirical generalisation should be accepted or rejected, many research projects depend on the collection of evidence. Depending on the nature of the evidence the decision may be made using standard statistical tests, such as the χ^2 or the t-test, or, less rigorously, in a more interpretative way simply by considering average or mean values and their standard deviations or by plotting suitable graphs or frequency distributions.[1] This is essentially a positivistic approach to research and the techniques and tools available are well understood and frequently used.

8.2.2   Creating a Theory

A research project may, on the other hand, require evidence to be collected before a theoretical conjecture can be established and subsequently expressed in terms of hypotheses and empirical generalisations which can be formally tested, perhaps at a later date in another project. An important technique for doing this is grounded theory (Glaser and Strauss, 1967) in which the researcher uses empirical evidence to establish directly the variables, concepts and relationships which will be combined in the theory.

8.2.3   Understanding and Explaining Phenomena

From the phenomenological point of view, evidence may also be collected in a less instrumental way in order to understand and explain phenomena. Here the researcher will have a much more open view as to how the evidence will be treated and what the evidence might reveal. Phenomenological evidence collection is considered in more detail in Chapter 6.

8.3   Approaches to Collecting Evidence

Several approaches to the collection of evidence are open to the researcher and the approach chosen will depend upon the research strategy and tactics being followed as well as the research question itself. For a masters or doctorate degree in business and management studies the research question is unlikely to be simply a matter of how much, i.e. establishing quantities of some sort, and thus the researcher usually has to probe the more difficult issues of how, why and when. A combination of evidence collection approaches is frequently required in one research project in order to support an eclectic research strategy.

8.3.1   Primary and Secondary Sources

Evidence may be collected from primary or secondary sources. Evidence is collected from a primary source when the researcher goes directly to the originator of the evidence. An example would be an interview with the managing director about the organisation's marketing strategy. A secondary source would be information that is already published or available indirectly, so in the previous example the researcher might be able to obtain essentially the same information from the annual financial statements. Thus secondary sources of evidence are available in some intermediate form, such as share market prices, interest and exchange rates, and are not delivered personally to the researcher. A number of databases containing useful evidence and information for research in business and management studies are available and the Internet and the World Wide Web are rapidly increasing in importance as sources of secondary evidence in business and management research.

8.3.2   Direct and Remote Evidence Collection

Primary evidence may be collected either directly or remotely. In direct evidence collection the researcher interviews the informant personally and records the responses directly. In contrast, remote evidence collection would correspond to a situation in which the informant completes a questionnaire without the interviewer being present. There are of course intermediate approaches, for example where the researcher interviews the informant on the telephone or engages in a dialogue with him or her by E-mail.

8.4   Valid and Reliable Evidence

One of the important challenges the researcher faces is to ensure, to the best of his or her ability, that the evidence that is being collected is valid and reliable. Often, in business and management research, individuals will plead a special case. An important method of ensuring that the evidence is valid and reliable is to use 'triangulation' which Loveridge (1990: 18) defines as 'using multiple methods to capture a sense of reality'. The word triangulation is taken from surveying in which a region is divided into a series of triangles based on a line of known length so that accurate measurements of distances and directions may be made by the application of trigonometry. In business and management research the term triangulation refers to obtaining evidence from multiple sources to ensure that a biased view is not being obtained from one informant. The essence of triangulation[2] is to attempt to corroborate any evidence that is supplied either by speaking to another individual or by asking for documentation that will support the initial view.

8.5   The Starting Point

In the first instance the approach to evidence collection will depend upon the result of the literature review and the research question or problem which this reveals. As stated in Chapter 5, if there is a strong theoretical basis for the research then the researcher may derive hypotheses and empirical generalisations and begin directly to collect evidence in a structured way for the purposes of formal testing. Where this is the case the literature review should also suggest the type of analytical tools which should be used to test the evidence, and the research should follow established precedents in this respect unless there is good reason for doing otherwise.

However, if the literature review does not reveal a strong and generally accepted theoretical framework, as is frequently the case in business and management research, then a grounded theory approach is required. As discussed in Chapter 3, grounded theory is an inductive approach to theory discovery or generation which allows a researcher to analyse a situation and synthesise the findings in such a way that a plausible or convincing theoretical explanation of the situation is offered. When using grounded theory the collection of evidence may be unstructured and there is considerable scope for creativity.

8.6   Evidence for Formal Testing

The formal testing of hypotheses and empirical generalisations usually requires numerical evidence that will be analysed statistically. Sometimes it is relatively easy to obtain numerical evidence while on other occasions it is more difficult.

8.6.1   Numerical Evidence

Where the evidence involves objects or characteristics that are, or can be represented numerically, such as units produced or consumed, sales figures, wage rates, or accident occurrences, to mention only a few, the evidence can be summarised using statistical techniques such as those described in Chapter 11. Standard tests of significance can then be performed.

Here the key issues are to identify the evidence required and to prepare an appropriate measuring instrument such as discussed in Chapter 12. The researcher needs to be careful that valid, reliable and up-to-date evidence is being supplied. This may not be easy as many organisations are reluctant to make their evidence public and researchers may have to deal with 'gatekeepers' who may not be as co-operative as the researcher would wish.

8.6.2   Non-Numerical Evidence

Sometimes issues relating to attitudes or perceptions, such as market conditions or management performance, which are usually not expressed in numbers, need to be investigated. In these cases techniques such as content analysis may be used to convert qualitative evidence into numerical form so that standard statistical tests may be used in the analysis.

Converting qualitative evidence into a numerical form is problematical and relies on assumptions concerning the homogeneity of the responses since counting the frequency with which a particular opinion occurs implies that each occurrence of that opinion is given equal weight. While positivists recognise these problems it is accepted that there is no better way to deal with such evidence. In recent years a number of computer packages, such as NUD·IST and ATLAS/TI, have been developed to facilitate the analysis of qualitative evidence.

8.6.2.1   NUD·IST
A popular computer package for text analysis is QSR NUD·IST (Non-numerical Unstructured Data Indexing Searching and Theorising) which the NUD·IST manual describes as 'a computer package designed to aid users in handling non-

numerical and unstructured data in qualitative analysis. NUD·IST does this by supporting processes of indexing, searching and theorizing.' Packages such as NUD·IST and ATLAS/TI enable the user to take several documents and then index and link them in a structured way that facilitates further analysis. One highlights a particular block of text and creates a reference to this block of text under a suitable heading. The different headings can themselves then be linked in a structured way and the eventual structure both helps the user to develop a conceptual paradigm and to draw out the original sections of text referring to different aspects of the argument. While this approach to the analysis of text-based evidence and the development of a theory is often welcomed by positivists, phenomenologists generally recommend a more hermeneutic approach to the interpretation of such evidence. In other words, close attention is paid to the text and an analysis is constructed after categories have been allowed to emerge from the textual material.

8.7   Evidence for Creating a Theory

When using a grounded theory approach, the researcher needs to draw on all available sources of evidence including quantitative and qualitative evidence from both primary and secondary sources. The emphasis is on first obtaining a broad view of the situation and then exploring key issues arising from the research question in depth.

At this level the evidence-collection process is creative, making it difficult to provide specific and detailed guidelines. However there are some general principles which may be helpful.

1   Both primary and secondary sources of evidence should be consulted.
2   Evidence should be collected from as many different informants as possible.
3   Informants should where possible represent a spectrum of individuals who may have quite different perspectives on the problem under consideration. It is important, for example, to involve both top management and relatively junior staff.
4   All evidence should be corroborated by means of some form of triangulation.

In the process of theory creation the evidence provides the raw material but it is the researcher's imagination and creative talents which lead to the development and formulation of the theory. While the evidence is critical, the way in which it is perceived, analysed, synthesised and understood will determine the extent to which it is used effectively.

8.8   Understanding and Explaining Phenomena

Evidence collection within the non-positivistic or phenomenological research paradigm is discussed in Chapter 6. The central issue is that the evidence will not be used for hypothesis testing and will less frequently be used for the purposes of creating a theory. Rather, the evidence will be collected in order to achieve a greater level of understanding or to develop an explanation of the observed phenomena.

8.9   Evidence Collection: Planning and Design

Whatever research strategy and tactics are used, the quality of the evidence will be improved if the research is well planned and designed.

8.9.1   The Basic Plan

As mentioned above, preparing a plan for the collection of evidence begins with the issues raised in the literature review and is directly influenced by the research problem or question. If the design is taken from other earlier work then the question is how to elicit the evidence from the informants. Some of the questions that should be considered include:

1   How to obtain access? In particular, how will the researcher gain acceptance to/by the organisations required and not be seen as an inconvenience?
2   How to be introduced to the right people in the organisation? Specifically the researcher needs to find out who are the gatekeepers to the required evidence and the departments or sections within the organisation.
3   Does the researcher have to collect the evidence personally or can some of it be collected remotely, i.e. by using questionnaires?
4   What arrangements can be made for triangulation to ensure the integrity of the evidence?
5   What sources of secondary evidence can these organisations supply?
6   Can external triangulation by means of, say, a trade organisation, a bank or a trade union be obtained?

Each particular project will produce its own planning issues and the above simply indicates some of the basic issues that arise in initiating a planning activity.

8.9.2   Access to Informants

Sometimes researchers find it difficult to contact organisations directly. On such occasions the researcher may try to use an intermediary to arrange an introduction. Members of staff of the university or business school may sometimes be helpful. Management consultants may be prepared to collaborate with researchers and thus introduce them to the appropriate organisations. On other occasions the researcher will not be able to find a sympathetic gatekeeper and he or she will just have to try another organisation.

If the researcher offers to help with an in-house project or offers to provide the informants with a copy of the results of the research, this may improve access to organisations. Once the researcher has obtained access to one organisation it is sometimes possible to have a friendly informant help the researcher obtain access to another suitable organisation. This approach, which is also discussed in Chapter 11, is sometimes called 'snowballing'.

8.9.3   Direct Evidence Collection

When evidence is being collected directly the researcher should present him or herself to the friendly gatekeeper and arrange for that person to effect the necessary introductions.

The researcher should employ an open and relaxed approach but may also use an interview schedule to keep the discussion on track. Direct evidence collection allows the researcher to probe the informant for more information where this is appropriate, but the researcher needs to know when not to require further explanations if the informant appears to be uncomfortable or unwilling to supply such evidence. The golden rule is never to force the pace by trying to obtain more evidence than is naturally and comfortably offered.

8.9.4   Indirect Evidence Collection

Remote evidence collection does not involve direct contact between the researcher and the informant and the most commonly used approach is the use of questionnaires as discussed in Chapter 9. Sometimes videos are made of consumers and used for later study although this raises a number of ethical questions. Various electronic means may also be used to establish contact with informants. While telephone interviews may be regarded as a form of remote evidence collection, the interactive nature of telephone conversations puts it somewhere in between direct and indirect approaches. E-mail is a form of asynchronous communication and therefore closer to remote evidence collection The main drawback of remote evidence collection is that it is difficult, if not impossible, to probe the informant.

8.10   Using the Internet and the World Wide Web

The Internet is a collection of several million computers located around the world, which are connected by real-time data communications networks. These computers allow virtually instantaneous communication between subscribers at a low cost. In addition many subscribers, especially those located in academic institutions, can arrange to access on-line libraries, academic papers, articles and other works of interest directly from their computers. This vast quantity of information is to a large extent available free of charge to any subscriber to the Internet.

To make use of the Internet a researcher needs to have access to a computer with a modem and to an Internet service provider. Once this is established, the researcher can explore hundreds of millions of pages of information. Most academic institutions provide this facility to their research students and in some cases it is possible to set up a link between the student's home computer and the institution's network.

Although the Internet consists of a wide range of facilities, by far the most popular and most widely used today is the World Wide Web. This is essentially the graphical interface to the Internet and users will require a Web browser to be able to search for and manipulate information on the Web. The two most popular Web browsers at the time of writing are Netscape Navigator and Internet Explorer.

The World Wide Web is referenced through *pages* of information, which are accessed via a Universal Resource Locator (URL) or address. Anyone having an account with an Internet Service Provider (ISP) can create their own web pages. Within universities and other academic departments it is usual to have pages for each department and members of those departments can put relevant information on to the department's Web page. The home page generally provides an index with which the user can navigate through the information available in the university. Highlighted words, phrases and icons provide *links* to other pages or sites.

There are basically two ways to access information on the World Wide Web. The first, and by far the quickest, is to know the universal resource locator (URL). For example, to access the Surrey University home page the address http:/surrey.com is entered. If an address is not known then one of the many *search engines* available on the Web is used to specify the required category. One of the most popular search engines is Yahoo.

Many university libraries and academic journals make papers and articles available on the Web, making it a rich source of information for the business and management researcher. In effect a substantial amount of literature may be reviewed directly through the use of the Web. It may also be possible to pick up empirical evidence in this way and researchers may share evidence and experiences through the use of E-mail.

However one of the problems associated with the use of the Web is the fact that there are not yet any really hard and fast rules about how to cite references properly. As a general approach researchers should provide sufficient information about the Web site to enable another person to access the same information subsequently.

8.11 Summary and Conclusion

There are different types of evidence and many different approaches to its collection for research in business and management studies. It is important for the researcher to understand the full range of options available so that no important source of evidence is omitted from the research programme.

The selection of a particular approach to the collection of evidence depends on the chosen research strategy and the particular research question being investigated. It is important to set time aside to plan the way in which the evidence will be collected and how informants will be obtained if this phase of the research is to be completed successfully.

Suggested Further Reading

Barley, S. R. (1996) 'Technicians in the workplace: Ethnographic evidence for bringing work into organisation studies', *Administrative Science Quarterly*, 41 (3) September: 404–41.

Easterby-Smith, M. Thorpe, R. and Leow, A. (1994) *Management Research: An Introduction*. Sage Publications, London.

Gofton, K. (1997) 'In search of a better way', *Marketing*, Marketing Guide Supplement, 13 March: vii–ix.

Heath, R. P. (1997) 'Seeing is believing', *American Demographics*, Tools Supplement, March: 4–9.

Kahn, R. L. and Canell, C. F. (1961) *The Dynamics of Interviewing*. Wiley, New York.

Knights, D. and McCabe, D. (1997) 'How would you measure something like that? Quality in a retail bank', *Journal of Management Studies*, 34 (3) May: 371–88.

Krueger, R. A. (1994) *Focus Groups: A Practical Guide for Applied Research*. Second Edn, Sage Publications, Newbury Park, CA.

Mark, R. (1996), *Research Made Simple*. Sage Publications, Thousand Oaks, CA.

Millar, R. and Hargie, O. (1991) *Professional Interviewing*. Routledge, London.

Morgan, D. L. (1993) *Successful Focus Groups: Advancing the State of the Art*. Sage Focus Editions, vol. 156.

Morse, J. (ed.) (1993) *Critical Issues in Qualitative Research Methods*. Sage Publications, Thousand Oaks, CA.

Moustakas, C. (1994) *Phenomenological Research Methods*. Sage Publications, Thousand Oaks, CA.

Payne, S. L. (1951) *The Art of Asking Questions*. Princeton University Press, Princeton, NJ.

Reason, P. (1988) *Human Inquiry in Action*. Sage Publications, London.

Sapsford, R. and Jupp, V. (1996) *Data Collection and Analysis*. Sage Publications, London.

Schuman, H. and Presser, S. (1981) *Questions and Answers in Attitude Surveys: Experiments on Question Form, Wording and Context*. Sage Publications, Newbury Park, CA.

Seror, A. C. (1996) 'Action research for international information technology transfer: A methodology and a network model', *Technovation*, 16 (8) August: 421–9.

Steier, F. (ed.) (1991) *Research and Reflexivity*. Sage Publications, London.

Notes

[1] A rather colourful description of this is 'eye-balling' the data.

[2] The term triangulation may also be used with respect to research tactics. In this case two or three different tactics are used and the researcher hopes that each of these will provide a similar result. Sometimes the term triangulation is used in the context of theories. Here the notion is that the researcher might use different theories to explain or understand a particular phenomenon.

9

The Questionnaire or Measuring Instrument

It is a good morning exercise for a research scientist to discard a pet hypothesis every day before breakfast. It keeps him young.

(Konrad Lorenz, *On Aggression*, 1963)

9.1   Introduction

This chapter discusses the use of questionnaires as measuring instruments in business and management research for the collection of evidence. It examines different type of questions, measurement considerations and questionnaire structure as well as the administration of a questionnaire survey. In the social sciences the term instrument, rather than questionnaire, is often used. Questionnaires can vary from being highly unstructured to being very structured.

In conducting questionnaire-based research there are three inter-related activities to consider, namely, the design of the questionnaire, the method by which the questionnaire is to be administered, and the choice of sample. It is not possible to provide a definitive way of doing questionnaire research. Each study will have peculiarities that make it unique.

This chapter discusses the key issues that have to be taken into account when collecting evidence through questionnaires.

9.2   Questionnaire Research

The main purpose of questionnaire research is to obtain information that cannot be easily observed or that is not already available in written or computerised form. Evidence from the questionnaire survey is then used for one or more of the following purposes – description, explanation, hypothesis testing.

The types of information sought when surveying individuals or objects, such as firms, usually include evidence on demographic and socio-economic variables. In addition, depending on the study, evidence may be sought on opinions or beliefs related to behaviours, experiences, activities and attitudes.

The philosophical attitude that underpins the use of a questionnaire for the purposes of evidence collection is that there exists a generalisable public opinion that is available to be tested through the use of these sorts of questions. This view is not totally accepted by all researchers. Marsh (1989: 269) points out that this assumes that: 'there is a general social will which is open to empirical discovery'. She questions whether it makes sense to aggregate, by the use of simple averages, a series of different and sometimes radical views. Jung (1995: 17) made the same point by noting that, 'Science works with concepts of averages which are far too general to do justice to the subjective variety of an individual life.' Clearly this objection has to be taken seriously as it represents a major concern about the validity of evidence which is collected through the use of questionnaires or measuring instruments. None the less the techniques described in this chapter are commonly used in business and management research at the masters and doctoral level and a thorough understanding of how this type of research is conducted is essential.

9.2.1   Questionnaire Design

The point of departure in the design of a questionnaire is a clearly defined problem and explicit terms of reference and objectives. There should be no ambiguity about the purpose of the study. That is, it is important to be clear about the phenomenon to be described and/or explained and the hypotheses to be tested. Once this has been achieved it will be possible to identify and define the concepts to be measured and how these are to be measured. At this point the first draft of the questionnaire can be designed.

The draft questionnaire is the product of qualitative research. This qualitative component is likely to include a search of the academic, trade and professional literature as well as the use of interviews, brainstorming and focus groups. Internalisation of how others have undertaken questionnaire–based research can be beneficial. The use of existing questionnaires or questions from them is permissible but it is important to establish where the copyright for these resides. Books by Beardon et al. (1993), Robinson and Shaver (1973) and Robinson et al. (1991) provide a source of established questionnaires together with information concerning their application, validity and reliability.

The above activities combine to influence decisions on the choice, wording and number of questions, as well as the nature of the questions, whether they are open or closed, the level at which to measure and the type of analysis to perform on the evidence. The layout of the questionnaire, its length and the time it takes to complete also has to be considered.

9.2.2   Pre-testing the Questionnaire

Pre-testing of the questionnaire needs to be undertaken before it is finally administered. The objective of such pre-testing is to detect possible shortcomings in the design and administration of the questionnaire (Emory and Cooper, 1991).

Approaches to pre-testing can be fairly informal where one consults friends, colleagues, experts and people of diverse opinions, or it could be more formal, involving a pilot study which is a replication, on a small scale, of the main study.

Pre-testing provides the opportunity to assess such things as the clarity of the instructions and questions, the covering letter, the comprehensiveness of the codes/categories chosen for the pre-coded questions, the quality of the evidence and the ability to perform meaningful analysis of the evidence obtained. The time taken to complete the questionnaire, the likely response rate, the cost of administering the questionnaire, which questions are irrelevant, which are relevant, and whether questions on key issues have been overlooked can also be assessed at this time.

There are no hard and fast rules concerning the design of a pre-testing exercise. Ideally the research candidate should attempt to ensure that the measuring instrument is pre-tested as far as possible. However there are a number of limiting constraints in the world of the masters or doctoral student, especially with regards to time and money which preclude the use of extensive pre-testing or a pilot study. None the less, for any substantial research study enough pre-testing needs to be done to provide the assurance that no serious problems are likely to be encountered in the main study.

9.2.3   Types of Questions

Questions can be either open ended or closed ended. The type of question chosen has implications for the type of evidence that can be obtained and therefore on the method of analysis of the evidence.

9.2.3.1   Open-ended Questions

Open-ended questions are typically used in exploratory studies where the researcher is not in a position or is not willing to pre-specify the response categories. The response is in the form of a narrative which has to be analysed qualitatively, but which may be converted into a form suitable for quantitative analysis. A popular technique for analysing narrative is content analysis. More recent advances have led to computer-aided methods becoming available to support qualitative evidence analysis. Software tools such as ATLAS/TI and NUD·IST are increasingly being used to assist in qualitative evidence analysis. A description of computer-aided methods and the corresponding software can be found in Weitzman and Miles (1995).

A disadvantage of open-ended questions is that they require the respondent to be articulate and willing to spend time on giving a full answer to the question. Questions of this type are typically used in personal interview surveys involving small samples.

9.2.3.2   Closed-ended Questions

Closed-ended questions are typically used in quantitative studies. The assumption is that detailed knowledge is available on the attributes of interest and therefore it is possible to pre-specify the categories of response. These can be pre-coded so as to be amenable to computer analysis using statistical packages such as SPSS and SAS, which are two of the more popular systems used to analyse questionnaire-based evidence.

Closed-ended questions are difficult to design but simplify the collection and analysis of evidence making the task of the respondent easier. Such questions are typically used in studies involving large samples.

9.3   Measurement Considerations

Questionnaire responses can be quantified by assigning numbers to the responses according to a given set of rules. This is what is understood by measurement. Measurement can be made at four levels: nominal, ordinal, interval and ratio. Variables that are measured at the nominal or ordinal level are often referred to as qualitative (or categorical) variables, while those variables measured at the interval or ratio level are referred to as quantitative variables.

9.3.1   Nominal Scales

Nominal scales, which are the least sophisticated level of measurement, are used to place individuals or objects into categories with respect to some characteristic. For example individuals can be classified on gender, or firms can be classified according to the industry in which they operate. Numbers can be assigned to categories, '1' for male and '2' for female, for example, while for the industry classification the SIC codes may be used to classify the responding firms. These numbers are no more than labels, and no ordering is implied. Therefore, the only meaningful quantitative analysis that can be performed on such evidence is to determine the frequency (or relative frequency) of occurrence of responses in each of the categories.

Question 1 in Part A of the questionnaire in Appendix B uses a typical nominal scale.

9.3.2   Ordinal Scales

Ordinal scales, the next step up in sophistication, are used when the respondent is asked for responses in the form of a rank ordering. While the evidence is again put into categories, the numbers assigned indicate the ordering of the categories. However, while there is order in the numbers assigned, the intervals between the numbers have no meaning. For example, a respondent is asked to rank order his or her preferences for say seven motor cars with a rank of '1' corresponding to the most preferred car and a rank of '7' corresponding to the least preferred car. The respondent gives Car A a ranking of '1', and Car G a ranking of '2'. It is therefore now known that Car A is preferred to Car G, but it is not known by how much more it is preferred, since the difference in the ranks does not provide information on the extent of the preference. Such scales do allow for more sophisticated analysis than is possible when using a nominal scale and it is meaningful to compute such non-parametric statistics as the median, quartiles and rank correlations.

9.3.3   Interval Scales

Interval scales possess the property that the difference between the numbers on the scale can be interpreted meaningfully. An example of an interval scale is the temperature scale where an increase of 1 degree Fahrenheit has the same meaning anywhere on the scale (but 100 degrees Fahrenheit is not twice as hot as 50 degrees Fahrenheit, i.e. ratios are not meaningful).

Evidence based on interval scales can be analysed by virtually the full range of statistical procedures such as the mean, standard deviation and Pearson's correlation coefficient.

Rating scales, such as the questions in Part B in Appendix B, are strictly speaking ordinal. However, in practice, especially in the marketing area, these are treated as being measured at the interval level. In fact, the more categories (say 1 to 9 as opposed to 1 to 5) that are used for the rating scale, the more likely the properties of 'true' interval variables will be exhibited by the rating scale (see Bryman and Cramer, 1992: 66). The questions in Part B of the questionnaire in Appendix B use a typical interval scale.

9.3.4   Ratio Scales

Ratio scales provide the highest level of measurement. For these scales the numbers on the scale possess all the properties of the nominal, ordinal and interval scales and in addition ratios of numbers on the scale have meaning.

Ratio evidence is the highest level of evidence and can be analysed by the full range of statistical techniques. For example, an increase of £1,000 in income has the same meaning whether it is an increase on £15,000 or on £30,000 and an income of £30,000 is twice an income of £15,000. Thus the scale possesses both the interval and the ratio properties. Further, it is possible to convert income evidence into a categorical scale by creating income categories, say 0 to 10,000, 10,001 to 20,000 and so on.

In general when collecting evidence one should always strive to measure at the highest level possible. In practice, however, surveys generally make most use of evidence at the nominal, ordinal and interval levels.

Questions 2, 3, 4 and 5 in Part A of the questionnaire in Appendix B are examples of ratio scales.

9.4   Structure of the Questionnaire

Questionnaires usually comprise sections. Typically these sections provide information through asking questions of the following types.

9.4.1   Background Questions

Background questions provide demographic and socio-economic information on the individual or firm. At the individual level these include evidence on age, gender, occupation, income, education level, while at the level of the firm it can include evidence on the industry in which the firm operates, the number of staff employed, their turnover and position in the company. All of Part A of the questionnaire in Appendix B collects typical background information.

9.4.2   Attitudinal Questions

Attitudinal questions provide information on the strength of feeling or opinion about objects, issues, activities and interests. For example, one may wish to determine the attitude of respondents towards privatisation, their jobs, management, internal marketing, computer-assisted learning techniques and so on. Attitudes can be measured through the use of single-item rating scales and multiple-items rating scales. Single-item scales are applied when a single question is used to measure the construct of interest whereas multiple-items scales are applied when two or more questions are used to measure the construct.

The most popular approach is to use a 5, 7 or 9 point rating scale such as the scale used in the sample questionnaire in Appendix B.

9.4.2.1 Single-item Scale

To what extent do you agree with the following statement?		
1	I expect ease of access for users to computing facilities to be excellent.	1 2 3 4 5 6 7 8 9

Box A   *Single-item scale*

The above question is unlikely to provide a sufficient working definition of the perception of the organisation's attitude towards its information systems. A better measure would be provided by a multiple-item scale comprising a number of questions relating to information systems each measured on a 9-point rating scale; in practice a minimum of three items is normally required. For each respondent, the respondent's scores for these questions are summed to obtain a measure of how the organisation is perceived with respect to this dimension. The technique described here is referred to as the technique of summated rating or more popularly as Likert's scaling. Typically Likert scales comprise a minimum of three questions to a maximum of 30 or so.

9.4.2.2 Multiple-item scale

For multiple-item scales the assumption of interval level measurement is more tenable. As can be seen from the three-items used to measure attitudes towards the information systems in Box B, the three-item Likert scale will total a minimum of 3 and a maximum of 27, so that the range is 25.

To what extent do you agree with the following statements?		
1	I expect users to be willing to find time to learn the system.	1 2 3 4 5 6 7 8 9
2	I expect the use of a service level agreement.	1 2 3 4 5 6 7 8 9
3	I expect the Information Systems Department to monitor its performance in delivering a service to the users.	1 2 3 4 5 6 7 8 9

Box B   *Multiple-item scale*

9.4.3 Activity and Usage Questions

Activity and usage questions provide information on the extent of involvement in activities such as water sports, radio listening, surfing the Internet and so on.

9.4.4   Sequencing of Questions

It is generally agreed that the best way in which to order the questions is to place general questions first, followed by specific questions and then attitudinal questions. Hard questions should be placed fairly early and interspersed with easy questions. Further, there is a need to ensure that the questions are structured in such a way that the respondent will find it easy to answer questions within a topic, and also not be burdened with questions that are irrelevant to him or her.

9.4.5   Funnel Questions

Funnel questions are used to provide a sequence within a particular topic using a set of questions in which each question is related to the previous question with successive questions having a progressively narrower focus.

9.4.6   Filter Questions

Filter questions are used to exclude the respondent from being asked questions that are irrelevant to him or her.

9.5   Questionnaire Administration

Methods for collecting evidence fall into two categories: self-completion and interviews. Self-completion methods include mailed and computerised questionnaires. Interview methods include personal or face-to-face interviews, and telephone interviews. There are advantages and disadvantages associated with each of the methods.

9.5.1   Mailed Questionnaires

Mailed questionnaires allow one to obtain a large sample with wide coverage, at a relatively low cost. It allows the respondent to complete the questionnaire in his or her own time, thereby ensuring that the responses are free from possible interviewer influence.

Questionnaires are mailed to a predetermined set of respondents with a covering letter informing the recipient of the nature of the study, its importance, what it will be used for, the time taken to complete the questionnaire, the date by which the questionnaire should be returned and the benefits to be gained from participating. It will invariably guarantee anonymity to the respondent and offer incentives such as a copy of the final report. A good covering letter can contribute significantly to increasing the response rate.

This method requires the questionnaire to be highly structured, with questions being predominantly closed-ended. The questionnaire should be simple to complete and not too lengthy, preferably not taking more than 20 minutes to complete. These factors are also important determinants of the response rate.

Response rates achieved for this type of survey are, in general, lower than for other survey methods. For a large survey, a response rate of 60 per cent is seen to be exemplary. Response rates as low as 1 per cent have been reported.

9.5.2   Computer-Administered Questionnaires

Computer-administered questionnaires are increasingly being administered electronically across the network through the use of E-mail or the Internet. The merits of this approach include its relative low cost, the ease with which it can be administered, elimination of interviewer bias, and the opportunity to do instantaneous evidence collection and analysis. Disadvantages of this approach include the sample being restricted to users of the network and the complexities of designing and programming the questionnaire, which is likely to require considerable time and money.

9.5.3   Telephone Interview Questionnaires

Telephone interview questionnaires are a low-cost form of personal interviewing that can be used to obtain information quickly. Costs are more than for mailed questionnaires but less than for personal interview questionnaires. It is possibly the most used method at present. Administration of this approach is relatively easy when compared to the use of face-to-face interviews, and as a consequence interview bias is less of a problem.

Despite most households having telephones, a sizeable number have unlisted numbers – in excess of 60 per cent in some areas. Omission of these from the sampling frame can result in serious response bias error. This problem has, to a large extent, been overcome by the use of random digit dialling.

It is important that the interviewee be convinced that the approach is genuine and that the interview will be short. The latter requires that the questions be brief, simple and focused. If open-ended questions are used, it is strongly advised that such questions do not exceed fifteen words and that the interviewee not be expected to give lengthy answers. For closed-ended questions the number of pre-coded options presented to the interviewee should not exceed five and these should in no way be ambiguous.

Response rates for telephone interviews are typically in the range from 35 per cent to 75 per cent.

9.5.4   Personal Interview Questionnaires

Personal interview questionnaires require a face-to-face conversation between interviewer and interviewee. Approaches can vary from being very informal to being very formal. In the former case the interviewer is given the freedom to interact freely with the interviewee. The questions are open ended and the interviewer is free to change the wording of questions and to add questions. At the other extreme there is a set of predetermined questions which is presented in pre-coded form, thereby ensuring that the answers to the questions are recorded in a standardised form across the sample.

This approach can be expensive in terms of interviewing time and travelling costs, as well as in terms of the time it takes to complete the whole process. There is the time needed to gain access to the informants, the need for training of the interviewers, the co-ordination and supervision of the fieldwork, and the time per interview which, typically, can take between 45 and 90 minutes. Each of the above incur monetary costs.

Thus, this approach is unlikely to be used with large samples where mailed or telephone questionnaires are probably more practical. Other problems associated with this approach include the lack of anonymity which could result in the interviewees not giving honest answers or giving socially desirable answers, thereby contributing to increased response bias.

There are many advantages associated with this approach which can, depending on the situation under investigation, outweigh its relatively high cost. It provides an opportunity to probe complex issues in a relaxed atmosphere. In such cases it is essential that use be made of suitably trained interviewers so that a quality response can result. Further, the interviewer is able to record additional pieces of information concerning the behaviour of the interviewee, which may be of assistance in subsequent analysis and interpretation of the interview evidence. Provided a large enough number of interviewers are used the evidence can be obtained quickly. Response rates are higher than for other approaches, typically between 50 and 80 per cent.

9.6   A Checklist for Using Questionnaires

The following is a step-by-step guide to conducting a survey in a firm.

Define objectives   Accurately define the purposes and objectives of the survey. Define the main research problem and its sub-problems if any. These should be stated as the survey's terms of reference.

Collect evidence   Decide how the evidence will be collected, i.e. personal interview, mail, computer, telephone, etc. Coding, entering and checking of evidence is also an issue here. How missing values and outliers are to be handled needs also to be considered.

Determine sample size and sample frame   Identify the list or lists that will provide the sample to be studied. Calculate the response rate and then use this to decide on the required sample size. The mathematics required for this is discussed in Chapter 12.

Produce questions   From the literature identify the key issues and potential questions and then form focus groups of six to ten informants to identify the key issues to be addressed by the survey and from these develop a list of appropriate questions.

Questionnaire layout   Having decided what questions to include, draft a questionnaire including the selection of an appropriate scale, structure, layout, length and wording.

Conduct a pre-test   Perform a pre-test using the questionnaire to determine initial responses. If a pilot study is used this may encompass between 50 or so individuals.

Revise the questionnaire   Using the results of the pre-test and or pilot study, revise the questionnaire so that it focuses more closely on the key issues.

Distribute measuring instrument   Distribute the finalised questionnaire or measuring instrument to the chosen respondents. Each respondent should be notified of the date by which the completed questionnaire is to be returned. Ensure that an appropriate covering letter is attached.

Collect results   The completed questionnaires should be collected and carefully vetted. It may be possible to discard partially complete questionnaires in favour of complete ones, depending on the response rate achieved.

Edit and code results   The results of the questionnaires should be coded appropriately, in order to make analysis and interpretation easier. Sometimes some editing has to be performed.

Analyse and interpret   The coded results should be analysed to determine the overall results of the survey. Careful analysis will reveal whether the survey was successful.

9.7   Summary and Conclusion

Questionnaire design is an art and invariably results in economic considerations forcing the researchers to sacrifice what they ideally require for what is practical in terms of the time and money available. It should be accepted that no survey is perfect. The key to a successful survey is the care taken in carrying out the time-consuming and costly preparatory work. This includes tasks such as clearly defining the purpose and objectives of the study, the running of focus groups, analysing transcripts of the focus group meetings, conducting fairly open-ended interviews with appropriate persons, and the development and thorough pilot testing of the questionnaire. Also there is the need to ensure that the sample is representative and of credible size.

Suggested Further Reading

Beardon, W. O. Netermeyer, R. G. and Mobley, M. F. (1993) *Handbook of Marketing Scales.* Sage Publications, London.

Briggs, C. (1986) *Learning How to Ask.* Cambridge University Press, Cambridge.

Fink, A. and Kosecoff, J. (1985) *How to Conduct Surveys: A Step-by-Step Guide.* Sage Publications, Newbury Park, CA.

Oppenheim, A. N. (1966) *Questionnaire Design and Attitude Measurement.* Gower, New York.

Robinson, J. P. and Shaver, P. R. (1973) *Measures of Social Psychological Attitudes.* Ann Arbor: University of Michigan Institute for Social Research.

Robinson, J. P., Shaver, P. R. and Wrightman, L. S. (1991) *Measures of Personality and Social Psychological Attitudes.* Ann Arbor: University of Michigan Institute for Social Research, Survey Research Centre.

10

The Case Study

It is a capital mistake to theorise before you have all the evidence. It biases the judgement.

(Spoken by Sherlock Holmes in *A Study in Scarlet*, by Sir Arthur Conan Doyle, 1892)

Perfection of means and confusion of goals seem – in my opinion – to characterise our age.

(A. Einstein, *Out of My Later Years*, 1950)

10.1 Introduction

This chapter introduces the use of the case study in business and management studies. It considers the case study as pedagogy, as an evidence-collection approach and as a separate research tactic in its own right for masters and doctoral degrees. The case study is an especially important research tactic and its use is on the increase for both masters and doctoral dissertations. Its importance is partly due to the fact that it may be used in a number of different ways that accommodate the complexity which is often an inherent part of the business and management research process.

10.2 Case Studies in Business and Management

Case studies contribute in important ways to our knowledge. They arise out of a need to understand and explain complex phenomena. Case studies allow the student or the researcher to retain a more holistic perspective than can be easily achieved through other approaches to cross-sectional or longitudinal studies. They allow for the meaningful exploration of the characteristics of real-life events, such as the managerial process, maturation of industries or power struggles in organisations.

However, the term case study is used in three distinctly different contexts to describe three different ways in which it can be used. Firstly, the case study can be used as a pedagogical device in the classroom, normally to explore and understand the way in which different situations and circumstances evolve over time. Secondly, a case study can be used to develop a framework for the collection of evidence, and finally it may be used as a research tactic.

10.3 Case Studies as Pedagogy

Although case studies have been an integral component of research in law[1] and medicine[2] for many years, they are relatively new in other fields of learning. In business and management studies the case study was pioneered by the Harvard Business School at the turn of the century and since then it has steadily grown in popularity.

The case study approach to teaching–learning is, in the view of Christensen and Hansen (1987), a pedagogy supporting a fundamental business education objective, which is to train people for professional business practice. By presenting situations that are often complex, ambiguous and even contradictory, the case study goes directly to the core of the skills required to cope with real-life situations in modern business. The case study is an excellent management development device as it encourages the blending of action and knowledge. Furthermore, the case study elicits a dynamic classroom discussion process, which, if correctly guided, leads to a learning process in which the participants discover new insights for themselves. This process of discovery, where individuals learn for themselves, may in fact be regarded as the most effective form of learning.

10.3.1 Action and Learning

The issue of action and learning is central to the use of case studies in teaching. Case studies can be discussed and analysed, and courses of action subsequently agreed in small and large groups, which is precisely how practical business issues are usually handled. The classroom and the syndicate group[3] provide the simulated business meetings in which the participant can learn the skills involved in listening to colleagues and assimilating their views, in presenting his or her own point of view, and in attempting to persuade others in the group to change their minds.

This action-oriented environment in which the case study is used also helps participants develop confidence in their judgement, as well as humility when colleagues do not accept their views.

10.3.2 Case Studies as a Teaching–Learning Device

From a teaching-learning point of view, a case study may be defined as a technique for presenting ideas, concepts or evidence, primarily for the purposes of stimulating discussion and debate.[4] Case studies can be used to address any subject area and range from single-page documents to lengthy tomes of dozens, scores or even hundreds of pages. It is one of the oldest ways of presenting ideas and concepts with its roots reaching back to earliest times when stories, sometimes in the form of myths and fables, were used as teaching–learning devices. The fact that the circumstances portrayed in these myths were fictitious, or at least exaggerated, did not in any way detract from their use as teaching-learning material. A teaching–learning case study need not be a complete or accurate rendition of a real-life situation, as its purpose is simply to present a framework for discussion and debate. Aesop's fable about the hare and the tortoise and Hans Christian Andersen's story of the ugly duckling are both case studies. In the business and management studies context, the case study called Robin Hood by Mintzburg et al. (1996) is a fable used to stimulate a discussion on the subject of stakeholders. In writing a case study the intention is to stimulate readers to identify the important issues and problems and to guide them in their search for a solution.

Teaching–learning case studies provide the pedagogical underpinning of the Masters of Business Administration at the Harvard Business School and other institutions of learning that advocate the Harvard approach, and the case study is the central, if not the only, learning activity. Virtually no use is made of other pedagogical approaches such as lectures or tutorials. In many other institutions this approach has much less support but may still be used to supplement other teaching–learning activities.

10.4 The Case Study in Research

In research the case study has two distinct features. Firstly, the case study can be used in establishing valid and reliable evidence. This evidence may be analysed from either a positivistic or a phenomenological perspective and subsequently synthesised in such a way as to produce a theoretical conjecture or even be used as evidence to support or contradict an already established theory. A positivistic analysis of a case study would include the collection of numerical evidence and the application of one or other technique of statistical inferential analysis. The techniques required for this type of analysis are discussed in Chapters 11 and 12. A non-positivistic analysis of a case study would require a holistic interpretation of the evidence because the focus is on learning about organisational process. The techniques required for this type of rigorous analysis are discussed in Chapter 6.

Secondly, the case study can be used as a vehicle for creating a story or narrative description of the situation being studied, in such a way that the resulting narrative represents a research finding in its own right and thus can be said to have added something of value to the body of knowledge. When used in this way the case study provides an explanation of the observed phenomena and demonstrates understanding of the subject of the investigation in its context and environment. Although this type of case study has to present a convincing argument, it does not necessarily have to be presented in quite the same rigorous way in which the case study is handled as an evidence-collection device for the positivist or the phenomenologist (see Section 10.11, p. 184). Used in this way the case study constitutes a comprehensive research tactic in its own right which may add something of value to the body of knowledge (Gummesson, 1991; Yin, 1989).

Figure 10.1 illustrates the two basic approaches to the use of a case study outlined above.

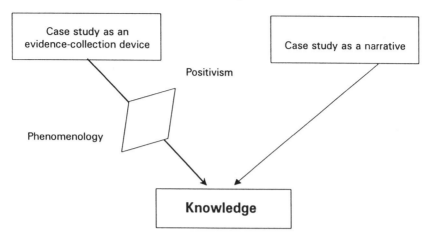

Figure 10.1   *The two basic approaches to the use of a case study as a research tactic*

10.4.1 Case Studies and Evidence Collection

Increasingly, case studies are being used by masters and doctoral students in business and management research as an evidence-collection approach which allows them to present a wide range of different sources of evidence and which does not in itself commit them to either a positivistic or a phenomenological strategy. Sometimes case studies are used as part of a grounded theory approach as described in Chapter 5, while on other occasions they are used in an attempt to validate an already established theory. In fact it is this versatility of the case study research approach that may be applied in a number of ways in a large number of situations that makes it so attractive to the business and management researcher.

10.4.2 Case Study Definition

It is important to establish a definition of a case study. As mentioned in Chapter 3, Yin (1989) regards a case study in much the same way that the natural scientist regards a laboratory experiment. According to Bell (1993) the case study approach is an umbrella term for a family of research methods having in common the decision to focus on an enquiry around a specific instance or event.

More formally, a case study may be defined as an empirical enquiry that *investigates a contemporary phenomenon within its real life context*, when *the boundaries between phenomenon and context are not clearly evident*, and in which *multiple sources of evidence are used* (Yin, 1989, 1993). In this context the case study is independent of the research strategy and thus may be used with positivistic orientated tools of analysis or with a more phenomenological approach.

The thinking behind the case study is that sometimes a full picture of the actual interaction of variables or events can only be obtained by looking carefully at a practical, real-life instance. The case study allows the researcher to concentrate on specific instances in an attempt to identify detailed interactive processes which may be crucial to understanding, but which are transparent to other research tactics such as the large-scale survey, focus groups, in-depth interviews, experiments and analysis of archival evidence.

However, there are other views of what constitutes a case study. According to Schramm (1971), the essence of a case study, i.e. the central tendency among all types of case study, is that it tries to illuminate a decision, or a set of decisions: why they were taken, how they were implemented, and with what result. This more focused view of the case study goes beyond the notion of it as an evidence-collection approach, as it also attempts to illustrate or explain the decisions and motivations that underlie the observed processes and is more suggestive of a phenomenological rather than a positivistic research strategy.

Whichever view is taken, it is the aim of the case study to provide a rich, multi-dimensional picture of the situation being studied. The case study can illustrate relationships, corporate-political issues and other patterns of influence in the particular context being researched.

10.4.3 Scope of the Case Study

As mentioned above, case studies are being increasingly used in business and management studies as an evidence-collection approach for several reasons including the fact that the scope of the case study is extensive, ranging from individuals, to business groups, to fiscal policy.

Cases concerning business decisions, processes, or organisational change have the inherent difficulty of knowing where to start and where to end. The question of the unit of analysis is critical to the research issues and needs to be related to the way the initial research questions have been defined. Thus, in a business context, the unit of analysis normally refers to the type of organisation that is to be studied, i.e. a firm or a division or a department or a project or a corporate function.

Confusion can arise in a number of ways when defining the unit of study. Time boundaries around the subject of the cases studied can often be a problem. However, time boundaries are essential as they help determine the limits of evidence collection and analysis. In addition, as most researchers want to compare their results with others, the unit of analysis, their definitions and time boundaries should not, where possible, be purely arbitrary or idiosyncratic. Thus in business and management studies it would be problematical if the researcher were to use case studies of an industrial conglomerate and a privately owned single-product firm for the purposes of comparison. It may also produce difficulties if the researcher attempts to compare two organisations in two different time periods – for example looking at the performance of supermarkets in the 1960s compared to supermarkets in the 1990s.

Although case studies may deal with unique situations, their results and conclusions may be compared, their characteristics studied and behaviour noted. It is important to bear in mind that most cases in business and management studies are, despite apparent simplicity, aggregates of complex organisational behaviour. From a research point of view, the case study approach emphasises the total or holistic situation as a combination of different factors and this orientation is most appropriate when dealing with the complexity of business and management research issues at masters and doctoral level.

The case study can focus on the description of the process, or sequence of events in which the behaviour occurs, the study of individual or group behaviour in its social setting. Comparison of cases can lead to the formulation of a theoretical conjecture, or in some circumstances the confirmation of hypotheses or empirical generalisations[5] (Yin, 1989). By using case studies it is possible to ascertain the number and variety of traits, qualities and habits combined in a particular instance. Case studies provide real-time information that can be as up to date as the researcher requires, making this approach ideal for contemporary issues and especially relevant in the fast-changing world of business and management studies.

Of course research tactics are not mutually exclusive. It is acceptable, for example, to have a survey within a case study. For example when studying how Peat Marwick Mclintock Management Consultants coped with their new office automation systems referred to as ICON, an opinion survey of the users was employed to help complete the evidence for the case study (Remenyi, 1990b). None the less, it is possible to identify some situations in which a specific approach or tactic, such as a case study, has a clear or distinct advantage over others. The case study comes into its own when a How?, Who? or Why? question is being asked about a contemporary set of events, over which the researcher has little or no control.

10.4.4 Depth of Enquiry of the Case Study

The depth of enquiry possible through the case study method is significantly greater than some other research methods such as surveys, focus groups, in-depth interviews, experiments and analysis of archival evidence. For example, although attempts are sometimes made to ascertain attitudes by means of questionnaires, the results are often unsatisfactory as one cannot do justice to the complexity of an attitude by ticking Yes or No or rating 1 to 5. Such methods of evidence collection that reduce responses to a scale of binary choices lose much of the richness of the circumstances or context being studied. As a general rule questionnaires alone are increasingly regarded as inadequate in providing the type of evidence for a doctorate in business and management studies. However at masters level a questionnaire approach by itself may be suitable.

The case study can go beyond a superficial evaluation of a point of view by obtaining information from an informant using multiple techniques, which can include the reasons for an opinion. For example, if a respondent is asked to rate a product on the grounds of quality in a case study context, he or she may reply with both a score on a pre-set scale and a list of explanations and or caveats qualifying the score. This additional information is clearly helpful to the researcher who may use it either to provide explanatory notes to illuminate the findings of the questionnaire, or as raw material for further content (Berelson, 1980), or correspondence analysis (Greenacre, 1984). Using content or correspondence analysis on evidence collected by means of a case study approach implies a positivistic strategy.

It would also be possible in a case study context to use hermeneutic approaches to analyse in-depth qualitative evidence that would be in keeping with a phenomenological strategy (Silverman, 1994).

10.4.5 Prejudices about the Case Study Method

Traditionally there have been prejudices against the case study method, especially in business and management research (Yin, 1989). It has been viewed as a less desirable form of empirical research methodology than surveys or experiments. Accusations include bias and a tendency to use incomplete evidence. But such views ignore the fact that bias can creep into any other research tactic, including experiments and surveys. Another accusation is that nothing can be deduced from a single case study. This ignores the fact that case studies, like experiments, can be generalisable and used to develop theoretical propositions, even if they do not represent a subsample of a particular population or universe. The researcher's goal is then to expand and generalise theories and not to enumerate frequencies.

Another objection is that case studies take too much time, are too expensive and generate too much documentation. Although case study research is frequently expensive at least in terms of the researcher's time, it is not absolutely necessary for case studies to be long, or for there to be excessive documentation. In fact a case study could be performed on a low budget using the telephone and without leaving the library[6] (Yin, 1989). It is not possible to lay down strict rules about the work required to produce a case study. However, many case studies in business and management research which are presented at masters level are between 15 and 30 pages in length and have been obtained by interviewing three or four informants in each organisation. At doctoral level, in general, the case studies tend to be longer, but not always so,[7] and the researcher would be expected to have collected evidence from more informants in each organisation. Of course the evidence collected from informants will have to have been triangulated by using other evidence sources and this is discussed later in this chapter.

Competent case study research, leading to real understanding and explanation in business and management, is difficult to perform. One of the main problems is that it is difficult to screen would-be case study researchers to ascertain their ability to do case studies. The subtle skills of listening and understanding the nuances in the evidence provided by the informants needed for undertaking case study research are not well understood. Therefore case study research is not an easy option and the business and management researcher needs to be prepared for a distinct challenge.

10.4.6 Case Studies and Experimental Logic

Because the case study follows the logic of an experiment,[8] rather than the logic of a survey, Yin (1989) argues that it is not necessary to replicate a case study many times.[9] Although case studies have some elements in common with experimental and observational science, Yin's claim deserves close examination. In the physical sciences there are two main groups of scientists, the theorists and the experimentalists.[10] A case study researcher is clearly closer to an experimentalist than a theorist, in that the case study requires the collection of empirical evidence. The researcher tries to get close to the phenomenon being studied in much the same way as a physical or life scientist does by collecting empirical evidence.

A single case study, like a single experiment, can establish the existence of a phenomenon, which in business studies may be adequate for the purposes of exploratory research.[11] Of course one case study, like one experiment, cannot provide sufficient evidence to be able to make robust generalisations[12] but in business studies this may not be essential. On the other hand, case studies differ from experiments in that case studies try to use passive observation and thus to leave unchanged by the enquiry the phenomenon being studied. While this is seldom possible, it is an objective of this evidence-collection tactic. Furthermore, as a passive observer (see Chapter 5) the case study researcher has little control over the situation being studied and this too makes it different from the experimental approach.

10.4.6.1 Rich and Complex Evidence

The logic of an experiment usually starts with the formulation of a theory followed by attempts to find evidence that either supports or refutes the theory. This may be done in case studies, although they may also be used as a vehicle for the collection of empirical evidence for the purposes of theory creation or theoretical conjecture development (Holland, 1993). Although the case study lends itself to evidence collection, it is most important to bear in mind Harre's observation (Harre, 1972) that 'we cannot describe the world in the absence of any prior understanding of it, in the absence of any theory'. It is important to note, however, that case studies are not designed primarily to measure the frequency of events, but rather to support or reject theoretical propositions or conjectures related to issues about the nature of the event, and in business studies this often relates to Who? Why? and How?

Much of the research work undertaken by academic business and management researchers specifically addresses issues such as who made what decisions, why these decisions were made and how these decisions were implemented, evaluated, terminated and so on. Therefore the case study evidence-collection approach is especially appropriate to this field of study.

10.4.7 Bias in the Case Study

Of course case studies are not perfectly objective due to the biases of both the supplier and the recipient of the information. Indeed, case studies are sometimes said to lack rigour and objectivity (McCutcheon and Meredith, 1993). The case study as an area of research is fraught with danger primarily due to the problem of subjectivity and bias. Not only are there problems in capturing evidence from witnesses, but there is also the problem of analysing or even reading evidence subjectively after it has been written down. Bias[13] is everywhere, but attempts may be made to minimise it, and clearly it is the primary function of the researcher to minimise or at least identify biases.

There are at least three difficulties in obtaining unbiased testimonials from observers:

1 the difficulties encountered by individuals in their being able to recall events accurately;
2 the difficulty individuals have in disclosing important feelings;
3 the suspicion individuals have about revealing information that might reflect poorly on themselves or their superiors.

Although all three of these difficulties exist in all areas of the social sciences, they are particularly noticeable in business and management studies, where an informant's career or even his or her job may be prejudiced by answering a particular question.

However, using multiple sources of evidence can substantially help to improve the validity and the reliability of the research. By studying every phase of the problem from as many aspects as possible, and by using different sources of evidence, the case study research strategy is a powerful approach in the hands of a skilled researcher.

Bias may be minimised by the process of triangulation. This involves a number of distinct activities. Firstly, multiple sources of evidence should be sought to support all important assertions. Thus if it is said in an interview that personal computers were first introduced in 1980, the researcher could ask to see minutes of the meeting approving their purchase. In some cases artefacts will also corroborate verbal evidence. In the case of personal computers, an inspection of the machines themselves could be used to date their acquisition – although it is rather unlikely that computers bought in 1980 will still be in use.[14] Secondly, corroborative evidence may be obtained from several different informants in the firm. The systems manager might say that the sales analysis system was a competitive information system. Discussions with, say, a general manager and a sales manager should then confirm this view. Opinions from outside the firm being studied, such as those of financial analysts and business journalists may also help reduce bias or at least put it in context. The final case study report may be sent to industry experts or to professional or trade associations for comment. From a practical perspective the more the evidence can be triangulated the greater the degree of validity it will be accorded. Of course, all of these techniques are time-consuming and expensive but they will help reduce bias.

Finally, on the issue of bias, it is naive to assert that any form of research,[15] or perhaps human activity generally, is without bias. Even in the physical and life sciences the researchers' bias is reflected in the subject researched, the experiments chosen, as well as the way the experiment is conducted. Thus bias cannot be totally eliminated but should be recognised and its implications acknowledged and accepted.

As the form of the case study is primarily narrative, accurate description is essential. All relevant facts need to be included, and circumstances having no bearing on the situation should be omitted.[16] There should be a logical sequence as well as continuity and cohesion throughout the narrative. Although simple language should be used where possible, terminology that has become accepted in the field of business and management studies may be incorporated.

10.5 The Case Study Process

Producing competent case study research is a process that needs to be understood and carefully followed. With a focus on the relevant steps in the process the results of a case study may be questionable or just invalid.

10.5.1 Uniformity when Recording Evidence

Business and management research usually involves multiple case study research, and thus uniformity of recording should be sought as this facilitates comparison between enterprises or situations, which allows the highlighting of similarities and differences. Unless there is some uniformity of recording, it is exceedingly difficult to see likenesses or differences, and much of the usefulness of the case study method, as well as its scientific value may be eliminated.

Case study research is often, mistakenly, thought to be rather informal because it is confused with case writing from a teaching–learning point of view. In fact, the case study research approach requires a distinctly formal approach. Before the research can proceed a protocol needs to be drawn up. The protocol is a formal and detailed master plan that specifies full particulars of the research, a summary of the questions to be asked during structured interviews (Braiden, Alderman and Thwaites, 1993), field procedures for the researcher, details of all types of evidence required, as well as the structure of the final report.

10.5.2 Case Study Protocol

Especially when you are using the case study as part of a positivistic research strategy,[17] a protocol is an important instrument for ensuring the reliability of the study. The protocol is in fact a detailed statement of what the research is trying to achieve, as well as a plan that indicates how the objectives will be met. In business and management research a protocol is always needed as the issues which are researched, especially by means of a case study, are often complex, and careful thought needs to be given to what is being attempted and how the researcher should go about it. The general rule is that the more time and attention which is given to the planning of the research the better the results are likely to be. A case study research protocol will have at least the following sections.

10.5.2.1 Protocol Overview
The protocol overview should include the main objectives and the detailed issues the researchers will focus on. A typical protocol overview is shown in Figure 10.2 (Remenyi, 1990b).

Objectives of the research

The main objective of the case study research is to obtain evidence as to how firms formulate and implement strategic information systems by a series of unstructured interviews which will allow informants the opportunity of supplying information on a wide range of issues related to formulation and implementation activities.

It is intended to allow the informants as much freedom in the interview as possible as it is critical to ensure that the interviewer does not prejudge in any way the evidence that the informants will offer. None the less, a list of possible discussion topics that the interviewer may use as an interview schedule has been developed. These topics are available to prompt the interviewer if the discussion requires some prompting or guidance.

Key issues on which the researcher needs to focus

There are two key issues of this research which are:

To establish how management formulates Strategic Information Systems (SIS), i.e. are highly systematised methodologies used or does the firm respond to other stimuli?
To discover what is involved in implementing SIS, i.e. are they implemented in much the same way as other systems or are there any significant differences?

Figure 10.2 *A protocol overview (Yin, 1989)*

10.5.2.2 Field Procedures

The researcher has to work in the real world, and thus cope with real world events during the evidence-collection plan. Respondents may drop out during the course of the study, corporate documents may not be available and many other unexpected problems may arise. Field procedures need to detail a number of issues including:

- defining who should be interviewed;
- how to access to the right people;
- ensuring resources are available including time, paper, tape recorders, etc;
- developing a procedure for obtaining assistance from other researchers;
- making a schedule of the required evidence-collection activities
- providing for contingencies.

A typical set of field procedures is shown in Figure 10.3.

10.5.2.3 Case Study Questions

At the centre of the protocol is a set of questions reflecting the actual inquiry. There are two characteristics that distinguish such a set of questions from those used in a more general survey. Firstly, the protocol questions are set for the researcher and not for the respondent. The questions are reminders or prompts to

At least three informants should be found in each case study. This triangulation is for purposes of data validation.

At least one informant per firm should be a senior manager, i.e. an individual who is either a member of, or reports directly to the board of directors.

Access to information should be obtained wherever possible by introduction through a trusted intermediary.

Initial contact with the respondent firm should be at the highest level possible.

A friendly gatekeeper or guide should be found as soon as possible.

Interviews should be tape-recorded.

Documentary evidence should be sought to support the verbal information.

An attempt should be made to secure multiple interviews per site so as to reduce travelling time.

Attempt to interview informants in their office rather than in an interview room.

Engage as many members of the staff as possible, including secretaries and support people, in general conversation about the firm.

Figure 10.3 *A set of field procedures*

the researcher concerning the information that has to be collected. Secondly, each question should be accompanied by a list of probable sources of evidence which cover interviewees' comments, documents, artefacts and observations.

It is important to remember that a particular protocol is designed for evidence collection from a single case and is not intended to serve the entire project. A typical set of case study questions is shown in Figure 10.4.

Has a generic corporate strategy been formulated?

Does top management have an understanding of the key IS/IT issues?

Has an information systems audit been performed?

Has the IS/IT strategy been matched to the generic corporate strategy?

Have projects been carefully planned and have these projects been documented in specific detail including cost benefit analysis?

Have these projects been thoroughly discussed with potential users before implementation?

Have strategic information systems been co-ordinated with other interfacing functions?

Have higher calibre operatives than usual been chosen?

Have computer users and managers received appropriate training?

Have computer users greater freedom to respond to exceptions when they occur?

Figure 10.4 *An interview schedule or a set of case study questions*

10.5.2.4 *Guide to the Case Study Report*
The guide to the case study report forces the researcher to think early on in the case study process about the audience for which the case study is intended.

The researcher should be concerned throughout the study with the design of the final report. An outline of the case study report should be included in the case study protocol. This protocol should also indicate to what extent documentary evidence would be used in the final report. Case studies often produce large amounts of documentation that may be used to produce an annotated bibliography and this, in turn, might be helpful to readers in suggesting what is available for further research.

An example of case study report guidelines is shown in Figure 10.5. This example has been somewhat abbreviated as it is possible to produce a much more detailed set of guidelines for the production of the type of write-up which may result as a result of the evidence collected during the case study interviews.

Case Study Report Guidelines

The following are the major headings that were established as the key focal points of the case study reports. These were established early in the research process so that they could be used as a supplementary aide-mémoire for the author in conducting unstructured interviews with informants.

Introduction and general background of the firm.
The state of IT within the firm.
The reasons for the current move towards strategic information systems (SIS).
The IS strategy:
a   What it actually is.
b   How it is formulated in the organisation.
The implementation of the strategic information system
What are the consequential effects of the SIS investment?
What conclusions have been drawn by the organisation themselves?

Figure 10.5   *Case study report guidelines*

10.5.2.5 Conducting a Pilot Case Study

The final step in preparing the framework for the evidence collection is to conduct a pilot case study. The pilot study, which may be much broader than the final study, can be a testing ground for both substantive and methodological issues, and it can help the researcher develop more relevant lines of questioning. The pilot may be so important that more resources are utilised at this phase than in the final collection of the evidence. This study can play the role of laboratory for the researcher.

A report based on the pilot case study may be written so as to highlight the lessons learnt about the research design and the field procedures. More than one pilot may be performed if the results of the first pilot are not found to be satisfactory. However, in business and management research there is usually time and considerable financial pressure to get the project started.

Because of the funding of masters and doctoral students in business and management studies, the pilot case study or studies are often selected on the grounds of convenience, access and geographic proximity.

10.6 Collecting the Evidence

For a masters or doctorate degree the case study approach to research requires comprehensive and intensive study of the subject and thoroughness is one of the first requisites. Evidence needs to be ascertained from the business enterprise or enterprises being studied and then be carefully scrutinised and interpreted. The collection of the evidence is a central issue in case study research.

10.6.1 Different Types of Case Study Evidence

Evidence can be obtained from documents, archival records and interviews as well as from any person who has knowledge of the subject, observations of the researcher, participant-observer interactions as well as physical artefacts. It is sometimes useful for the researcher to read the published annual financial accounts or, if the organisation is privately owned, published promotional material, before collecting evidence from within the organisation. If the researcher is working in an organisation listed on the stock exchange, then there will usually be an abundance of information available that can be obtained through sources such as the financial press or from stockbrokers. However, evidence should be carefully weighted, tested and sifted to eliminate fictitious and false statements as well as, where possible, personal rationalisations and bias.

There are six important sources of evidence used in case studies:

1   documents;
2   interviews;
3   direct observations;
4   participant-observation situation;
5   physical artefacts;
6   archival records.

Several overriding principles are critical to the collection of evidence for a case study, including multiple sources of evidence, development of a case study database and a chain of evidence. All of these are important in the management and the validation of the evidence collected.

10.6.2 Documents

Documents are primarily used to corroborate and augment evidence from other sources. They are helpful in verifying spellings and titles. They provide specific details that can support the verbal accounts of informants. They can set the context for interviews or discussions within the organisation being studied. In business and management studies the most recent set of published financial accounts can be used to begin a discussion with an in-company focus group. Inferences may be made based on the number of copies made of certain documents such as marketing proposals, etc. In fact some case study researchers have been criticised for over reliance on documentary evidence, and in business and management studies the researcher can collect a large volume of documents.

It should always be remembered that these documents were written for a reason other than research and thus they may not necessarily accurately reflect the situation. For business and management researchers the emphasis may be placed on obtaining copies of proposals, contracts, accounts, personal correspondence between informants, as well as corporate publicity material.

10.6.3 *Interviews*

Interviews, which may be open-ended, focused or in the form of surveys, are one of the most frequently used sources of evidence especially for the business and management researcher.

With an open-ended interview the researcher asks the respondent for the facts of a matter as well as his or her own insights into certain occurrences. If the emphasis of the interview moves substantially towards obtaining insights then the respondent is referred to as an informant. Although informants are useful, it is important to be particularly cautious about such information due to the possibility of bias.

A focused interview is one in which the informant is interviewed for a short period of time, for example an hour. Although such an interview will frequently be reasonably open-ended and informal in manner, the researcher will be following an interview schedule or set of questions.

Interviews are an essential part of case study evidence. However, they are verbal reports only and as such are subject to the problems of bias as well as poor and inaccurate articulation and listening. Thus interview evidence should be corroborated wherever possible by the process of triangulation (Jick, 1979). Corroboration may be verbal, by other members of the firm, by documents, by observation or by the firms' suppliers or clients.

The personal interview is becoming the most frequently used method of evidence collection by business and management researchers. It also allows the researcher to feel a degree of intimacy with the informant as he or she will have actually met and be known to them. By conducting a personal interview the researcher will probably have visited the organisation and will perhaps have been shown around the premises. This type of visual contact is also useful for the purposes of triangulation.

10.6.4 *Direct Observation*

All evidence other than observation is essentially hearsay and its reliability needs to be examined. Observation is thus one of the most valuable ways of collecting reliable evidence. The researcher may, for example, observe locations, individual behaviour, behaviour at meetings, morale, dress codes, and corporate culture, to mention a few examples (Silverman, 1994). Observed evidence is clearly stronger than hearsay evidence (Silverman, 1997).

By visiting the case study site the researcher has the opportunity to observe directly the surroundings as well as relevant interaction and behavioural and environmental conditions. These observations are yet another useful source of evidence and an important way to triangulate. Observations may be so important that it is necessary to take photographs or to make a video of the case study site (Lumley and Benjamin, 1994).

10.6.5 Participant-Observation Situation

An example of the use of the technique of participant-observation was given in Chapter 3 – the involvement of the researcher participating in the work of the organisation which he or she was studying. This approach suffers major problems due to bias and therefore needs to be used with considerable care. In business and management studies it is a particularly useful approach when used in conjunction with other research tactics to obtain a comprehensive view of an organisation as part of a case study. However, it is not always easy for a researcher at the masters or even at doctoral level to be given this level of access to an organisation.

10.6.6 Physical Artefacts

Physical artefacts include books, technological devices, tools, instruments and ledgers. A computer printout may be considered an artefact. A printout might show what type of work was done, how long it took, how much processing was required, etc. The presence of books on MS-DOS 2,[18] for example, would be evidence of the organisation having used personal computers for more than 15 years. This could be useful to describe the level of computer literacy in the organisation.

10.6.7 Archival Records

Archival records include staff service and payroll records, old correspondence, old product or service descriptions and so on. They may exist on paper or microfiche or computer tape. The importance of such evidence will vary enormously from case to case. Often archival evidence is highly quantitative. The same general caution about the original purpose of the information applies to archival records as well as to documents in general. Sometimes business and management students need archival records but by and large their interests are frequently more current and it will only be occasionally that an archive will need to be taped.

10.7 Principles for Good Practice

The benefits of the evidence collected from the above six sources can be maximised by following the three principles of evidence collection. These principles help with the problems of construct validity and reliability:

1   use multiple sources of evidence;
2   create a case study database;
3   maintain a chain of evidence.

10.7.1 Use Multiple Sources of Evidence

Although case studies have been conducted using only a single research entity such as one organisation or one government department, it is clearly essential to use multiple sources of evidence when examining or producing the one case. One of the strengths of the case study method is its use of multiple and different sources that can corroborate evidence found from each of the different sources. This process is part of triangulation (Loveridge, 1990) and makes the finding of a case study much more convincing.

An example of triangulated evidence is obtaining a view about the corporate strategy from the managing director, the workers in the factory and from a stock exchange broker or the organisation's bank manager. The evidence may then be corroborated by reference to annual accounts and also to articles published in the business press.

Multiple sources of evidence tend to help with the problem of construct validity because this provides several measures of the same phenomenon. The multiple nature of evidence collection also allows the researcher to attempt to find information convergence.

10.7.2 Create a Case Study Database

A case study database is a critical part of the evidence supporting the case study research strategy. There are two aspects to the case study database: the evidence collected and the reports written by the researcher.

A researcher creates a formal, retrievable database of the evidence collected so that other researchers can easily review the original material. The main item in the database will usually be the case study notes. These notes should be organised and categorised and as complete as possible. They should be available in the original medium i.e. in writing, as well as supported by tape recordings if these were used.

A large number of documents will be collected and the researcher will find it useful to organise the filing of these into primary and secondary systems. It is also essential to cross-reference the documents for subsequent retrieval. Large amounts of numerical data could be included in the database, which should be held on disk or tape. In Chapter 13, the period of time for which this database and supporting records should be retained by the business and management researcher is discussed.

As a by-product of the case study database, some of the summary material written by the researcher will become part of the text of the dissertation. In effect, this database forms the start of the writing-up procedure discussed in Chapter 14.

10.7.3 Maintain a Chain of Evidence

The principle of maintaining the chain of evidence states that an external observer or reader of the case study should be able to follow the argument and the derivation of the evidence from the original research design and questions to the eventual conclusions. The observer should be able to trace the argument both forwards and backwards. The chain of evidence principle also states that no evidence should be lost or omitted. If these rules are followed then the case study will have addressed the methodological issues of determining construct validity and the overall quality of the case will have been enhanced.

10.8 How to Judge Case Study Design

From a positivist point of view, case study design may be judged on the basis of four tests, which are *construct validity, internal validity, external validity* and *reliability*.

10.8.1 Construct Validity

Construct[19] validity refers to establishing correct operational measures for the concepts, ideas and relationships being studied. More formally, construct validation is a scale evaluation criterion that relates to the following question: 'What is the nature of the underlying variable or construct measured by the scale?'

To meet the test of construct validity the researcher should be sure to have covered two steps:

1 carefully identify ideas, concepts, relationships and issues which are to be studied;
2 demonstrate that the selected measures to be used in the research actually address the ideas, concepts, relationships and issues being studied.

For example, if the research aims to determine the extent of awareness of Porter's Generic Strategies Model in those making strategic information systems decisions, it is necessary to demonstrate that the questions will actually measure this. Three tactics are available to increase construct validity.

1 triangulation;
2 establish a chain of evidence to show how each link in the chain relates to the next;
3 draft a case study reviewed by key informants who have detailed knowledge if the relevant ideas, concepts and relationships.

Construct validity is an important issue because criticisms are often made of the validity of research in business and management studies. These criticisms are mainly to do with the suggestion that spurious effects can easily creep into this type of research, which do not directly relate to the phenomenon that is believed to have been studied. This is indeed a fair comment and is one of the reasons why rigorous research in business and management studies is so challenging.

10.8.2 Internal Validity

Internal validity is of concern in all causal and explanatory studies of the relationship between different events. Thus according to Rosenthal and Rosnow (1991) internal validity may be defined as the degree of validity of statements made about whether x causes y. In demonstrating internal validity it is necessary to consider plausible alternative explanations of the apparent relationship between x and y.

In case studies in business and management this problem is generalised to the broader situation, whereby the researcher may be inferring that a particular result was caused by a particular phenomenon, without necessarily having all the evidence. It is seldom possible to have all the evidence available. Internal validity may be asserted if not in fact proved, by examining possible alternative explanations of the phenomenon. The evidence may be inspected to see if it converges[20] and whether the result is the only plausible outcome of the evidence. Internal validity is demonstrated by sound argument, as has been discussed in Chapter 3, and this is a fundamental pillar on which the validity business and management research is based.

10.8.3 External Validity

External validity is concerned with knowing whether the researchers' findings are generalisable to a wider universe beyond the immediate research environment. For positivists this is a central issue, while phenomenologists are less concerned with external validity and more concerned as to whether the research is authentic and properly represents the events being studied.

This issue has traditionally been a major barrier to the use of case studies by positivists. Critics contrast case study evidence with sample evidence from a survey and claim that the case study does not have sufficient rigour or breadth of evidence But this is a misunderstanding of the nature of the research being conducted when dealing with case studies. Survey and case study research have quite different objectives and are in no way interchangeable. Survey research relies on accumulating numerical evidence and interpreting it using only statistical generalisation, whereas case studies rely on in-depth evidence that is evaluated on the basis of analytical generalisations. In analytical generalisation, the researcher is striving to associate a particular set of results to some broader theory, and thus the sample size is not such a relevant issue (Yin, 1989).

At the same time, generalisation from a case study, although possible in a certain sense, is by no means automatic except in the limited sense that if the phenomenon exists in one place it is likely to exist elsewhere. For theory development there is a need to test conclusions by replicating the study in other organisations. The logic of replication in case studies is the same as that which underlies replication in experiments (Yin, 1989). Most business and management researchers who use the case study approach would not attempt to argue that their findings are generalisable in the same sense as a physical or life scientist would, or for that matter as a social scientist who had conducted a large-scale survey would.

10.8.4 Reliability

Research reliability refers to the issue of whether the evidence and the measures used are consistent and stable. This is especially important if the findings of the research are to be applicable to other situations and not only to the original environment or environments in which the research was conducted.

A positivist using multiple case studies will claim reliability but a phenomenologist will not regard this issue as pertinent. To the positivist the purpose of ensuring reliability is to reduce or minimise errors and bias in conducting the study. On the other hand, some phenomenologists will argue that all situations and organisations are different and thus the same results cannot ever be obtained again, and consequently reliability *per se* is not a central issue.

10.9 Single versus Multiple Case Study Design

Sometime a single case study is sufficient while on other occasions multiple case studies are preferred or even necessary. There are an increasing number of dissertations being concluded on the basis of a few case studies. The idea that a large number of observations of a phenomenon is not necessary is well expressed by Gummesson (1988) when he said:

> It no longer seems so 'obvious' that a limited number of observations cannot be used as a basis for generalization. Nor does it appear to be 'obvious' any longer that properly devised statistical studies based on large numbers of observations will lead to meaningful generalizations.

This view continues to gain support and credibility.

10.9.1 Single Case Study Design

A single case may be regarded as analogous to a single experiment. Thus a single case study may be sufficient when a well-formulated theory is to be tested. If the theory specifies a clear set of propositions, as well as circumstances in which it is believed that these propositions will be true, then a single case could be used to confirm, challenge, or extend the theory. Business and management studies has been slow to accept a single case study as representing sufficient evidence at doctoral level. However, there is now broadening of this approach, which demonstrates a growing acceptance that some knowledge may be generated from research in one location. A single case study would have to draw on the principles of ethnography as discussed in Chapter 3. It would be important for the researcher to spend a considerable amount of time with informants in the organisation being studied and it would be essential for there to be proof of careful triangulation of the evidence collected. None the less, in most circumstances a single case study approach should be regarded as high risk by a business and management researcher.

10.9.2 Multiple Case Study Design

Multiple case studies have advantages and disadvantages over single case studies. Evidence from multiple case studies is more compelling and the results are more robust.

Multiple case studies should be considered in the same light as multiple experiments in that they follow the logic of replication. In the hands of a positivist, the sampling logic requires identifying the target population followed by the use of a statistical sampling procedure to select an appropriate subset to be surveyed. This approach is applicable when the frequency or prevalence of a particular phenomenon is being measured. The result of the survey is assumed to reflect the characteristics of the universe from which it was drawn. Inferential statistics are then used to establish confidence intervals that determine reasonable bounds for the particular findings.

However, as stated before, in general case studies should not be used on their own to assess the incidence of phenomena. Case studies cover the phenomenon and its context, and as a result they generally yield a large number of possible relevant variables. This means that a large sample of case studies, which is not in keeping with the case study philosophy, would be required to allow for statistical inference.

If all case studies produce the same result then there is compelling evidence for the initial set of hypotheses. If some of the cases produce contradictory evidence then the initial hypotheses should be reconsidered and then re-tested with other cases.

Multiple case study design is now very common for business and management studies. Of course the question which continually plagues researchers is how many case studies need to be undertaken and there is no simple answer to this. Many masters degrees will address a very small number of cases, perhaps two or three. For doctorate degrees, sometimes five to ten are required,[21] but as mentioned above there are an increasing number of instances where one case study has been deemed sufficient.

10.9.3 Flexibility within Case Studies

As in all research the design of a case study may not be complete at the outset and may be altered or revised after the initial stages. A pilot case study may of course be used, and this may reveal inadequacies in the original design. However, the theoretical bases of the case study approach should not be materially shifted. If the evidence collected during the case study process does not conform to the theoretical conjecture this does not detract from the value of the research. In fact, it is perfectly adequate for a masters or a doctoral dissertation to assert that the hypotheses or empirical generalisations are rejected.[22]

The flexibility of the case study approach refers to the ability to change cases if they are found to be inappropriate. This is analogous to changing an experiment if it is found to be unsuitable to prove the hypothesis. However, changing the theory is quite a different matter and to do this means restarting the research project from close to the beginning

10.10   Case Studies in Use

As mentioned earlier, case studies may be used as part of a grounded theory approach or they may be used to validate an already established theory.

10.10.1   Case Studies and Grounded Theory

When using case studies as part of a grounded theory approach the researcher is attempting to find empirical evidence from which to develop a theoretical conjecture. A process of induction described in Chapter 5 underpins this procedure.

10.10.2   Validating Established Theory

When case studies are used to validate an already established theory, the first step is to articulate the theory that is to be tested. The next step is to select cases and to design an evidence collection protocol. Then the case studies are conducted and individual case reports written. Each report should show how each proposition was demonstrated. Cross-case conclusions may be drawn.

An important step in this approach to research is the establishment of a thorough theoretical framework. This framework should state the conditions under which a particular phenomenon is likely to be found, as well as the conditions under which it is unlikely to occur. This framework becomes the vehicle for generalisation to new cases in the same way that cross-experimental designs are used.

According to Yin (1989) there are nine basic steps in the case study approach to research:

1   develop theory;
2   select cases;
3   design evidence collection protocol;
4   conduct case studies;
5   write case reports;
6   draw cross-case conclusions;
7   modify theory;
8   develop policy implications;
9   write cross-case report.

After defining the problem and designing the case study, the next step is to prepare for the collection of evidence. The skills required for collecting evidence for a case study are much more demanding than for experiments and surveys and include the ability to ask suitable questions, the ability to listen, being adaptive and flexible, having a firm grasp of the subject, being unbiased and not having preconceived notions.

10.10.3   Quantitative and Qualitative Case Studies

As has already been stated several times in this book, it is a misunderstanding to assert that the case study method of research is by its nature qualitative. In many instances purely descriptive evidence may be converted into quantitative evidence to which statistical techniques can be applied. The main technique for this is content analysis, which is referred to in Chapters 3, 6, 7 and 9. It is worth noting that what is qualitative evidence today may be quantitative evidence tomorrow.[23] To an experienced researcher, quantitative and qualitative techniques are complementary rather than antithetical. But there will always be qualitative evidence that cannot or should not be quantified. It is indeed questionable, for example, to ask informants to quantify on a scale how they feel about certain types of advertisement.

It is worth noting that even in the physical and life sciences there are several disciplines such as geology, botan*y, zoology, and psychiatry, which are substantially based on qualitative evidence and information.

10.11   The Case Study as a Narrative or Story

In addition to being an evidence-collection tactic as described in the above sections, the case study also plays an important role as a knowledge generation approach in its own right.

The result of a case study is often written or told as a story.[24] Stories have from time immemorial been the repository of knowledge and the main vehicle for transmitting knowledge from one generation to another throughout the world.

At the end of the twentieth century story-telling is still the principal way our society introduces its children to its culture. Aesop's[25] 'The Hare and the Tortoise', Hans Christian Andersen's 'The Ugly Duckling', and Charles Perrault's 'Cendrillon', Cinderella,[26] are essentially lessons in fundamental community values and as such their storylines are knowledge about our culture.

But in what way can stories, especially as represented by the case study, be regarded as research? The telling of a story requires the presentation of the facts or the evidence, in such a way that it is intelligible and of course engaging to the listener or the reader. This requires the writer/story-teller to process the evidence and structure it in such a way that a convincing proposition is established. The listener or reader is then offered an explanation of how the issues are resolved. In effect this is a direct equivalent to the research process.

The initial proposition of the story involves the definition of the ideas, variables or concepts and the relationships between them. Then the story presents the situation in which some event will take place, which may be seen as the equivalent in the research process of the theoretical conjecture.

The way the propositions and situation develop in the story and the way they are challenged are similar to the testing of the hypotheses; the resolution of the challenges described in the story is equivalent to producing the findings.

Thus it is clear that the telling of a story has a similar structure to that of the research process and thus story-telling may be regarded, at least in some cases, as the creation of knowledge.

Stories may be rendered well or badly. A well-rendered story clearly explains its meaning in such a way that the listener or reader understands the message. The story needs to make sense or put another way, it needs to resonate with the listener or reader. Consequently, in physics quantum mechanics theorists had to face considerable difficulties, as their new ideas did not easily resonate with the established thinking. In this respect the establishment view was well summarised by Einstein (1931) when he said:

> Quantum mechanics is certainly imposing. But an inner voice tells me that it is not yet the real thing. The theory says a lot, but does not really bring us any closer to the secret of the 'old one'. I, at any rate, am convinced that He is not playing at dice.

The better the rendition of the story the less the ambiguity in the meaning of the story and thus the more resonance it will usually have for the listener or reader. However, the story will always be told from the point of view of the story-teller or writer and thus there may be different stories told about the same event or series of events. Thus the story as described here is quintessentially a phenomenological research tool.

From an academic point of view the arguments presented here may be necessary, but are not sufficient, to claim that a story is a knowledge creation activity *per se*. Perhaps the essential point is that there is a commonality shared by the creation of knowledge in all fields of studies. This is the essence of the argument presented by Rosenthal and Rosnow (1991) when they said:

> although it would be wrong to claim that art and poetry are the same as science, scientists and philosophers have long been aware of the basic unity of the creative act as found in the arts and poetry and that in the sciences (e.g. Garfield, 1989a, 1989b; Nisbet, 1976). Twenty-five hundred years ago, Plato likened the creative work of the astronomer to that of the painter. Just as art and poetry are grounded in aesthetics (i.e. a sense of the beautiful) scientists are conscious of the beauty and the poetry of their theoretical conceptualisations and empirical relationships.

In business and management studies the question of whether the story is a knowledge creation activity needs to be addressed in terms of the arguments expressed in Chapter 2 concerning the dialectic. If the story or the case study is useful and it contributes to an understanding of the world or explains interesting phenomena, then the case study's or story's value will be acknowledged and it will become an integral part of society's knowledge base. On the other hand, if the story or the case study offers little or no contribution to society's understanding or its ability to explain then it will not be regarded as knowledge. Business and management studies are replete with such story-telling. Townsend (1984), and Harvey-Jones (1988) are two of the better known narrators of their business experiences who have published their stories in full-length books. In addition to this there is a plethora of short case studies written in academic journals (Chand, 1994; Kayes, 1995; Al-Arjani, 1995; Remenyi, 1996; Kawalek and Leonard, 1996; Nandhakumar, 1996; Molnar and Sharda, 1996; Bussen and Myers, 1997; Subramanian and Lacity, 1997; Remenyi and Cinnamond, 1996).

In simple terms, case studies or stories that are useful contribute to knowledge, while those that are not useful do not. The question that then arises is, 'to what extent has a useful case study or story to be true?' Although it is rather unlikely that a hare ever ran a race against a tortoise, Aesop's fable clearly contains universal knowledge. The fact that a hare and a tortoise have been anthropomorphised does not detract from the validity of the values portrayed in the story. In terms of knowledge content the story is useful. And in a sense this idea of narrative or story-telling being a route to knowledge brings the case study back to its pedagogic origins as a teaching–learning device. However, as an approach to research and the methodological options available, this type of story could not really be regarded as empirical but rather a theoretical treatise. None the less case study research used in this way offers many opportunities to the business and management researcher especially when addressing the more complex aspects of the field of study.

10.12 What Makes an Exemplary Case Study?

There are five general characteristics required for exemplary case study research:

1 it should be significant;
2 it should be complete;
3 it should consider alternative perspectives;
4 it should display sufficient evidence;
5 it should be composed in an engaging manner.

In the business and management research context a significant case study is one which is of general interest to business and management professionals, i.e. the stakeholders as described earlier in this book. The case study should be of importance to decision making as well as important to policy formulation.

For a case study to be regarded as complete the boundaries of the research need to have been given considerable attention. This means there has to be a careful and rigorous definition of the research problem as well as the determination of the research questions. If there is any muddled thinking in this respect then the case study approach may not add anything of value to the body of knowledge. This is a particular challenge to business and management researchers as many issues in this field of study have very broad boundaries that overlap with those of other areas and concerns, functions and disciplines.

Exhaustive effort should have been expended in collecting the relevant evidence and for an exemplary case study the evidence should have been considered from as many perspectives as possible. This involves extensive triangulation and the consideration of the evidence from the point of view of rival propositions.

In addition an exemplary case study will judiciously and effectively present a compelling or convincing argument. Where at all possible the identity of the organisation and the main individuals described in the case setting should be disclosed.

It is useful to have case studies reviewed by peers and by participants in the firms being studied. If the comments are helpful then they could be published as part of the report. This procedure is a way of corroborating facts and evidence. The feedback from the firm will add to the case study's construct validity. However, these reviews can produce considerable delays, and the time required obtaining feedback should be planned for at the outset of the research programme. When composed in this way the case study can make engaging and convincing reading.

10.13 Summary and Conclusion

The term case study refers to a least two entirely different issues in the business and management field of study. As a teaching–learning device it is a highly effective and well-established technique. As a research approach it is a particularly powerful technique in answering who, why and how questions. The use of multiple sources of evidence allows the researcher to provide a convincing argument as an answer to these questions. It is not essential to the validity of the case study research method that a case study should be generalisable. The relatability[27] of a case study is as important as its generalisability. Like other research tactics the case study needs to contain a convincing argument as the basis of its contribution to the body of knowledge.

As the case study is normally presented as a story it is more than an evidence-collection approach. When a case study is carried out both systematically and critically, aiming at the improvement of our understanding and our ability to explain, and when, by publication of its findings, it extends or expands the boundaries of existing knowledge of the subject area, then it is a valid tactic for research in business and management studies.

As the case study approach to research can, in the hands of a skilled researcher, produce excellent results, its use is on the increase in most areas of business and management studies.

Case studies are sometimes said to be a soft tool because they may not rely on the hard science of mathematics or statistical analysis. However, it is also probably true that the softer a research technique the harder it is to add something of value to the body of knowledge! This is based on the notion that it is often, although not always, more difficult to develop a convincing argument than it is to perform a statistical test.

As a general rule case studies are a preferred research tactic when how or why questions are being examined, when the researcher has little control over events, and when the focus is on a contemporary phenomenon within some real-life context. This is the reason for the growing popularity of the case study among business and management researchers.

It is not possible to give an exhaustive account of case study research in one chapter of a book. Thus, this chapter has focused on some of the key issues but the researcher at masters and doctoral level in management and business studies will need to explore these issues further. The suggested further reading will help with this endeavour.

Suggested Further Reading

Bromley, D. (1986) *The Case Study Methods in Psychology and Related Disciplines.* John Wiley, Chichester.
Douglas, J. D. (1986) *Creative Interviewing.* Sage Publications, Newbury Park, CA.

Fink, A. and Kosecoff, J. (1985) *How to Conduct Surveys: A Step-by-Step Guide*, Sage Publications, Newbury Park, CA.

Jick, T. D. (1979) 'Mixing qualitative and quantitative methods: triangulation in action', *Administrative Science Quarterly*, December, Vol. 24: 602–11

Kirk, J. and Miller, M. (1986), *Reliability and Validity in Qualitative Research*. Sage Publications, Newbury Park, CA.

Lincoln, Y. and Guba, E. (1985) *Naturalistic Inquiry*. Sage Publications, Newbury Park, CA.

Loveridge, R. (1990) 'Triangulation – or how to survive your choice of business school PhD course', *Graduate Management Research*, 5 (3): 18–25.

Maanen, J. van (ed.) (1995), *Representation in Ethnography*. Sage Publications, Thousand Oaks, CA.

Miles, M. (1979) 'Qualitative data as an attractive nuisance', *Administrative Science Quarterly*, 24: 590–601.

Miles, M. B. and Huberman, A. M. (1984) *Qualitative Data Analysis: A Source Book of New Methods*. Sage Publications, Newbury Park, CA.

Rubin, H. and Rubin, I. (1995) *Qualitative Interviewing: The Art of Hearing Data*. Sage Publications, Thousand Oaks, CA.

Schuman, H. and Presser, S. (1981) *Questions and Answers in Attitude Surveys: Experiments on Question Form, Wording and Context*. Sage Publications, Newbury Park, CA.

Silverman, D. (1994) *Interpreting Qualitative Data: Methods for Analysing Talk, Text and Interaction*. Sage Publications, London

Strauss, A. L. and Corbin, J. (1990), *Basics of Qualitative Research: Grounded Theory Procedures and Techniques*. Sage Publications, Newbury Park, CA.

Weisberg, H. F., Krosnik, J. A. and Bowen, B. D. (1996), *An Introduction to Survey Research Polling and Data Analysis*. Sage Publications, Thousand Oaks, CA.

Whyte, W. F. (1985) *Learning from the Field: A Guide from Experience*. Sage Publications, Newbury Park, CA.

Yin, R. K. (1989), *Case Study Research – Design and Methods*. Sage Publications, Newbury Park, CA.

Yin, R. K. (1993), *Applications of Case Study Research – Design and Methods*. Sage Publications, Newbury Park, CA.

Notes

[1] According to the Microsoft Bookshelf 1997, Christopher Columbus Langdell, Dean of the Law School at Harvard, introduced the case study method of teaching law as early as 1869.

[2] In medical research case studies take a different form and are usually applied to the study of diseases, one of the most notable being the discovery of the relationship between smoking and lung cancer. A number of people suffering from the disease (lung cancer, say) are identified and matched with a number of controls. The controls are chosen so that they match the cases with regards variables such as age and occupation, which are believed to be relevant to the development of cancer, but are not of interest to the particular study. Factors are then sought that are more commonly found among the cases than among the controls. In the lung cancer study it was found that those with the disease were much more likely to be smokers than those without the disease.

[3] The syndicate group whereby four to eight students work together has become a key feature of most business school education today.

[4] Discussion and debate are seen here as the primary catalysts of the learning process. This view owes its origin directly to the notion of the dialectic that has been discussed in Chapter 2 and which is at the heart of the research process, especially in business and management studies.

[5] Although it is possible to envisage circumstances where a case study may be used to test hypotheses or empirical generalisations as Yin (1989) suggests, in the field of business and management studies this is rather unlikely. In general the case study is better used as an approach to developing a grounded theory from which a theoretical conjecture may be developed which leads to hypotheses and empirical generalisations. The testing of hypotheses and empirical generalisations requires evidence from a reasonable number of incidences if they are to be rejected in the formal scientific sense of the word.

[6] Conducting a case study in the library and through contacting individuals on the telephone is unlikely to deliver a sufficiently insightful account of a situation to allow it to qualify for rigorous

academic research especially in business and management studies. It might just be possible to use this approach at the masters level but it is certainly unlikely to succeed for a doctoral degree.

[7] The issue of quality and quantity is always present when discussing length of work. And quantity will not substitute for quality when it comes to research; any attempt to so do will always be apparent and most if not all examiners will immediately reject this.

[8] Although there are numerous ways of conducting case study research, action research is one well-established approach. The following comment by Baskerville and Wood-Harper (1996) illustrates well the reason for considering this an experiment. 'Action research is a method that could be described as a paragon of the post-positivist research methods. It is empirical, yet interpretative. It is experimental, yet multivariate. It is observational yet interventionist. To the arch-positivist it should seem very unscientific. To the post-positivist it seems ideal.'

[9] Although Yin is enthusiastic about the fact that the case study follows the logic of the experiment, this notion only holds true in a limited sense. The case study is quite unlike the experimental approach described in Chapter 5 under the heading of deliberate intervention. Rather, the similarity between the case study and the experiment lies in the fact that they both differ from other established methods of collecting evidence in the social sciences. The case study and the experiment are empirical procedures that observe real situations.

[10] This of course is also true of the social sciences in general, and even of business and management researchers.

[11] Although it cannot be stated as a universal rule, some examiners would regard exploratory research as too superficial to be worthy of a doctorate. However, a piece of well-conducted exploratory research should not have a problem at masters level.

[12] If the researcher is following a phenomenological approach, then the question of robust generalisations is just not an issue.

[13] An interesting comment on the general nature of bias is made in the 1997 electronic version of the *Encyclopaedia Britannica* in a paper entitled, 'The social sciences: sociology: status of contemporary sociology: scientific status', which states,

Bias, in more than one direction, is sometimes presumed to be a chronic affliction of sociology. This may arise in part from the fact that the subject matter of sociology is familiar and important in the daily life of everyone, so that there exist many opportunities for the abundant variations in philosophical outlook and individual preferences to appear as irrational bias.'

Of course business and management studies are at the end of the day a subset of sociology and are therefore affected by the problems that afflict the greater subject.

[14] There may be other secondary artefacts that can also supply useful evidences such as invoices and statements of purchase.

[15] Life science uses double blind methods to minimise bias. Life and physical sciences insist that the experiments be replicable so that bias is illuminated or at least reduced to a minimum. This type of approach is not applicable in the world of the business and management researcher and the only safeguard which the masters and doctoral students can apply is that of triangulation. Some business and management researchers will actually argue that there is no point in trying to reduce, let alone eliminate, bias. They suggest that the only acceptable course of action is to recognise up front the potential bias and to allow the recipients and the other stakeholders of the research to evaluate for themselves the impact of the actual bias on the results.

[16] In their search for high-quality learning–teaching experiences Harvard includes red herrings in their case studies so that students may learn to distinguish between the relevant and the irrelevant.

[17] A phenomenologist might argue that a strict research protocol could interfere with the ability of the researcher to encourage the informant to reveal the evidence that is important. The argument is that a research protocol could reduce the creativeness of the evidence-collection process.

[18] MS-DOS is the trademark of the Microsoft Corporation.

[19] A construct may be defined as the operationalisation of a concept or variable in such a way that it may be used in a research project. According to the Merriam-Webster *Collegiate Dictionary* the word construct means to make or form by combining or arranging parts or elements. Rosenthal and Rosnow (1991) define a construct as an abstract variable, constructed from ideas or images, which serves as an explanatory term.

[20] Evidence converges when different sources have few if any contradictions and generally support each other and thus offer a credible picture.

[21] One external examiner recently declared that he considered it necessary for the doctoral degree candidate to undertake 100 case studies. This is indeed a very extreme view and would hardly be achievable by any one researcher in an acceptable period of time. By the time 100 case studies were completed the research question would almost certainly be irrelevant.

[22] The issue of the evidence not supporting the theoretical conjecture or the hypotheses or the empirical generalisations causes considerable unnecessary concern for some students. By rejecting the theoretical conjecture etc., something of value may well have been added to the body of knowledge. The researcher is not expected to be right, whatever that might be, but rather to conduct competent research and to report faithfully his or her findings and to be able to argue convincingly why the business and management community should accept the findings.

[23] There have been technological breakthroughs in various fields, including genetics and astronomy, which have allowed scientists to measure in a way impossible before.

[24] A story is an account or a rendition of an event or a series of events in such a way that it has meaning to the listener or reader. According to the Meriam-Webster's *Collegiate Dictionary* (1997), an account is a statement or exposition of reasons, causes, or motives and a rendition is an interpretation or translation of events. Ultimately all research will be reduced to a story of some sort or another. Numbers such as means or standard deviations do not talk. Only words can really convey the meanings of the numbers in any useful way

[25] Aesop is the supposed author of Greek fables dating back to the sixth century BC. These are the oldest known fables in the western world. However, his actual identity has never been established and it is believed that the title 'Aesop's Fables' may simple be a convenience for a collection of folktales of that period.

[26] The familiar English version is a translation of Charles Perrault's 'Cendrillon', a European folktale, published in *Contes de ma mere l'oye* (1697), the theme of which appears in numerous stories from all over the world with more than 500 versions having been found in Europe alone. One of the oldest known accounts of the theme is a Chinese version from the ninth century AD.

[27] The idea of relatability refers to how easy it is to tell the story of the case study, as well as how easy it is to hear the message or the lessons which the case study writer is trying to relate.

11

The Sample

There are three kinds of lies: lies, damned lies and statistics.

(B. Disraeli in: *Mark Twain, Autobiography*, edited by Charles Neider, 1959)

Now, what I want is Facts. Teach these boys and girls nothing but Facts. Facts alone are wanted in life. Plant nothing else, and root out everything else. You can only form the minds of reasoning animals upon Facts: nothing else will ever be of any service to them. This is the principle on which I bring up my own children, and this is the principle on which I bring up these children. Stick to Facts, sir!

(C. Dickens, spoken by Mr Gradgrind, in *Hard Times*, 1854)

11.1 Introduction

This chapter discusses the issue of selecting a sample in business and management research both from a positivistic point of view as well as from the perspective of the phenomenologist. The sampling issue is important because it is seldom possible for a researcher to be able to collect evidence from all members of the population being studied. Most frequently the researcher has to choose or select a subset of all the possible informants[1] in the target population. This selection is referred to as choosing a sample.

11.2 Definition of a Sample

From the point of view of a positivist, empirical research normally requires the selection of those individuals who are to provide the information. This set of individuals is called the sample. The sample normally comes from a larger group of individuals or objects, called the target population. Ideally the sample is chosen so that no significant differences exist between the sample and the population in any important characteristics. In other words, the sample serves as a model for the population, and thus, from a statistical analysis of the sample data, it is possible to generalise to the whole population with a specified degree of confidence.

There are, however, challenges associated with sampling. It is important that the sample is representative of the whole population, for if it is not, then the results may be biased and will not be representative of the population. Whether a sample is considered representative or not is in the final analysis a subjective assessment by those carrying out the survey or those using the results of the survey.

Sampling also has to deal with problems of variability. Even if considerable care is taken to avoid bias, the sample will not be exactly the same as the total population. If another sample were chosen in precisely the same way, it would be different. This limits the accuracy of the sample, and therefore how much confidence can be placed in statements that can be made about the whole population.

11.2.1 *Choice of Sampling Frame*

In the use of a sample one of the first considerations is to obtain a working definition of the population to be studied, which constitutes the sampling frame. This is a comprehensive list of individuals or objects from which the sample is to be drawn. For example, the membership list of a major association of data-processing professionals or, perhaps, the membership list of the Institute Marketing Managers could form the sampling frame. Other examples of sampling frames are the electoral register, the 'Yellow Pages' telephone directory, or companies listed on the New York stock exchange.

11.3 Types of Sample

Sampling techniques fall into two broad categories, namely non-probability samples, which are the domain of the phenomenologist, and probability samples, which are used by the positivistic researcher. For a *non-probability sample* statistical techniques may not be used in the analysis of the evidence. Examples of non-probability samples include *convenience samples, judgement samples, quota samples* and *snowball samples*. In *probability sampling* the assumption is that each individual has a known, not necessarily equal, probability of being selected. Examples of probability sampling include *simple random sampling, systematic sampling, stratified sampling, cluster sampling,* and *multi-stage sampling*. Probability samples can be rigorously analysed by means of statistical techniques.

11.3.1 *Non- Probability Samples*

From the point of view of a phenomenologist, the selection of a random sample is seldom if ever relevant. Thus non-probability sampling which is based on some sort of subjective assessment of the sample is an appropriate approach.

In non-probability sampling the subjective judgements of the researchers are used in selecting the sample. Clearly, this could result in the sample being biased.[2] Non-probability samples are particularly relevant in exploratory research. The more popular non-probability sampling methods are described below.

11.3.1.1 *Convenience Samples*
Convenience samples comprise those individuals or organisations that are most readily available to participate in the study. Such samples are extensively used in universities or business school research, where the samples often comprise a group of students or sometimes executives attending short post-experience courses at the time the research is being pursued.

11.3.1.2 Judgement Samples

Judgement samples, also called purposive samples, are samples where individuals are selected with a specific purpose in mind, such as their likelihood of representing best practice in a particular issue. The composition of such a sample is not made with the aim of it being statistically representative of the population. Such samples comprise individuals considered to have the knowledge and information to provide useful ideas and insights. This approach is extensively used in the exploratory research stage and is invaluable in ensuring a 'good' final questionnaire.

11.3.1.3 Snowball Samples

A snowball sample is one where the researcher uses an informant to help him or her find the next informant. Thus the researcher asks the informant if he or she can introduce the researcher to another person or organisation who is in a position to provide useful information or insights into the issues being researched. Sometimes this is the only way in which a researcher will obtain access to appropriate informants.

11.3.2 Probability Samples

In obtaining a probability sample, use is made of some random procedure for the selection of the individuals or organisations. This is done in an attempt to remove the possibility of selection bias.

11.3.2.1 Simple Random Sampling

In simple random sampling each member of the population should have an equal chance of being selected. This can be achieved by numbering the individuals in the sampling frame, and then selecting from these using some random procedure produced manually or on a computer.

11.3.2.2 Systematic Sampling

A systematic sample is selected from the sampling frame of size N in the following manner. Having decided what size sample n is to be selected from the sampling frame, calculate:

$$\left[\frac{N}{n}\right] \text{ where } [\ ] \text{ denotes the largest integer } I \le \frac{N}{n}$$

Now select a random number i, say, in the interval $1 \le i \le I$. The sample size n then consists of the ith, $(i + I)^{th}$; $(i + 2I)^{th}$ and so on, up to the $(i + (n-1)I)^{th}$ item from the sampling frame.

Should there be some pattern present in the sampling frame, then such samples will be biased. For example, a systematic sample from the daily sales of a supermarket could result in picking out sales figures for Saturdays only.

11.3.2.3 Stratified Sampling

In stratified sampling the population is subdivided into homogeneous groups, called strata, prior to sampling. Random samples are then drawn from each of the strata and the aggregate forms the stratified sample. This can be done in one of two ways:

- The overall sample size *n* can comprise items such that the number of items from each stratum will be in proportion to the size of the stratum.
- The overall sample size can comprise items from each stratum where the number of items from each of the strata are determined according to the relative variability of the items within each of the strata.

The first approach is the one invariably used in practice.

11.3.2.4 Cluster Sampling

In cluster sampling, the population is considered to be made up of groups, called clusters, where the clusters are naturally formed groups such as companies, or locational units.

A cluster sample from a large organisation could be achieved by treating the various departments of a company as the clusters. A random sample of departments could then be chosen and all individuals in the departments sampled. In other words a census of the selected departments (clusters) is performed.

11.3.2.5 Multi-Stage Sampling

An extension of cluster sampling is multi-stage sampling. The simplest multi-stage sample involves random selection of the clusters in the first stage, followed by a random selection of items from each of the selected clusters. This is called two-stage sampling. More complex designs involve more than two stages. For example, in selecting a sample of accounting software users in accounting practices in England and Wales, a random sample of geographic areas may be made from the Institute of Chartered Accountants in England and Wales (ICAEW) membership list. Then, from within the areas, a number of accounting practices may be randomly selected, and finally, in the third stage, a random sample of software users is selected from each of the previously selected practices.

11.4 Size of Sample

Determination of the sample size is a complex problem. Factors which need to be taken into consideration include: type of sample, variability in the population, time, costs, accuracy of estimates required, and confidence with which generalisations to the population are made.

Formulae exist for computing sample size, based on sound scientific principles. In practice, the sample sizes resulting from the application of the formulae are not slavishly adhered to. Often, the samples chosen are of a size that fits in with company policy or are regarded as credible through having been used by others conducting similar studies in the past. Such an approach is acceptable (Lehmann, 1989).

11.4.1 Statistical Determination of Sample Size

This section describes two situations encountered in practice. The first situation concerns how to determine the sample size for estimating a population mean to a specified margin of error, or accuracy, with a specified level of confidence. The second situation shows how to determine the sample size needed to estimate a population proportion (or percentage) to a specified margin of error, or accuracy, within a specified level of confidence.

11.4.2 Sample Size to Estimate the Mean

Suppose the true average of an information system's response time is to be estimated. In order to estimate this, a random sample of response times is taken and the average of these used.

The question is now what size of sample is needed to be 95 per cent confident that the sample mean will be within E units of the true mean, where the unit of measurement of E can be in, say, seconds or minutes? E is therefore the accuracy required from the estimate. Under the assumption that the population from which the sample is being made is very large, the sample size is given by:

$$n = \frac{4\sigma^2}{E^2} \qquad (1)$$

where σ is the population standard deviation of response times.

In practice σ is inevitably unknown and will have to be estimated. This can be done by using response times for a pilot sample of size n_p, say, in the sample standard deviation formula:

$$S = \sqrt{\frac{\sum (x_i - m)^2}{n_p - 1}}$$

where the x_is are the n_p pilot response times, and m is the numerical average of the sample response times.

A simpler approach, often used, is to estimate σ from the range of the pilot sample values. This is done according to the following formula:

$$S_R = \frac{\max(x_i) - \min(x_i)}{4} = \frac{range(x_i)}{4}$$

Some texts suggest division by 6. This is likely to result in an under-estimation of 5. Of course a purely subjective estimate of σ is also possible.

Should it be required to estimate the mean to the same accuracy E as before, but now with a confidence level of 99 per cent, then the sample size is given by:

$$n = \frac{9\sigma^2}{E^2}$$

where σ can be estimated as described above.

11.4.3 Sample Size to Estimate a Percentage.

Suppose a firm wished to estimate the actual percentage, p, say, of its customers who purchase software from a competing company. Suppose further that it required to know what sample size is needed to be 95 per cent confident that the estimate of p resulting from the sample will be within E per cent of the actual percentage, p. Then the required sample size is:

$$n = \frac{4p(100-p)}{E^2} \qquad (2)$$

As before, the formula is based on the assumption that the population from which the sample is drawn is very large.

The caveat in this case is that p is not known, as it is the parameter being estimated. In practice the value of p used in the above formula can be estimated in a number of ways. It can be estimated subjectively, i.e. guessed, or it can be taken from a pilot sample or taken to be 50 per cent. The latter results in the most conservative sample size estimate.

For a 99 per cent confidence level:

$$n = \frac{9p(100-p)}{E^2}$$

where p can be estimated as described above.

11.4.4 Sample Size Correction Factor

As previously stated, the above formulae hold strictly true only when the target population is infinite or very large, and will provide good approximations when the calculated sample size n is small relative to the target population size N. By small it is understood that the sample size is 10 per cent or less of the population size. That is,

$$\frac{n}{N} \times 100 \langle 10\%$$

In situations where the sample size (n) as determined by the formulae in equations (1) and (2) above exceeds 10 per cent of the population size (N), n has to be adjusted downwards by applying a sample size correction factor (see Lehmann, 1989: 301). In this case the required sample size n' is given by:

$$n' = n \times \frac{N}{N+n-1}$$

where $N/(N + n - 1)$ is the sample size correction factor and the use of a sample of size n' will provide the desired accuracy E.

The need for correction often arises in practice. For example, it is likely to occur should a firm decide to conduct an internal survey among staff using the computer network. In practice, all that needs to be done is to apply the sample size calculation under the infinite population size assumption and then if $(n/N) \times 100$ is greater than 10 per cent the calculated sample size n has to be multiplied by the sample size correction factor.

Another situation which arises is the need to calculate the accuracy E', say, associated with a specific confidence level given a sample size n', say, where $n' > 10\%$ of N.

For estimating the percentage accuracy associated with 95% confidence and sample size n':

$$E' = \sqrt{\frac{4P(100-P)}{n'} \times \frac{N-n'}{N-1}}$$

and for estimating the accuracy of the mean associated with 95 per cent confidence and sample size n':

$$E' = \sqrt{\frac{4\sigma^2}{n'} \times \frac{N-n'}{N-1}}$$

Examples of the application of these formulae can be found later in this chapter.

Sample size calculations for more complicated sampling schemes (e.g. stratified sampling) can be found in Lehmann (1989) and Churchill (1994).

11.5   Example 1: Marketing Ventures Ltd

Marketing Ventures Ltd has a regular client base of 15,000 world-wide. In the UK alone there are more than 11,000. The firm wishes to conduct a survey to establish how its customers perceive the after sales service. It is realised that the total number of customers is too large to be able to survey all of them. Therefore it is agreed to use a sample of customers spending more than £10,000 per annum. After much discussion it was decided that in the first instance only the customers in the UK would be surveyed. There are 3000 clients.

Management have asked the survey team to design the measuring procedure so that they can have 95 per cent confidence that its results will be accurate to within 2 per cent.

1   How large a sample should the survey team recommend?
2   How will the sample size change if management change their mind and want to have 99 per cent confidence that the survey team's results are accurate to within 1 per cent?
3   After completing the customer survey Marketing Ventures Ltd want to extend the survey to include all the other users in the UK. How big should the sample be if management want 5 per cent accuracy and a confidence level of 95 per cent.

There are two ways in which a sample size can be calculated. Firstly there is the issue of measuring a percentage of a population, and secondly there is the issue of measuring a mean on a scale.

11.5.1 Measuring a Percentage of a Population

Firstly it is necessary to decide how many respondents have to be surveyed in order to be able to state that a particular percentage of the population have a particular view. This percentage should be stated in terms of an accuracy level and a given degree of confidence. For example, 70 per cent of the population found the system to be effective. This is estimated to 5 per cent accuracy at a confidence level of 95 per cent.

The calculation of sample size requires a relatively subjective procedure in that it requires estimates of variables for which there may be no recent experience.

Before calculating the sample size, it is necessary to know approximately what proportion of the whole population is likely to hold this view. The proportion of the population holding this view is designated P. Once P has been estimated then the formula may be expressed as per the following:

If E is level of accuracy expressed as a percentage and P is proportion of population likely to hold the view expressed as a percentage, then at 95 per cent confidence, the sample size which is designated n is:

$$n = \frac{4 \times P(100 - P)}{E^2}$$

The 95 per cent confidence level determines the 4 in the formula. The P in the formula is expressed as a percentage. In the absence of knowledge of the order of magnitude of P, the most conservative estimate is 50 per cent which will produce the largest sample size.

The calculated result shows how many respondents should return questionnaires to obtain the required accuracy with 95 per cent confidence. If a response rate of 50 per cent is expected, then twice as many as calculated should be dispatched.

In situations where the population size N is finite and is known, should the n calculated by the above formula exceed 10 per cent of N then the appropriate sample size is determined by applying the correction factor noted above to n.

11.5.2 Measuring the Mean on a Scale

The objective is to decide how many customers have to respond to be able to state that the mean score of a rating scale is accurate to a specified level and to a given degree of confidence. For example, using a scale of 1 to 9, the aim would be to state that the mean score for an attribute was, say, 5.0, to a 5 per cent degree of accuracy, with a confidence level of 95 per cent, where the 5 per cent accuracy has to be expressed in units of the rating scale.

Before calculating the sample size it is necessary to estimate the potential variability of the score for the population. This is the standard deviation of the score. As the scale takes values between 1 and 9, in the absence of better information it is suggested that the variability, i.e. standard deviation, be estimated by taking the range of the values and dividing by 4. In the above case this would be 9 minus 1 divided by 4, i.e. 2.

In this case the accuracy has to be expressed in terms of the units of the scale ratings being used. Thus a 5 per cent level of accuracy should be translated in units. In the absence of any better information the mid-point of the scale should be used and 5 per cent of 5 is 0.25 units.

The above two estimates are then used in the following equation. If E is the number of units of accuracy, S is the standard deviation and n is the sample size, then at 95 per cent confidence,

$$n = \frac{4 \times S^2}{E}$$

In situations where the population size N is finite and is known, should the n calculated by the above formula exceed 10 per cent of N then the appropriate sample size is determined by applying the correction factor given above to n.

11.5.3 Marketing Ventures Ltd Solution

1   The size of sample required to be able to measure customer satisfaction with the service to 2 per cent accuracy with 95 per cent confidence.

1.1   *Sample size to estimate a percentage.* In the first instance calculate a sample size assuming an infinite population.

$$n = \frac{4 \times 50(100 - 50)}{2^2} = \frac{4 \times (2500)}{4} = 2500$$

Check whether the calculated sample size exceeds 10 per cent of the population size. If so then a correction should be made which will reduce the sample size.

Since $\dfrac{n}{N} \times 100 = \dfrac{2500}{3000} \times 100 = 83.7\%$ and therefore is $\rangle 10\%$

The above formula substantially overestimates the required sample size. Apply the sample correction factor to calculate the appropriate sample size under these circumstances.

$$n' = n \times \left(\frac{N}{N+n-1} \right)$$

where n' is the appropriate sample size:

$$n' = 2500 \times \left(\frac{3000}{3000 + 2500 - 1} \right)$$

$$n' = 2500 \times (0.546)$$

$$n' = 1364$$

Therefore if 1364 responses are received and the percentage of the sample which holds a view is calculated and quoted then there is 95 per cent confidence that the percentage quoted is accurate to within 2 per cent .

1.2 *Sample size to estimate the mean response.* Again start by applying the formula assuming finite sample size. Thus,

$$n = \frac{4 \times S^2}{E^2}$$

To estimate S, the standard deviation:

$$S = \frac{\max(X_i) - \min(X_i)}{4} = \frac{9-1}{4} = 2$$

therefore $S^2 = (2)^2 = 4$

To express E in terms of the measurement scale's units (the measurement scale goes from 1 to 9) take $E = 5 \times 0.02 = 0.1$ (0.02 corresponds to 2 per cent which is the required accuracy). Hence:

$$n = \frac{4 \times (4)}{(0.1)^2} = \frac{16}{0.01} = 1600$$

Again, if the calculated sample size exceeds 10 per cent of the population size then a correction should be made to reduce the sample size.

$$\text{Since } \frac{n}{N} \times 100 = \frac{1600}{3000} \times 100 = 53.3\% \text{ and therefore is } \rangle 10\%$$

the sample correction factor is applied, giving

$$n' = 1600 \times \left(\frac{3000}{3000 + 1600 - 1} \right) = 1600 \times 0.65 = 1040$$

2 The size of sample required to be able to measure customer satisfaction with the service to 1 per cent accuracy with 99 per cent confidence.

2.1 *Sample size to estimate a percentage.* Proceed as in 1.1 above but using the appropriate formula:

$$n = \frac{9 \times p(100 - p)}{E^2} = \frac{9 \times 50 \times 50}{1^2} = 16,650$$

Since 16,650 is more than 10 per cent of the population size, applying the correction factor the result is:

$$n' = 16,650 \times \left(\frac{3000}{3000 + 16,650 - 1} \right) = 2543$$

2.2 *Sample size to estimate the mean response.* Proceed as in 1.2 but using the appropriate formula:

$$n = \frac{9 \times S^2}{E^2} = \frac{9 \times (2^2)}{(0.1)^2} = 3600$$

Again there is a need to apply the sample correction formula. Thus,

$$n' = 3600 \times \left(\frac{3000}{3000 + 3600 - 1} \right) = 1637$$

3 The size of the sample required to be able to measure customer satisfaction including all the other users in the UK to a 95 per cent confidence level and to 5 per cent accuracy.

3.1 *Sample size to estimate percentage.* In this case we have *n=400*, thus,

$$\frac{n}{N} \times 100 = \frac{400}{11,000} \times 100 = 3.6\%$$

Since the sample size is less than 10% of the population size there is no need to apply the correction formula.

3.2 *Sample size to estimate the mean.* In this case it is necessary to express E in terms of the measurement scale units. Thus in section 1.2, E = 5 × 0.05 = 0.25 (0.05 corresponds to the 5% required accuracy). Also the standard deviation S = 2 as in 1.2 above. Hence:

$$n = \frac{4 \times S^2}{E^2} = \frac{4 \times 4}{0.0625} = 256$$

11.6 Example 2: Sludge Pumps Inc.

Sludge Pumps Inc. is a large engineering firm in the south of England. The firm decided to conduct a survey to establish what the customers believed the service level was. The survey was sent to 1,150 customers and only 256 were returned. The firm would like to know the degree of accuracy and the degree of confidence that it may associate with the results of the questionnaire.

11.6.1 Sludge Pumps Inc. Solution

The total population is denoted by *N* and the number of valid responses to the returned questionnaires is n'. Therefore *N* = 1150, *n'* = 256 and thus *n'* > 10% of *N*, so the correction factor should be applied.

1 Estimating the percentage accuracy associated with 95 per cent confidence, sample size *n'*.

$$E = \sqrt{\frac{4p(100 - p)}{n'} \times \frac{N - n'}{N - 1}}$$

$$E = \sqrt{\frac{4 \times 2500}{256} \times \frac{1150 - 256}{1150 - 1}}$$

$$E = \sqrt{\frac{10,000}{256} \times \frac{894}{1149}}$$

$$E = 5.5\%$$

Note: if *n'* is small relative to *N* then $\frac{N - n'}{N - 1} = 1$

2   Accuracy achieved when estimating the mean.

$$E = \sqrt{\frac{4(4)}{256} \times \frac{(1150 - 256)}{11,501}} = \sqrt{0.0047} = 0.22$$

If the average was 5 then the accuracy expressed as a percentage of the mean would be 0.22 / 5 × 100 = 4.4 per cent.

11.7 Summary and Conclusion

This chapter has discussed the issues relating to the question of sampling and the calculation of an appropriate sample size. This is an important issue for those researchers who are following a positivistic strategy to their research and it is believed that the information in this chapter will provide such a researcher with a useful guide to the subject. It is hoped that the use of practical examples to show how the mathematics of sample size is calculated will help make clear how these formulae can be used. Students who do not have a mathematical background will probably need to obtain assistance from specialists, at least in so far as checking that the formulae have been used in an appropriate way.

Suggested Further Reading

Fleiss, J. L. (1986) *The Design and Analysis of Clinical Experiments*. John Wiley, New York.
Mead, R. (1988) *The Design of Experiments: Statistical Principles for Practical Applications*. Cambridge University Press, Cambridge.
Moroney, M. J. (1992) *Facts from Figures*. Pelican, Middlesex.
Phillips, J. L. (1982) *Statistical Thinking*. Freeman, New York.
Porkess, R. (1988) *Dictionary of Statistics*. Collins, London.
Rees, D. G. (1991) *Essential Statistics*. Second Edition, Chapman and Hall, London.
Spiegal, M. R. (1992) *Statistics – Schaums' Outline Series*. McGraw Hill Book Company, New York.

Notes

[1] In this context an informant may be an individual in his or her own right or may be a representative of an organisation. Of course it is also possible to select a sample from an impersonal list such as a list of all the firms quoted on the London Stock Exchange.

[2] In business and management research it is often the case that a biased sample is required. If the researcher is interested in developing guidelines for managers then he or she is only interested in learning from organisations who may be considered to be good or excellent performers. Even when the researcher wants to study poor performance in order to learn what mistakes to avoid, then the sample that he or she would seek would also be biased.

12

Statistical Analysis

Like dreams, statistics are a form of wish fulfillment.

(Jean Baudrillard, *Cool Memories*, 1987)

He uses statistics as a drunken man uses lamp-posts for support rather than illumination.

(Andrew Lang, cited in Alan L. Mackay, *The Harvest of a Quiet Eye*, 1977)

12.1 Introduction

This chapter discusses the role of statistical analysis in the research process for masters and doctorate students in business and management studies. By its nature statistical analysis is only relevant to those research candidates who are following a positivistic strategy to their research. This chapter does not attempt to present a detailed or technical account of statistical analysis. Rather it presents an overview of the issues and the techniques available to the researcher. What this chapter achieves is to introduce the key concepts and ideas that lie behind the statistical analysis of evidence so that not only will it be known what tests to use but also why they are being used and what the statistics actually mean.

12.2 Background

When presented with a mathematical formula or even a statistical table, the eyes of many business and management researchers glaze over, the subject under discussion is changed rapidly and there is relief all around. Yet mathematics gives enormous power to those who appreciate it. This chapter will not attempt to explain the details and complexity of how a particular statistical test or formula is used. These details and formulae can be found in the many books on statistics that jostle for position on the shelves of bookshops. Rather, it will try to convince the reader that mathematics is important for the analysis and interpretation of evidence in the business and management world; that it enables us to deal with and to solve problems that otherwise would be quite intractable; and that in this day and age of modern computers and computer packages it no longer requires a degree in statistics to be able to use the most modern and powerful statistical methods.

It is also important to stress at the outset that evidence is never collected without the researcher already having some notion of what is expected in the evidence. If large amounts of evidence are simply gathered and then run through a statistical package it is unlikely to generate anything but large amounts of incomprehensible numbers. What should be done is think carefully about the problem at hand and decide on what may be going on. The evidence collection can then be planned in such a way as to be able to test ideas as carefully as possible, and to look at the evidence and see whether or not the patterns that are expected are indeed there. Only then should statistical analysis be used to ensure that the patterns observed are not simply there by chance, but really do reflect the underlying processes that the researcher is attempting to understand. All too often, statistics are used, in the words of Andrew Lang quoted at the beginning of this chapter, 'as a drunkard uses lamp-posts for support rather than illumination'.

12.3 The Origins and Basis of Statistics

Modern statistics has its origins in the study of games of chance. If two dice are thrown in a game of craps, what is the chance of throwing a six? Is it easier to get a six by throwing a two and a four or by throwing two threes? In such situations it is never possible to predict, with certainty, what the outcome will be. However, it is possible to predict with great precision what will be the relative probability of various outcomes. Provided the dice are not loaded the chance of throwing two threes is 1 in 36, the chance of throwing a two and a four is 1 in 18. This follows immediately because it is only possible to throw two threes in one way while a two and a four can be thrown in two ways so that the latter outcome is twice as likely as the former.

In statistics, then, the basic unit of analysis, the fundamental concept which underlies all else, is the notion of probability distributions of various outcomes, But it is necessary to think clearly about what is meant by 'probability'. Take the spinning of a coin and the question, 'What is the probability of getting heads rather than tails?' Most people would say 50 per cent or 1 in 2. But try to be more precise and ask what this means. There are several ways in which the answer could be expanded further.

One way would be to say that the result is just as likely to be heads as to be tails. But this only says the same thing in different words and what is probably meant is that the definition as given has to be taken, that it cannot be explained further.

Another explanation might be to say that if a coin is thrown many times, the result will be heads on about half the throws. To test this, a penny was thrown one million times (admittedly with the aid of a computer pretending to be a penny) and the result was 500,737 heads and 499,263 tails. The proportion of heads was 50.07 per cent, which almost, but not exactly, equals the expected 50 per cent. So how close to 50 per cent is it necessary to be before it can be said that heads and tails are indeed equally likely?

Still another explanation might be that if someone throws a coin, it is worth betting that it will land heads only if the odds offered are better than 1 to 1.

These answers represent three ways of looking at probability. The first, *a priori,* approach says that the concept cannot be reduced further and so it simply has to be accepted that a thing called probability exists. The next step is to define laws for combining probabilities, derive theorems about probabilities (much as is done with Euclidean geometry at school) and then try to match our theoretical predictions with the outcome of whatever experiments are done.

The second, empirical or experimental approach says that probability should be defined in terms of *long-run frequencies*. This is certainly a useful way to think about probability and is the way most people do think about it. In the first edition of his book *Logic*, the English philosopher John Stuart Mill wrote (Bulmer, 1979: 5):

> Why in tossing up a half-penny do we reckon it equally probable that we shall throw heads or tails? Because we know that in any great number of throws, heads and tails are thrown equally often; and that the more throws we make, the more nearly the equality is perfect.

But this long-run approach is not without its problems. One might agree that there is a definite probability that it is possible to get run over by a bus tomorrow: but if this does happen, it is hardly likely that the experiment will be repeated many times.

The third way of looking at probability, which might be called the casino definition, is particularly suited to those who gamble. While it is not appropriate to suggest that Mill led a dissipated life, he explicitly rejected the frequency definition in the later editions of his book and gave the following definition instead (Bulmer, 1979: 6):

> We must remember that the probability of an event is not a quality of the event itself, but a mere name for the degree of ground which we have for expecting it. Every event is in itself certain, not probable: if we knew all, we should either know positively that it will happen, or positively that it will not. But its probability means to us the degree of expectation of its occurrence, which we are warranted in entertaining by our present evidence.

This would seem to be a useful definition for actuaries and insurance brokers.

In science you should always follow the approach that best suits you. In the first, *a priori* view of probability, an unbiased coin is simply defined as one for which the probability of heads is 0.5 and the laws of probability are used to work out whether 500,737 heads in one million throws is a reasonable outcome given the hypothesis that the coin is unbiased. In other words, in the physical and life sciences, a hypothesis is stated, an experiment is performed and then the resulting evidence is looked at to see if it is in reasonable agreement with the expectations: if it is not the hypothesis should be reconsidered and possibly the evidence as well.

Testing hypotheses not only makes for more rigorous statistics but helps the researcher to remember that the reason mathematics is used is not to generate large amounts of obscure numbers, but to help to formulate clear and precise hypotheses to test.

Sometimes the second, the long-run frequency idea, is the most useful. If it is difficult to decide on how to assign frequencies or probabilities, or indeed to decide on what might be the important factors in an experiment, the question to ask is: What would be expected to happen if this experiment is repeated many times?

The third, casino, approach can also be useful because it reminds us that the random nature of our observations arises, at least in part, from our lack of knowledge of the precise factors affecting our experiments. Given some information, it might then be possible to make certain predictions concerning the outcome of an experiment. But more information might lead us to change the prediction and this reflects well the provisional nature of scientific knowledge.

12.4 Representing Evidence

Evidence may be represented by graphical summaries such as bar charts and histograms, tabular summaries such as one-way and two-way relative frequency tables and by numerical summaries such as the mean and the standard deviation.

12.4.1 Bar Charts and Histograms

The first step is to decide how to represent the kinds of outcomes that there are in statistics and the standard way, familiar to everyone, is to use bar charts or frequency histograms. A chart is drawn in which the height of each bar is proportional to the frequency with which that outcome occurs or, by dividing each bar by the total number of observed events, to estimate the probability with which that outcome occurs.

The bar chart can be used for category or qualitative data, and emphasises the relative size of the numbers in the data. Figure 12.1 shows a bar chart of the number of units sold by five different companies. It is easy to see, from the height of the bars, which product sells most.

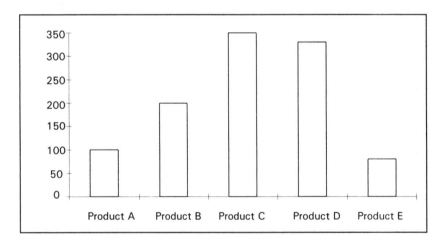

Figure 12.1   *The number of units sold by five different companies*

The histogram, which is a close relation of the bar chart, is used to summarise quantitative data. It is a bar chart where the widths of the bars are of significance as well as the heights, for instance the number of people in different age groups. Figure 12.2 is a histogram showing the number of organisations in different risk groups.

It is possible, though a bit confusing, to use histograms where all the bars are not of equal widths. If the histogram is well behaved, usually with a peak in the middle of the distribution, tailing off towards the sides, a new observation can be taken to see whether it falls within a reasonably likely part of the distribution or if it is an outlier – when there is something unusual about this particular observation which demands further investigation. But this may be tedious to do and it is preferable to be able to summarise the distribution in a more convenient way.

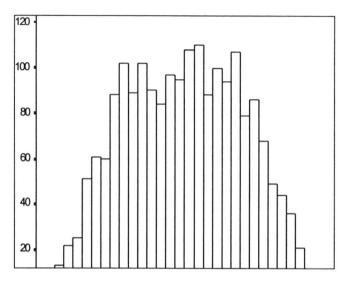

Figure 12.2   *The frequency of organisations falling within net profit groupings*

12.5 Measures of Distribution

Distributions can be summaries in terms of certain key characteristics. In statistics this has traditionally been achieved by using such summary measures as the mean, the median and the standard deviation. Range and quartiles are other dimensions that are sometimes used.

12.5.1 The Mean

The most common measure of location is the mean. This is calculated by making a series of measurements and then adding up the results of the measurements and dividing by the total number of measurements. Everything in mathematics can also be described in words, but as the descriptions rapidly become cumbersome and even tedious, mathematicians have added their own words and symbols to language so that things can be described more concisely and easily. The mathematical sentence, corresponding to the above description of the mean, is then:

$$m = \frac{\sum_{i=1}^{n} x_i}{n} \qquad (1)$$

which, expressed in words, simply reads 'the mean is equal to the sum of the values of x from i equal one to n divided by n'.

12.5.2 The Median

Another measure of location is the median, which is the measurement that falls in the middle of the distribution so that there are as many items below it as above it. An example of a situation in which it might be appropriate to use the median rather than the mean could be an experiment to measure the time it takes for individuals to complete a task.

Starting with 11 individuals and measuring the time it takes each one to finish a task, the mean time to complete the job can be calculated. But if the last person takes a long time to finish, most of the time might have been spent waiting for this last person. To obtain the median time, on the other hand, it is only necessary to know the time at which the sixth person finishes, after which the experiment can be stopped.

A further advantage of the median is that if there are outliers in the evidence, that is to say, a few points that are very much larger or very much smaller than the others, these points will influence the mean greatly. For example, the mean of 2, 4 and 6 is 4 and the mean of 2, 4 and 100 is 53, while in both cases the median is 4.

12.5.3 Standard Deviation

Having decided where the evidence is located, the next thing to know is how widely it is scattered about this central measure of location. One way to do this would be to take the difference between each number and the mean and then work out some sort of average value of this deviation. However, care is required because the mean of the numbers 1, 2 and 3 is 2, the deviations from the mean are −1, 0 and 1 and the mean deviation is 0! This clearly does not capture the spread in the numbers. To get around this problem the deviations are calculated as before, the numbers are squared, the squared numbers are added together, the result is divided by the number of points and then the square root of the answer is taken. Squaring the numbers ensures that all differences contribute positively to the answer. In the example the squared deviations are 1, 0 and 1, the sum is 2; divide this by 3 to get the mean of the squared deviations and the answer is $\sqrt{2/3} \approx 0.8$. However, this also makes it clear that words are rapidly becoming limiting in helping to write down these ideas concisely and so they are instead expressed mathematically as:

$$s = \sqrt{\sum (x_i - m)^2 / (n - 1)} \qquad (2)$$

If we read the formula from right to left, we understand it as saying that the standard deviation is the root-mean-square deviation from the mean[1].

The more widely scattered the evidence is around the mean the greater the standard deviation. The standard deviation tells how much scatter there is in the evidence. Since the mean is most interesting as the best estimate of the 'true' value, it is also necessary to know how accurate the estimate of the mean is. Clearly, the more measurements made the better the estimate of the mean and it can be shown that the standard error, the standard deviation of the mean, is:

$$s.e. = s / \sqrt{n} \qquad\qquad (3)$$

Immediately the power of expressing thoughts in a concise mathematical way can be seen. For example, take a series of measurements for which the standard deviation of the mean is ± 10 per cent. It is decided that a better level of precision is required, say ± 5 per cent. Then equation (3) says that to halve the error limits it is necessary to take four times as many measurements and it can then be decided if this is worthwhile or indeed feasible.

12.5.4 Range

The median often provides a simpler measure of the location of the distribution than does the mean; similarly it might be appropriate to choose to use the range rather than the standard deviation as a measure of the spread in the evidence. The range would then simply correspond to the largest value minus the smallest value, but again if there are outliers in the evidence they would influence the range greatly. It might then be preferable to use the interquartile range which would be the difference between two points, the lower corresponding to a point below which one quarter of the points lie (the lower quartile) and the other to a point above which one quarter of the points lie (the upper quartile).

12.6 Distributions

Having decided how to represent and describe distributions we find out that there are a few common, and therefore important, distributions which arise in statistics. The first is the binomial distribution, which is the case whenever there are only two possible outcomes: heads or tails, true of false, girls or boys, and so on. The binomial distribution then shows the probability of having two boys in a family of eight children, three heads if a coin is spun seven times, and so on. The Poisson distribution is the limiting case of the binomial distribution when the probability of one of the outcomes is very small. Indeed Poisson discovered the distribution named after him when he studied evidence on the number of Prussian army officers who were kicked to death by their horses each year. In addition to these there are a number of other fundamental distributions, but the most important of all is the normal distribution in which the distribution of outcomes follows the familiar bell-shaped curve.

The reason for the importance of the normal distribution follows from what is known in statistical circles as the *central limit theorem*, which says that the sum of a large number of independently distributed random numbers is nearly always normally distributed. The height of a child depends on genetic make-up, the parents' genetic make-up, diet, the amount of exercise taken, whether or not the parents suffered from various diseases in childhood and so on. The result is that the heights of a large number of children will nearly always be normal and led Francis Galton (*Encyclopaedia Britannica*, 1997) to say, 'The Law of Frequency of Error ... reigns with serenity and in complete self-effacement amidst the wildest confusion. The huger the mob and the greater the apparent anarchy the more perfect is its sway.' When the evidence is analysed statistically it can nearly always be assumed that the errors are normally distributed.

12.7 Testing Hypotheses

Before the various options that are available are considered for statistical testing of the evidence, it is useful to consider precisely what is being asked of the evidence. To be clear it is also necessary to be rather formal, so let us consider a test to decide if a coin is biased so that it is more likely to fall heads than tails.

The first point is that the experiment would not be being conducted unless there was some reason to believe that the coin is in fact biased so that the hypothesis being examined is that *there is a biased coin*.

Evidence is collected by spinning the coin 100 times which produces a result of 65 heads and 35 tails. This seems to confirm the hypothesis, but even if the coin is not biased it is possible, if unlikely, that this could be the result. Being cautious people, we set up a null hypothesis, which is the denial of what is being shown, by asking 'Could this outcome have occurred if the coin were not biased?' and hope to be able to disprove the null hypothesis.

Since the distribution of heads or tails follows a binomial distribution a statistical package is used to ask 'What is the probability that there could have been 65 or more heads in 100 throws if the null-hypothesis is true?' In this particular case it turns out that the probability of getting 65 or more heads in 100 throws is about 1 in 500. It is concluded that the outcome was unlikely to have arisen by chance and that it is likely therefore that the coin is biased.

To summarise: it is assumed that something is happening and it is necessary to see if the evidence supports this. Since it is all too easy for human beings to see what they want to see, rather than what is actually there, it is assumed that nothing is happening. A decision is made as to whether the observed result could have arisen by chance, and if the answer is no, then the pursuance of the hypothesis is justified. It is important to stress that this does not 'prove' the hypothesis true, only that something is there and the hypothesis provides a useful point from which to start.

What happens when the null hypothesis is not disproved? Suppose the coin was thrown only 20 times and there were 13 heads. The proportion of heads (65 per cent) is exactly the same as before. But on looking up the statistical tables we will find that this could have happened by chance if the null hypothesis is true, with a probability of about 1 in 7. All that can then be said is that the null hypothesis has not been disproved; it cannot be said that the original hypothesis is false. The evidence is therefore neutral on the truth or otherwise of the original hypothesis.

12.8   Type I and Type II Errors

This can be formalised further by noting that there are two kinds of error: the null hypothesis can be rejected when it is true (Type I) or be accepted when it is false (Type II). When experiments are designed it is important to try and ensure that the probability of making a Type I error is small – this is referred to as the significance level of the test. If the probability of making a Type I error is less than 1 per cent it is described as having a 1 per cent significance level, and if less than 0.1 per cent as having a 0.1 per cent significance level. Since the aim is to be able to reject the null hypothesis, the smaller the significance level the better. If the significance level is greater than 5 per cent it is generally accepted that the result is not significant; if between 5 per cent and 1 per cent it is given one star,[2] between 1 per cent and 0.1 per cent two stars; and below 0.1 per cent three stars.

In order to determine the probability of making a Type II error, an alternative hypothesis is required: in the case of the coins example it might be said that the alternative hypothesis is that the expected number of heads is 80 out of 100. It is then possible to decide on the probability of observing 65 heads if the true expected value is 80 heads and this is specified as the power of the test.

In general the alternative hypothesis is not well defined but it needs to be considered when deciding on the sample size in experiments. In the case of the coins it might be said that if the bias is small, so, for example, the expected value is 51 heads and 49 tails, that this is not of interest. However, if the bias is large, so the expected value is 80 heads and 20 tails, it is of interest. If the significance level is set to, say, 5 per cent, and the power of the test (1 minus the probability of making a Type II error) is set at say 90 per cent, the computer program will then calculate how big a sample is needed in order to test the evidence at the 5 per cent significance level and with 90 per cent power.

12.9   Comparisons

It is often necessary to test two sets of measurements to determine if the mean values differ. For each set of measurements the mean response can be calculated and a test can be done to determine whether the means differ significantly. For example, if the mean and standard errors of the means for the first set of evidence are m_1 and s_1, and for the second set are m_2 and s_2, then the difference in the means is $d = m_1 - m_2$, and the standard error of the difference is:

$$e = \sqrt{s_1^2 + s_2^2}$$

It is presumably hoped that d differs significantly from zero so a null hypothesis is made that the true value of d is equal to zero, and this is tested to see if it could have arisen by chance. If it is assumed that e is normally distributed then the absolute value of d should exceed $1.96 \times e$ with less than 5 per cent probability which is the same as saying that if d/e is greater than 1.96 the null hypothesis at the 5 per cent significance level can be rejected. The procedure is then straightforward: calculate the difference to test, divide it by the standard error of the difference and determine the significance level from a table of a standard normal distribution.

For a normal distribution the test statistic exceeds 1.96 with 5 per cent probability and 2.63 with 1 per cent probability, so that from the second column in Table 12.1 the difference between actual and expected sales is significant at the 5 per cent but not at the 1 per cent level.

Table 12.1   *The expected and actual sales of 10 salespersons*

Month	Expected sales	Actual sales	Difference
Jan	538	687	149
Feb	483	611	128
Mar	536	679	143
Apr	521	648	127
May	545	716	171
Jun	474	603	129
Jul	430	616	186
Aug	472	630	158
Sep	474	723	248
Oct	487	662	175
Nov	446	627	181
Dec	596	648	52
Mean	500.2	654.2	153.9
Std.	47.5	40.1	46.6
Mean diff.	154.0		
Std. Diff.	62.1		
t	2.48		3.30

For large samples this works well, but if the sample size is small a problem arises because, although the estimate of the mean is sound, for small numbers the estimate of the standard error is always significantly underestimated. This difficulty was solved by William Gossett, who wrote under the *nom de plume* of 'Student'. Gossett showed that even for small numbers of evidence points it is still possible to test the ratio of d/e, and he provided what is now called Student's t-distribution which is used instead of the normal distribution. For the *t.d.*-test it is necessary to know the number of degrees of freedom which is given by the number of evidence points minus the number of parameters estimated from the evidence, in this case 2 since two means have been used. If the number of points, and therefore the number of degrees of freedom, is sufficiently large the t-distribution is the same as the normal distribution and the original result will be returned.

For the evidence in Table 12.1 a *t*-test with 18 degrees of freedom (20 points minus 2 means) should be used for which the critical values are 2.10 and 2.88. Note that these are slightly greater than the values for the normal distribution so that the *t*-test is more conservative than the test assuming normal distributions. However, the difference is still significant at the 5 per cent level.

12.9.1 Paired and Unpaired t-Tests

The test described above is called an unpaired *t*-test because it has been assumed that the two sets of measurements are made on separate individuals, organisations or other sampling units. If it is possible to make both measurements on the same person, organisation or sampling unit, a more powerful test can be developed. Instead of testing the difference between the means, the difference between each pair of means is calculated and then the standard deviations of the mean of the differences is calculated. This is called a paired *t*-test since it has been possible to treat the evidence points in pairs.

Since the expected and actual sales are measured for the same people, the difference between each pair of means is taken, the mean *difference* is calculated, which turns out to be the same as the difference between the means, but then the standard deviation of the *differences* is calculated. Since there are 10 differences and one mean, the number of degrees of freedom is now 9. For a *t*-test with 9 degrees of freedom, the critical values are 2.26 and 3.25 at the 5 per cent and 1 per cent levels respectively so that the difference is now significant at the 1 per cent level. The paired T-test therefore gives a more powerful test but of course can only be applied when the observations are made on the same individual, organisation or sample so they can be analysed in pairs.

12.10   Tests of Association

Another commonly encountered problem is to decide if there is an association between two factors in an experiment. For example, it might be necessary to know if men and women differ in their relative earning power. Suppose the number of men and women in a village who earn more or less than, say, £20,000 per year are counted and the results in Table 12.2 are returned.

Table 12.2   *The number of men and women earning more or less than £20,000 p.a.*

	Men	Women	Row totals
< £20,000	130	105	235
> £20,000	160	85	245
Column totals	290	190	480

The requirement is to know whether income is associated with gender. Starting from the null hypothesis that income and gender are *not* associated then the probability that a man earns more than £20,000 is the probability that one of the sample is male (290/480) times the probability that one of the sample earns less than £20,000 (235/480). The number of men who are expected to earn less than £20,000 *if there is no association between gender and income* is therefore:

$$E(\text{men earning} < £20,000) = \frac{290}{480} \times \frac{235}{480} \times 480 = \frac{290 \times 235}{480} = 142$$

This can be repeated to get the expected numbers in each cell of the table noting that in each the row total is multiplied by the column total and the result is divided by the grand total. To see if the expected and observed values differ significantly, it can be noted that

$$\chi^2 = \sum \frac{(O_i - E_i)^2}{E_i} \qquad (4)$$

follows a χ^2 distribution with $(R - 1) \times (C - 1)$ degrees of freedom, where R and C denote the number of rows and columns respectively. In this particular case there is one degree of freedom, the χ^2 statistic is 5, and the table of the χ^2 distribution indicates that a value greater than 5 with one degree of freedom corresponds to a probability of 2.5 per cent so that the association between income and gender is significant at the 5 per cent but not at the 1 per cent level. The probability that the observed evidence could have arisen by chance, *if the null hypothesis is true*, is then less than 5 per cent, which means the null hypothesis can be rejected and it can be concluded that there is an association between income and gender.

12.11 Regression

So far pairs of numbers have been compared or associations between different categories have been looked for. However, it might also be necessary to consider problems in which the variables are continuous where it is hoped to identify trends in the evidence. For example, to ascertain if more beer is sold when the weather is hot the first step would be to plot a graph of the amount of beer sold against the temperatures as shown in Figure 12.3 and Table 12.3.

A straight line could be drawn that is considered to 'best fit' the evidence and then whether the slope of the line is upward or downward could be determined. This is just what regression does but it does two particular things. Firstly it gives the 'best fit' line and secondly it enables the error in the slope to be determined so that it can be seen if the slope differs significantly from zero. Again the null hypothesis would be that the amount of beer sold does not depend on temperature so that if the slope does not differ significantly from zero it is not possible to establish an association.

Table 12.3 *The amount of beer sold and the average temperature for each month*

Temperature (°C)	Beer sold (gallons)	Fitted (gallons)
33	250	267
35	270	273
30	260	257
28	240	251
29	240	254
32	250	264
36	300	277
31	275	261
27	250	248
30	260	257
22	240	232
26	250	245

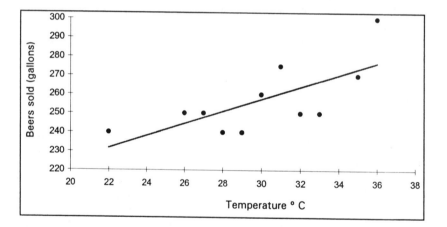

Figure 12.3 *The amount of beer sold and the average temperature for each month*

To determine the best fit line the computer software assumes, in this case, that a straight line is being fitted so that the equation of the line is:

$$y = a + bx \qquad (5)$$

where *a* is the intercept on the *y* axis and *b* is the slope of the line.

The software then calculates the values of *a* and *b* for which the root-mean-square value of the deviations from the line is a minimum which is directly analogous to the calculation of the standard error of the mean.

The line shown in Figure 12.3 is then the best fit line and the evidence in Table 12.4 shows the best fit values of the slope and the intercept on the *y* axis as well as their standard errors. The slope of the lines is 3.21 and this is significant at the 1 per cent level (*p*-values less than 0.01). Since the slope is 3.21, sales increase by 3.21 gallons for every degree centigrade rise in temperature. The software also gives 95 per cent confidence limits for the slope, which range from 0.98 to 5.43 gallons per degree centigrade.

Table 12.4 *The slope, intercept and statistics for the best fit line*

	Coeff.	Std. Error	t-stat	p-value	Lower[3] 95%	Upper 95%
Intercept	161	30	5.3	0.00032	94	228
Slope	3.21	1.00	3.2	0.00925	0.98	5.43

12.12 Correlation

An alternative measure of association for evidence such as this is the correlation coefficient. For example, for the question 'Does profitability go up or down with size of organisation?' the correlation coefficient[4] is calculated as

$$r = \frac{\sum (x_i - \bar{x})(y_i - \bar{y})}{n s_x s_y} \qquad (6)$$

If there is a perfect positive correlation between *x* and *y* then $r = 1$; if there is a perfect negative correlation then $r = -1$; and if there is no correlation then $r = 0$. For the evidence in Figure 12.3 the correlation co-efficient is 0.50 so that the correlation is positive as expected from the previous analysis.

12.13 Analysis of Variance

The next most important kind of evidence that needs to be analysed, arises when there is a series of categorical independent variables for each of which a continuous dependent variable is measured. In the example given in Table 12.5 the salaries of men and women in each of two companies have been measured.

The requirement is to know if salary depends on gender, or on the organisation paying the salary, and if there is any interaction between the two. In this case the ANOVA techniques can be used which are similar in concept to regression techniques. Essentially what the programs do is to calculate the mean value for each category and then tests can be performed to see which of the factors significantly affects the outcome. The ANOVA given in Table 12.6 shows that the particular organisation significantly affects the income whereas the gender of the employees does not. The mean values for each level of companies and gender can then be plotted in order to confirm the observation.

Table 12.5   *Salaries of men and women in two different companies*

Organisation	Males	Females
A	3712	5165
A	3964	4140
A	4132	6743
A	3719	5308
A	5061	3822
B	7793	7632
B	6776	6207
B	7533	4493
B	7184	8135
B	7583	5253

The program first subtracts the mean of all of the evidence. It then calculates the sum of the squares of the differences from the means for each factor (sums-of-squares, SS, in Table 12.6). Each sum of squares is divided by the number of degrees of freedom for that factor (2 − 1 for each of companies and gender) to get a mean square. It turns out the ratio of two mean squares follows an *F*-distribution and the table gives the significance level for each factor.

Table 12.6   *Analysis of variance for the evidence shown in Table 12.5*

Source of Variation	SS	df	MS	F	P-value
Companies	26044466	1	26044466	25.01512	0.00013
Gender	15624.05	1	15624.05	0.015007	0.90402
Interaction	4742406	1	4742406	4.554973	0.04864
Within	16658385	16	1041149		
Total	47460882	19			

Having decided that there is a difference between the companies, we can plot the mean salary for each organisation (averaged over gender), which shows (in Figure 12.4) that organisation B pays significantly more than organisation A.

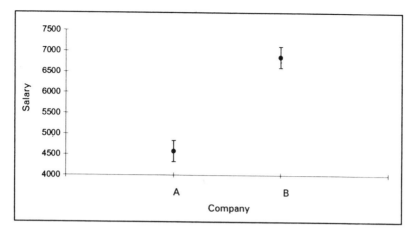

Figure 12.4 *The mean salaries paid by the two companies*

Plotting the mean salaries for gender shows that on average men and women do not earn significantly different salaries. This can be seen in Figure 12.5.

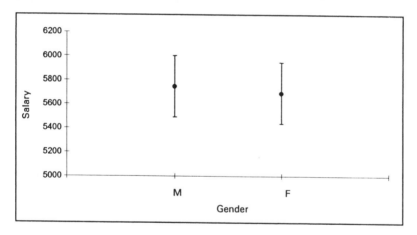

Figure 12.5 *The mean salaries paid to men and to women*

However, there is an interaction between gender and companies. Figure 12.6 shows the salaries paid to men and to women by each organisation. Although men and women earn, on average, the same salaries, it can be seen that organisation A pays women more than it does men while organisation B pays men more than it does women, and this is reflected in the 'interaction' row in Table 12.6.

What the ANOVA does is to test for each factor separately, averaging over all other factors, and then testing for interactions between the factors. With only two levels (men and women, organisation A and organisation B) for each factor (gender and organisation) the analysis could almost be done simply by plotting graphs. In a more complicated analysis with several factors, each with several levels, the ANOVA quickly enables the factors or interactions that are significant

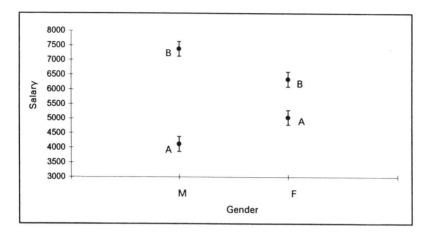

Figure 12.6   *The mean salaries paid to men and to women by the two companies*

to be identified and then the means to be examined in each case to decide why that factor or interaction influences the result.

12.14   Multivariate Analysis

There are a number of more sophisticated multivariate analysis techniques available to the researcher. Two of the most frequently used are factor analysis and correspondence analysis. These techniques are extremely powerful and they can make a major contribution to the research. Frequently they provide insights which are not otherwise obvious to the research. According to Dunbar (1996):

> Statistical analysis, which uses mathematical techniques to separate out the influence of different factors, has made possible a dramatic rise in the number of non-experimental empirical studies, especially in the second half of the present century.

12.14.1   Factor Analysis

Factor analysis is a mathematical or statistical technique or procedure that can assist the researcher in conceptualising a problem especially with regards to data reduction and the exploration of underlying dimensions.

According to Kerlinger (1969) it is a method for determining the number and nature of which underlie the dimensions (or factors) among large numbers of measures of the concepts or constructs being evaluated or explored.

Factor analysis is a technique used to locate and identify fundamental properties underlying the results of tests or measurements and which cannot be measured directly. (A factor is a hypothetical entity that is assumed to underlie the results of the tests.) It is therefore a technique that can be used to provide a parsimonious description of a complex multi-faceted intangible concept such as the quality of service or the relationship between individuals in an organisation.

The mathematics underpinning factor analysis is the analysis of the inter-relationships between variables as measured by their correlations. The mathematical analysis required is substantial and thus a dedicated software package is needed, together with a reasonably powerful personal computer. Factor analysis is available with most large statistical software packages.

In using factor analysis there are traditionally four steps to be performed by the researcher with the computer results which are:

1   Consult the Kaiser-Meyer-Olkin (KMO) measure of sampling adequacy as it offers some idea of how relevant the factor analysis is for the evidence being used. The rule for the use of this statistic is that if the KMO is less than 0.50 there is no value in proceeding with the technique. The greater the value of the KMO the more effective the factor analysis is likely to be.

2   Examine the eigen-values. Only factors with an eigen-value of greater than one are used in the analysis. The reason for selecting eigen-values greater than one is that this suggests that the factors concerned, which are linear combinations of the original variables, will explain more variability than any one of the original variables on their own.

3   Study the rotated factor matrix. Examine each factor separately, looking for the input variables that influence the factor, which have a loading of 0.5 or more.

4   Attempt to combine the meaning of the variables identified in 3 above into an underlying factor or super-variable which will explain the combined effect of these individual variables, and will become the invisible factor the analysis attempts to isolate. What is being sought is a relatively simple description of the complex effect of several of the original variables.

12.14.2   Correspondence Analysis

Benzecri developed correspondence analysis in France in 1969, while its popularisation in the English-speaking world is to a large extent due to Greenacre (1984). In addition, the work of Hoffman and Franke (1986) has been influential in the marketing area.

Two lessor known works (Underhill and Peisach, 1985, and Bendixon, 1991) provide excellent examples of applications of correspondence analysis. These papers have strongly influenced the manner in which the output from the correspondence analysis computer program, is presented and interpreted.

Correspondence analysis is a multivariate analysis technique that can be used to analyse and interpret cross-tabulations of categorical data. More specifically it can be used to determine the nature of the dependency between the rows and the columns of the contingency table resulting from the cross-tabulation. The only constraint on the cell entries in the contingency table is that they be non-negative.

The main output from a correspondence analysis is a graphical display that is a simultaneous plot of the rows and columns of the contingency table in a space of two or more dimensions. Those rows with similar profiles are plotted 'close' together, as are columns with similar profiles.

The number of dimensions needed for a perfect representation of a contingency table is given by the minimum of (R–1) and (C–1), which for a large contingency table will clearly not be helpful. The idea is to find a lower dimensional representation of the table, preferably two or at the most three dimensions, which will provide an 'adequate' summary of the results.

The decision concerning the number of dimensions to retain for interpretation purposes is made on the basis of the variation, or inertia as it is more likely to be called, that the retained dimensions explain. In practice the focus is usually on the two or three primary dimensions. The ANACOR program within the SPSS package can be used to perform a correspondence analysis.

12.15   Summary and Conclusion

Statistical analysis has played a central role in business and management studies at the masters and doctoral level. This is especially true for the positivistic approach to research. This chapter has discussed those statistical techniques that are thought to have the greatest application in this area. The focus has not been technical, but rather has been to describe what can be achieved.

For more detail about the techniques described, there is a list of useful software in Appendix D.

Suggested Further Reading

Davidson, F. (1996) *Principles of Statistical Data Handling.* Sage Publications, Thousand Oaks, CA.
Freund, J. E. (1972) *Mathematical Statistics.* Prentice-Hall, London.
Green, P. E. (1978) *Analyzing Multivariate Evidence.* Dryden Press: Hinsdale, IL.
Hays, W. L. (1988) *Statistics.* Holt, Rinehart and Winston, Orlando, FL.
Manly. B. (1986) *Multivariate Statistical Methods: A Primer.* Chapman and Hall, London.
Siegel, S. and Castellan, Jr, N. J. (1988) *Nonparametric Statistics for the Behavioral Sciences.* McGraw-Hill, New York.
Sprent, P. (1990) *Applied Nonparametric Statistical Methods.* Chapman and Hall, London.
Traub, R. E. (1994) *Reliability for the Social Sciences.* Sage Publications, Thousand Oaks,CA.
Winer, B. J. (1971) *Statistical Principles of Experimental Design.* McGraw-Hill: New York.
Wright, D. B. (1996) *Understanding Statistics.* Sage Publications, London.

Notes

[1] A better estimate of the population standard deviation is obtained by dividing by $n-1$ rather than by n.

[2] Marking a result with one star (an asterisk is usually employed for this purpose) is a convention that indicates that the finding is significant at the 5 per cent level while two stars are used when the finding is significant at the 1 per cent level.

[3] This is the 95 per cent confidence limit and this provides a range within which it is possible to be 95 per cent sure that the true value lies.

[4] The correlation coefficient merely establishes whether there is a linear link between two variables and does not reflect on the cause and effect issue.

III   REPORTING RESEARCH

13

Ethical Considerations

Education is the art of making man ethical.

(Georg Hegel, *The Philosophy of Right,* no. 58, 1821; tr. 1942)

The average Ph.D. thesis is nothing but a transference of bones from one graveyard to another.

(L. J. Peter, *The Peter Prescription: How to Make Things Go Right,* 1972)

13.1 Introduction

The objective of this chapter is to outline the main issues that the researcher needs to consider concerning the issue of ethics in his or her research.

As ethics involves consideration of right and wrong (Singer, 1994), it is difficult to write this chapter without sounding prescriptive. However, it is specifically not the intention of the author to attempt to offer a definitive set of guidelines for the masters or doctoral researcher to apply. Rather it raises a number of issues that should be considered if a major research project for a masters or doctoral degree is not to be queried on the grounds of questionable ethical practices.

13.2 Research and Trust

University researchers, especially those working towards a masters or doctoral are in a privileged position. In the case of doctoral candidates, such researchers are working towards the highest degree which a university offers by examination, and this degree will not only give them a qualification but will actually change their status in society by giving them a title. Further, universities place a high level of trust in the candidates for these degrees. Universities generally assume that master and doctoral candidates will perform their work to the highest ethical standards and thus, except for the advice offered by their supervisors or promoters,[1] these researchers in the business and management field, are generally left alone to work independently.[2] In the field of business and management studies, universities usually require no other verification of the ethical standards used during the research work other than a certificate stating that the research is the personal work of the degree candidate. This is despite the fact that it is relatively easy to cheat with the results of business and management research.[3]

In addition to the trust placed in business and management research candidates by the university, business people and others will generally be prepared to discuss their affairs with university degree candidates much more frankly and openly than they would with other people, including non-academic researchers. Therefore it is generally considered important that business and management researchers respect the confidentiality of the source of any evidence or information that is supplied to them by informants. This is especially true if there is any question of the evidence having any competitive or commercial sensitivity.

13.2.1 Implications of a Breach of Trust

When trust is breached by some sort of unacceptable behaviour on the part of the researcher, universities normally take the matter seriously. It is worth pointing out that in the few cases where a university withdraws a degree from a graduate it is generally because some major ethical irregularity has occurred during the candidate's pursuit of the degree. This of course is an unusual occurrence.

13.3 Some Central Issues

There are a number of key issues that need to be carefully addressed and carefully thought through by the masters and doctoral researcher if the integrity of the research is to be ensured. These include, but are not limited to, what should be researched, how the research should be conducted, who is paying for the research and what should happen to the results of the research. Of course, what is considered ethical will vary enormously from individual to individual and from institution to institution and thus this chapter can only suggest some tentative thoughts on important issues. In addition many of the ethical matters concerned do not have clear boundaries and thus there are many grey areas of which the researcher should be aware.

13.4 What Should be Researched?

As already discussed in Chapter 2, what should be researched is an important issue for the masters and doctoral student. From a broad societal or macro point of view there are a number of research subjects that may cause ethical concern among certain groups of people. These include genetic engineering, total or whole body transplants, the use of animal organs in human transplant surgery, germ-line gene therapy (Equinox, 1996), strategic defence techniques such as those which have been labelled 'Star Wars', nuclear weapons, and artificial intelligence (Remenyi and Williams, 1996). However, from a business and management perspective the areas of concern would be related to less lofty issues, such as the implications of employment of new technologies on those employed in the production function in the factory, or for that matter those in the office. There could also be concerns surrounding marketing practices which might infringe on privacy, or which might exert excessive influence or coercion on prospective buyers. Research into ways of controlling and manipulating the workforce could be considered questionable. Information systems that have a built-in bias in favour of financial institutions such as banks or insurance companies, at the expense of their clients, would also be questionable, and research in this field might be considered not quite ethical.

In general there are a large number of business and management research issues that cannot be questioned on the grounds of ethical considerations, and it is probably sensible for research candidates to stay within these parameters. If they do not it is important for the researcher to be aware of the objections that could be raised by those who might query their conduct on ethical grounds.[4]

13.5 How the Research Should be Conducted

In business and management studies *how* the research should be conducted is perhaps of greater concern in an ethical sense to the typical masters and doctoral candidate than the question of *what* is being researched.

There are three major aspects of this *how* question. In the first place there is the issue of the collection of evidence, in the second there are the problems associated with processing the evidence, and finally there is the use of the findings.

13.5.1 Evidence Collection

When researching in the business and management field at doctoral level, experiments are unusual, especially in the UK. Rather, research is performed by collecting evidence from informants either through the use of questionnaires or through interviews using an interview schedule, or perhaps through participant observation or action research approaches or methodologies.

13.5.2 Openness with the Informants

In business and management studies the informants or participants in the study need to know a number of things and to be given a series of assurances (Sekaran, 1992). The main issues are as follows:

1 It is imperative that the researcher does not have any hidden agendas[5].
2 It essential that the researcher be fully open and honest with the informants and participants. This means that the informants and participants should be made aware of exactly why the evidence is required and exactly what will be done with it once the research has been completed.
3 It is necessary for the researcher to declare if he or she has any connections or relationships with organisations or individuals that could in any way be construed to be competitive to the informant or to his or her organisation. Thus anything which could remotely relate to a conflict of interest needs to be specifically dealt with in advance of any evidence being revealed.[6]
4 Where an informant does not wish to have his or her name associated with the evidence, this request should be respected.[7]
5 The researcher should not obtain evidence from informants under duress. Thus it would not be acceptable for a researcher to have the managing

director of an organisation insist that the staff complete a questionnaire if the individuals involved did not wish to so do. The informant should be told that he or she can withdraw from the interview at any time without any recriminations.

It is usual for the informants or participants to be aware of the final use of the evidence, and if at any stage the researcher wants to change how the evidence will be used, or to use it for additional purposes, it is important that he or she seeks the permission of the informants to do so.

13.5.3 The Integrity of the Evidence

The verification of evidence is important. The researcher may feel that the evidence has not been honestly presented by the informant and in such cases an attempt should be made to verify it. To present in an unquestioning way evidence which the researcher feels is suspicious would not be acceptable. Thus the researcher needs to be actively honest rather than passively honest in the presentation of his or her evidence and research findings.

It is also sometimes possible that the researcher has misunderstood the evidence and this should be checked. For example, when using the case study method of evidence collection, the researcher may offer the transcript of the case to one or more of the informants to establish that the situation was correctly understood and properly recounted in the written version.

It is sometime believed that the original source of the evidence, for example a transcript of an interview, or copies of the original questionnaire, should be kept for a period of time, say somewhere between two and five years, to allow other researchers access to the data.[8] A good example of the need to retain data is in the case of the controversy surrounding the research conducted by Sir Cyril Burt (Medawar, 1986) and which led to profound changes in the education system in the UK. Wadeley (1991) suggests that if Sir Cyril Burt had retained his data and made it publicly available, then the issue of whether or not he falsified the data would have been easily resolved.[9]

13.6 Processing the Evidence

The researcher needs to give considerable attention to the ethical issues related to processing of the evidence. If the evidence is quantitative then the concerns are to do with numerical and mathematical accuracy, which is relatively easy. Any attempt to window dress or manipulate and thus distort the evidence is of course unethical, as is any attempt to omit inconvenient evidence. In statistical terms this does not mean that outliers have always to be included in the numbers, but it does mean that the occurrence of such outliers should be reported as part of the findings and a reason supplied for not including them in the statistics.[10] In the case of qualitative evidence, the issues are more complex and sometimes more difficult as the researcher has more subjective evidence to work with. Here the question of giving appropriate importance and thus weight to statements and opinions becomes a central issue and the researcher needs to take great care to balance his or her approach. This is a difficult line to tread as it is important that the research should not be overwhelmed with personal biases. It is not a useful or rational strategy to fabricate evidence or deliberately to misinterpret it, as a masters or doctoral degree does not rely on the candidate finding or proving a particular result. Even when hypotheses or theoretical conjectures are rejected, the research is perfectly valid and there is no reason why such findings should not lead to the awarding of the degree.

Subconscious bias on the part of the researcher is a problem. Of course triangulation may be used to help in this respect, but in the final analysis an argument based on a judgement is always required (Collins, 1994). This may not be easy to make with personal prejudices playing an overtly influential and important role. The bias problem has been well described by Hubbard (1979) when she said:

> The mythology of science asserts that with many different scientists all asking their own questions and evaluating the answers independently, whatever personal bias creeps into their individual answers is cancelled out when the large picture is put together. This might conceivably be so if scientists were women and men from all sorts of different cultural and social backgrounds who came to science with very different ideologies and interests. But since, in fact, they have been predominantly university-trained white males from privileged social backgrounds, the bias has been narrow and the product often reveals more about the investigator than about the subject being researched.

With regards research findings, it is important that these are honestly presented and not produced in such a way as simply to support the opinions or prejudices of the researcher. This is indeed hard to accomplish. Ideally the researcher is trying to apply 'disinterested intellectual curiosity' (Trevelyan, 1993), but this is almost impossible as was pointed out by Gould (1980a) when he said, 'Science is not an objective, truth-directed machine, but a quintessentially human activity, affected by passion, hopes, and cultural biases. Cultural traditions of thought strongly influence scientific theories.' Sometimes, if not frequently, personal bias is so subtle that the researcher is not even aware of it. In fact, many would argue that a researcher should not attempt to compensate for bias, but should simply state clearly the possible biases involved and allow the readers to compensate for these themselves.

13.7 Using the Findings

Although the researcher will ultimately have little control over this issue, it is important that the intention of the research is that the findings will be used for ethical purposes. Thus research conducted for the purposes of perpetrating a fraud, for example, has no place in a university or business school.

Furthermore the findings of business and management research conducted by masters and doctoral students need to be placed in the public domain. This is in keeping with the general spirit of a university, as well as being in recognition of the fact that most universities and most businesses are funded to a large, or at least substantial, extent from public money. Sometimes an informant will give a researcher access to evidence on the grounds that it should not be immediately released into the public domain. This practice is not really in the spirit of academic research. Some universities, although they allow restrictions to be placed on the publishing of evidence of this type, will not allow the degree to be finally awarded, and thus the candidate will not graduate, until the research evidence and findings are released into the public domain. Other universities simply impose a time limit, such as one year, after which the findings are placed in the library.

Of course it is expected that research conducted for a higher degree will only be presented to a single university towards the award of a single degree. It would not be considered acceptable for the findings to be used for a number of different degrees at different institutions.

13.8 Funding the Research

Doctoral research is often funded by the individual candidates themselves with, in many, if not most instances, subsidies from the state in one form or another. Only a limited amount of doctoral research is sponsored by private interests, such as commercial organisations. In the case of privately funded academic research it is important that the interests of the funder do not influence the research approach or the findings of the work in any way. Thus the central issue here is the possibility of there being a conflict of interest. If doctoral research has been funded then it is essential for the candidate to declare this explicitly to the university and to the supervisor at the outset of the work. All informants who supply evidence for the research should also be aware of this. Of course the external examiner or examiners should also be informed of such arrangements.

13.9 Performance of the Work

There are a number of ethical issues relating to the more routine aspects of research work than those mentioned above and these include plagiarism, fudging references, measuring-instrument construction, choosing a sample, assistance from others, misrepresentations of work done, to mention only a few points.

13.9.1 Plagiarism

Occasionally plagiarism is a problem as sometimes candidates may rely too heavily on the work of others, to the extent of copying large tracts of work without acknowledging the source. This is obviously considered unethical and can lead, in extreme cases, to candidates being excluded from the university. As a general rule, although research candidates are required to rely heavily on the ideas of others at the outset of the research, these ideas need to be appropriately referenced. In addition, a dissertation, although it should include some quotations from other works, should not be too reliant on this type of printed evidence. It is sometimes said that a quotation from another piece of work should not be more than 50 to 100 words in length. Of course these are not hard and fast rules, but rather rough guidelines which if approximately followed will help avoid arguments.[11]

Sometimes it is argued that there is an element of plagiarism present when a candidate attempts to replicate an experiment conducted in another country or conducted in another set of circumstances. This view is somewhat controversial, and provided there is no outright copying of a previous dissertation the author would not accept that replicating an experiment is essentially an act of plagiarism, especially if the original work is correctly referenced.

13.9.2 The Theft of Ideas

Ideas can be stolen. A researcher may overhear others talking about possible areas of research or preliminary findings and pursue these research ideas without reference to their origin. When this happens unpleasant circumstances arise, especially if ideas are stolen from research students or junior members of staff by senior members of staff. This is a particularly difficult area as it is not possible to have much control over ideas and thinking. According to the *Guardian Weekly* – 'Le Monde' section (1988):

> Now in the past two decades, the ethics of the scientific profession (at least among mathematicians) have become so degraded that wholesale plundering of ideas (and particularly at the expense of those in no position to defend themselves) has become almost the general rule among scientists. It is at any rate tolerated by all, including in the most glaring and ubiquitous of cases.

Ideas can also been stolen by referees who see them in academic papers that they have been asked to review. It is also possible to have an idea stolen by members of funding boards who are given early access to new ideas that require money to proceed.

The only safe position to take to prevent any possible accusation of stealing ideas is for a researcher to acknowledge any and all sources of ideas, be they from journals or books, or from verbal presentations, conversations or discussions. To prevent ideas being stolen, the best course of action is not to discuss interesting thoughts within earshot of colleagues until the ideas are reasonably well developed. This will help reduce such incidents, although clearly it will not eliminate them. It is difficult to protect ideas from unscrupulous referees.

13.9.3 Fudging References

Related to plagiarism, but not quite of the same severity, is the issue of quoting an authority without having actually read the original reference, but rather having seen it published in someone else's work. It is considered unacceptable to do this. Any reference made in a dissertation to the work of another should only be made if the research candidate has read the original him or herself. However it is acceptable to use the 'cited by' approach. Thus if the eminent scientist Albert Einstein is quoted in a book by Joe Bloggs, the candidate may use Einstein's words provided he or she states that the quotation was cited by Joe Bloggs in this book and a full reference is given to this work.

13.9.4 Measuring-Instrument Construction

Constructing a measuring instrument can be a critical part of research in the business and management field and there are many ethical issues around how this is handled and how the evidence collected with the measuring instrument is treated.

Increasingly, personal questions are becoming unacceptable. Issues of age, race, sex, educational standard achieved and so on are no longer regarded as issues about which researchers can expect to obtain information. In fact some would argue that this has become an ethical issue.

Researchers are sometimes tempted to state that the questionnaire is anonymous, while at the same time placing some sort of indicator on the document to allow its origin to be determined. The justification that can be given for this is that it enables the researcher to chase up those who have not completed the questionnaire. Such practice is generally considered to be unacceptable.

Using leading questions that have a high probability of being answered in the manner desired by the researcher is also ethically questionable.

13.9.5 Choosing a Sample

The choice of sample can dramatically affect the results of the research and thus is an important issue. However, it becomes an ethical issue if the sample is manipulated to show a desired result. This may come about in two ways:

1 The researcher may choose only informants whom he or she knows will have opinions the researcher espouses.
2 The researcher may discard evidence from informants who do not comply with his or her views.

Samples need to be established honestly, which means they may produce results that will not necessarily support the views and/or prejudices of the researcher. Inconvenient or conflicting evidence should be directly addressed and not hidden or ignored.

13.9.6 Assistance from Others

The amount of assistance which a masters or doctoral candidate may obtain from others is a delicate issue. There have been cases where even minor help has resulted in questions being asked by examiners and this has produced problems that have delayed the awarding of the degree. An example that comes to mind is where a candidate had a science student write a computer program to help with the analysis of some evidence. This caused an examiner's enquiry. However, this particular incident occurred a few years ago and would probably not be treated in the same way today.

A potentially more serious incident took place recently where a masters student approached a member of staff with a request for help in writing his dissertation. The candidate said that due to pressure of work in his salary-earning job he was unable to complete the dissertation on time and he would pay a large sum of money for help. The implication was that the member of staff would actually write the dissertation for him. Clearly this was totally unacceptable and the offer was declined.

There is much anecdotal evidence of considerable assistance being given to degree candidates. Of course supervisors may extensively assist candidates in a number of ways, but care needs to be taken so that the dissertation does not become predominantly the work of the supervisor rather than that of the student. Research degree candidates and their supervisors sometimes publish joint chapters and this is a perfectly acceptable way in which they may work together and through which the supervisor may give considerable help to the student.[12]

If the candidate seeks help from professionals such as statisticians, then the question of whether a payment is made may become an issue. Many universities would regard paying for help of this kind as being ethically questionable.

13.9.7 Misrepresentation of Work Done

Because of the high degree of trust placed in researchers it is not difficult for them to exaggerate the amount of work actually done. Candidates can purport to have conducted 30 interviews when they have actually only had 20. Interviews and questionnaires can be fabricated.

The amount of work undertaken for the literature review may also be exaggerated. Researchers may say that they consulted texts when they did not. This can lead to misunderstanding of quotations especially with regards to their context.

Any such misrepresentation is clearly unacceptable and furthermore is highly dangerous. Candidates can be found out and this type of misrepresentation would probably lead to the termination of their registration at the university.

13.10 Responsibility to the Greater Community

So far this chapter has only addressed the researcher's ethical responsibility to the integrity of the research itself and to the university at which the researcher is registered. There is however another important dimension to the ethical issue and that is the researcher's responsibility to the greater community or the society of which he or she is part.

13.10.1 Discovery of Unacceptable Practices

A major ethical issue that a researcher may face relates to the discovery or uncovering of some misconduct within the organisation being researched. This of course is not likely to be revealed through survey research, but rather through case study research. There are three levels at which this may occur and these relate to:

1   unlawful or illegal conduct;
2   unsatisfactory practices which endanger staff;
3   embarrassing revelations.

13.10.1.1   Unlawful or Illegal Conduct

It is possible for a research degree candidate, when conducting an in-depth case study, to discover unlawful or even illegal practices. An example of this would be the discovery that some sort of criminal act was being perpetrated on the firm by the employees, or perhaps by the employees on the firm's customers.

Such a circumstance presents a difficult situation for the researcher. The law requires that the presence of criminal acts or serious fraudulent practices should be reported to the authorities and it is essential that the researcher comply with the law. This of course may well mean the end of the research exercise for the degree candidate with the organisation and people involved in this unfortunate situation. If this happens during an important case study then the researcher's work may be set back by a considerable amount of time. However, this inconvenience, no matter how great, should not lead to the researcher refusing to comply with the law.

13.10.1.2   Endangering Staff

In some respects an even more difficult circumstance may arise where the researcher discovers, for example, that some important business practice essential to worker safety or to customer safety, is not being complied with. What is happening or not happening may not be a criminal act in terms of any legislation, but none the less the organisation may be behaving totally unacceptably. The difficulty here is that although nothing actually illegal is taking place, the situation as discovered by the researcher is highly unsatisfactory.

There are many grey areas in these circumstances and thus it is hard to give any general advice. All that may really be said is that the researcher needs to discuss carefully these situations with his or her supervisor and that an appropriate course of action should be taken. This will usually mean taking the discovery of the questionable situation up with senior officials of the organisation concerned. As already stated, such a course of action may well mean for the degree candidate the end of this part of the research exercise with the organisation and people involved.

13.11   Summary and Conclusion

Academic research is a challenging, but also a rewarding activity. Ensuring that research is conducted in an acceptable way and that its findings add something of value to the body of knowledge, is extremely demanding. It is not surprising therefore that few people succeed as competent academic researchers, especially at the doctoral level. The difficulty of research may have been in the mind of H. G. Wells (1925) when he said, 'Fools make researchers and wise men exploit them.' Of course those who succeed at research do sometimes achieve fame and fortune, win Nobel prizes, register new inventions or start up biotech companies and make millions of dollars,[13] although it should be admitted that this is a relatively rare occurrence experienced by only the best in the field.

The subject of ethics is one of considerable controversy and sometimes different individuals take strongly opposing positions. According to Ewing (1965), 'Ethics, like other branches of Philosophy, is a subject where very wide differences of opinion exist between competent authorities.'[14] In a general sense what is right and wrong is a question which has puzzled humankind and many of our greatest philosophers for millennia (Aristotle, 1976; Kant, 1948; Mill, 1863; Russell, 1946). There are no clear universal answers to the questions of ethics or morals, even within a relatively homogeneous cultural group such as western society (Lacey, 1982). As Wittgenstein (cited in Redpath, 1990:36) pointed out, 'We feel that even if all possible scientific questions can be answered, the problems of life have still not been touched at all' – and morality is one of the central 'problems of life'. Even within a single institution such as a university or a business school there may be substantially conflicting views about what is right and wrong. The problem is that although everyone will immediately agree that it is unethical to cheat, there will inevitably be disagreements as to what actually constitutes cheating. Increasingly, though, ethics is a subject which is attracting attention from managers, consultants and academics (Wheatley, 1992) and thus it is likely that this will produce a better and wider understanding of the issues involved.

It is however interesting to note that Bertrand Russell (1976), perhaps in one of his more playful moods, pointed out the highly subjective nature of ethics by saying that, 'Ethics is in origin the art of recommending to others the sacrifices required for cooperation with oneself.'

It is perhaps unfortunate, although in fact realistic, that Russell sees ethics as a sacrifice. As pointed out above, cheating by the individual is not a rational stratagem in research. Either the researcher will be caught and the penalty will be high, or the research itself will sooner or later be discredited. It is interesting that from the point of view of the body of knowledge cheating is irrelevant as it simply places the work in the category of poor or wrong findings and at the end of the day no one will care much. This was well expressed by Gould (1988) when he said, 'Fraud [in science] is not historically interesting except as gossip.' And Oscar Wilde (1891) attempts to dispense with the issue of ethics in a rather cavalier way by saying that, 'No artist has ethical sympathies. An ethical sympathy in an artist is an unpardonable mannerism of style.'

Irrespective of the plight of the artist, it is crucial to our modern world that there is a high standard of ethics, as without this it would not be possible to operate the highly sophisticated, large-scale, high-technology society which now exists. The operation of railways, airlines, local and international banks, police forces – to mention only a few fundamental institutions – would not be possible without a highly honed sense of morality and ethics and thus a mutually agreed view of what is right and wrong.

Irrespective of any particular individual's view of what is right or wrong many would agree that some notion of ethical behaviour is important in research. The authors believe that this is the case and suggest that one way to ensure a high standard of ethics in research is to focus on the three principles of medical research (Jenkins, 1996), which may be translated in business and management research as follows:

1   ensure a high degree of respect for the autonomy of the individual;
2   work towards the benefit of society as a primary motivation of research;
3   respect justice.

Research ethics is a challenging subject that the research candidate has to face, and which, if not addressed correctly, may cause the result of the research work to be considered tainted or even invalid. It is therefore necessary for the research candidate clearly to understand the ethical restraints which his or her community places on the way he or she conducts the research work and publishes the results. It is hoped that the above discussion will be helpful in setting a course through this difficult maze.

Suggested Further Reading

Andersen, J. (1997) 'What cognitive science tells us about ethics and the teaching of ethics', *Journal of Business Ethics*, 16 (3) February: 279–91.
Bulmer, M. (1982) 'When is disguise justified? Alternatives to covert participant observation', *Qualitative Sociology*, 5 (4), Winter.
Connolly, L. S. (1997) 'Does external funding of academic research crowd out institutional support?', *Journal of Public Economics*, 64 (3) June: 389–406.
Morris, M. H., Marks, A. S., Allen, J. A. and Peery, N. S., Jr (1996) 'Modelling ethical attitudes and behaviours under conditions of environmental turbulence: The case of South Africa', *Journal of Business Ethics*, 15 (10) October: 1119–30.
Sapsford, R. and Jupp, V. (1996) *Data Collection and Analysis*. Sage Publications, London.
Wyld, D. C. and Jones, C. A. (1997) 'The importance of context: the ethical work climate construct and models of ethical decision making: an agenda for research', *Journal of Business Ethics*, 16 (4) March: 465–72.

Notes

[1] Promoter is a term used by some universities, especially in continental Europe, in place of supervisor. In some senses it more correctly reflects the function of the person who is assisting the doctoral candidate obtain his or her degree.

[2] Despite this high level of trust, or perhaps because of it, there is a certain amount of anecdotal evidence to suggest some candidates during the course of their degrees perpetrate unethical practices. However, it is generally believed that those involved in such behaviour are in a small minority.

[3] The trust placed in business and management researchers is perhaps a result of the trust placed in research produced in the physical and life sciences. Because experiments performed in the physical and life sciences have to be repeatable, it is difficult to cheat or produce fraudulent results and thus business researchers may have picked up attitudes resulting from this.

[4] It is of course essential that the research topic chosen be of some importance within the discipline, as a frivolous research topic would not be accepted.

[5] There may perhaps be one acceptable exception to this rule. Where a researcher is interested in studying issues related to the honesty and integrity of organisational behaviour it would not be reasonable to expect an informant to declare that he or she behaved in a dishonest way. Thus some sort of device would have to be used which would not be transparent to the informant. Clearly a research study into the ethical practices of research degree candidates would require such treatment as it would be unreasonable to expect such researchers to admit to any questionable activities which would put their degrees at risk.

[6] The issue of conflict of interest can lead to problems with part-time students who are currently in employment and who wish to study an aspect of their work on a generic basis and who therefore

may need to solicit evidence from competitors. It is considered unacceptable practice for such students not to declare their employment affiliation, a situation which has sometimes led to substantial difficulties.

[7] Respecting the confidentiality of an individual informant in business and management research is important as sometimes special or privileged evidence will be supplied to a researcher, which, if its source was known, could have an adverse effect on the informant's career.

[8] In the physical and life sciences data or evidence will often be kept indefinitely and the work will not be considered valid unless this data is available so that others can easily replicate the experiment.

[9] Sir Cyril Burt, who held a professorship at University College London, had a significant influence on education in the UK and this led to the eleven plus assessment system. It is now believed that his evidence was possibly falsified. In fact Gould (1988) claims that 'Cyril Burt included faked data compiled by the non-existent Ms Conway.' Burt actually said that he did not dispose of his evidence but that it had been destroyed as a result of a bombing raid during the 1939–1945 war.

[10] This point is somewhat controversial and some researchers would argue that all evidence collected has to be included in the final figures for the analysis.

[11] Although there is only anecdotal evidence to support the claim, it is said by colleagues both in the United Kingdom and in North America that there are quite different cultural interpretations of the notion of plagiarism. Degree candidates from the developing countries seem to have a much less clear notion of the issue and its importance.

[12] In the Department of Earth and Planetary Science at McGill University in Montreal, it is now customary for the supervisor and the PhD candidate to write the 'dissertation' as a series of joint chapters which are also submitted for publication to academic journals (Salvi, 1994). Here there is no suggestion that the work is exclusively that of the student, but rather a joint effort and thus the supervisor takes on the role of a promoter of the degree candidate. This arrangement clearly recognises the reality of the shared nature of doctorate-level research, which exists in many universities but which is not often openly admitted.

[13] Some of the biotech companies make large sums of money especially as much of the basic research has been done with government money before the project is commercialised.

[14] Professor Trefor Jenkins of the South African Institute of Medical Research points out that this is not true in the case of medical research ethics where there is considerable agreement about what is right and what is wrong. However, although this may be true in general, there are still a number of issues, especially in areas such as genetic engineering and whole body transplantation, where there is considerable controversy.

14

Writing up the Research

Even such earnest and inquiring thinkers as Tolstoy and Dostoievsky could not see that science was more than a comparatively insignificant activity.

(L. Sullivan, *The Limitation of Science*, 1952)

An immense and ever-increasing wealth of knowledge is scattered about the world today; knowledge that would probably suffice to solve all the mighty difficulties of our age, but it is dispersed and unorganized. We need a sort of mental clearing house for the mind: a depot where knowledge and ideas are received, sorted, summarized, digested, clarified and compared.

(H. G. Wells in *The Brain: Organization of the Modern World*, 1940)

14.1 Introduction

This chapter addresses the issues related to writing up the research and producing the dissertation. A well written-dissertation is important as it is primarily through this written work and papers in scientific journals that the work will be presented to the academic community as well as to the rest of the world.

14.2 Defining the Work Required

The amount of work required in writing a dissertation varies substantially, depending upon the degree being undertaken, the nature of the research and the institution where the work is being carried out.

In general a masters degree in business and management will require a dissertation which will clearly demonstrate that the candidate has a firm grasp of the subject, as well as some knowledge of research methodology. Such a document could be presented in five to eight chapters with anywhere between 75 and 100 pages[1] in one-and-a-half-line spacing. Depending on the number of diagrams, etc., this would represent somewhere between 10,000 and 20,000 words. Dissertations which are undertaken as part of a masters degree by course work will normally be shorter than those dissertations for degree by research only.

A doctoral degree would typically involve a substantially greater amount of work. In addition to the criteria noted above for a masters degree, a doctorate also requires that the work conducted by the candidate has added significantly to the body of knowledge. Typically, a doctoral dissertation would include a similar number of chapters although there would normally be an additional chapter discussing the limitations of the research. A doctoral dissertation would generally require between 200 and 400 pages. This represents approximately 50,000 to 100,000 words. It is important for the candidate to avoid a dissertation that is too lengthy as documents containing more than 500 pages[2] are sometimes sent back by examiners to be shortened.

Typically, the chapters of a masters or doctoral dissertation will fall under the following headings:

1   Introduction
2   Literature review
3   Research questions
4   Methodology
5   Evidence collection and analysis
6   Interpretation
7   Summary and conclusion

The precise requirements for dissertations vary substantially from institution to institution and research candidates should establish these from their own university or business school. Researchers should also consult, in their library, other recent masters and doctoral dissertations which have recently been passed and are now available for students to consult.

14.3   Strategies for Writing Up

There are at least two different strategies for writing up the dissertation. The first, which is sometimes called the final lap approach, is to collect all the literature references, all the evidence and the analysis, and then write the dissertation. Here the writing is done as a single task at the end of the research process when all the other contributory work has been completed. This could be regarded as the 'just-in-time' write-up.

The second strategy is to write up the work as it is in progress and to begin as soon as the research has been started. This approach is recommended in most cases as it makes more manageable the time-consuming and difficult task of writing. Whichever strategy is chosen it is important for the research candidate to keep detailed records of literature which has been read and quotations which will be used, as well as a concise record of the evidence collected. In addition, the researcher needs to maintain a detailed record of the results of whatever analysis has been used on the evidence. The better the recording of the research work in progress, the easier the writing of the final dissertation will be.

14.4   Knowing when to Finalise the Dissertation

A question often raised by research candidates is 'When is the research ready to be written up or to be finalised?' The authors know of doctorates that have taken up to fifteen years to finish and this is neither desirable nor necessary.

In practical terms the research is ready to be finalised when the supervisor or promoter agrees that the candidate has achieved the research objectives. In the case of a masters degree the candidate needs to convince the supervisor or promoter that he or she has mastered the subject and has an understanding of research methodology. For a doctorate, the candidate needs to convince the supervisor or promoter that he or she has fulfilled the criteria needed for a masters, but also that the work adds something of value to the body of knowledge.

Clearly these decisions are subjective and depend on the standards set by the institution at which the degree is being done. An indication that the candidate is ready to finalise his or her work may be the demonstration of a high degree of expertise in the field of study. If the candidate has already had papers published or accepted for publication in refereed journals, has presented his or her work at academic conferences, presented seminars to peers or to faculty, or has had a book on the research accepted for publication, these would be clear indicators that he or she is in a position to finalise the dissertation.

14.5 Technical Considerations

Every institution has an explicit or implicit set of standards to which the dissertation should be laid out. These relate to the type style, the size of the fonts, how the figures and tables are numbered and what sort of referencing convention should be used. This varies so much among institutions and even departments that no generalised guidelines may be given, but it is important to comply with these regulations and it is essential to establish what these standards or rules are. If there are no set standards, then the candidate should present a sample of how he or she wishes to write up the research and have his or her supervisor or promoter approve the style well in advance of producing the major portion of the work.

14.6 Producing Academic Papers on the Way

Sometimes, even at the masters level, a research candidate may produce a sufficiently novel finding to warrant publication in a refereed academic journal. At the doctoral level a research candidate may be able to write two or three papers. For example, at doctoral level the candidate might write a theoretical paper relating to the conceptualisation of the research problem, a paper discussing some element of the methodology and the evidence collection, and a paper which reports on the research findings. It is important for doctoral candidates to have published in peer-reviewed journals and they should attempt to write up the key aspects of their work for publication in academic journals.

The following is a summary of advice collected by the authors of this book from the editors of three academic journals; would-be authors of academic papers will find this advice useful.

14.6.1 Fundamentals

Novice authors sometimes do not realise that a paper should only be sent to one journal at a time. It is important to comply with this requirement because there will be substantial embarrassment if the paper is accepted for publication by two journals simultaneously. If a journal refuses to accept a paper for publishing, then the author is free to send it to another journal if he or she so wishes.

Authors need to be realistic about the length of time it can take for a paper to be reviewed. Some journals can obtain comments from referees in a few months (*Sloan Management Review*), whereas others can take up to a year. This means that authors who wish to maintain a publishing rate of two to three papers per year need to have six to ten papers submitted to various journals at any one time.

There is considerable difference between journals concerning copyright, with some insisting that they retain the copyright. Furthermore, the matter of copyright is becoming increasingly difficult as journals move towards electronic media using the Internet and the World Wide Web (Kourrie and Introna, 1995).

14.6.2 Relevance, Rigour and Impact

Three key issues concern an editor when considering an academic paper. These are relevance, rigour and impact.

Relevance refers to the requirement that the academic paper should address issues which are of interest to the target audience of the journal. Rigour is concerned with whether or not the research reported in the paper has been carried out using an appropriate and sound research methodology. The issue of impact concerns the reasons why top scholars or practitioners would be interested in the paper and motivated to read it and this requires a high degree of originality.

14.6.3 Writing Style

Many editors advise contributors to ensure their papers are readable, well organised and exhibit good writing style. Some journals accept the use of graduate-level mathematics in the paper with the proviso that it has to be essential for the understanding of the subject. It is sometimes necessary to demonstrate that a paper appeals to professionals as well as to academics. Because many journals want their contributors to remain anonymous to their reviewers, to ensure there is no bias or favouritism, authors should not reveal their identity anywhere in the manuscript (*MIS Quarterly*).

14.6.4 Choose the Proposed Journal Carefully

Ensuring a match between the fields covered by the prospective journal and the work to be published is important in selecting a journal. It would usually be a waste of time to send papers on the future of artificial intelligence or techniques in database design to a journal which publishes in the field of computer security systems.

Papers that contribute to a continuing debate in a journal usually stand a better chance of being published. Therefore consider whether the proposed paper

Papers that contribute to a continuing debate in a journal usually stand a better chance of being published. Therefore consider whether the proposed paper contributes to an ongoing interest of the journal. If this is the case, it is worthwhile ensuring that the paper refers to work already published in the chosen journal.

It is important that the paper should comply with the established style and research methodological paradigm of the journal. Thus if the journal usually only publishes empirical work it may not accept a theoretical paper.

14.6.5 Instructions to Authors

Obtain a copy of the instructions to authors that specify how the paper should be presented to the journal. These should be read carefully and the instructions complied with. They differ from journal to journal and many authors do not notice the difference. It is important to comply with the journal's length requirements. If the paper is too long or too short the journal may reject it. The inclusion of an abstract and key words is important as they set the tone and focus the mind for the ensuing paper.

Papers submitted in the wrong format, such as single spacing when double spacing is required, or with the wrong referencing convention, can create a negative impression from the start. In fact some journals automatically reject all papers which do not fully comply with the instructions to authors.

14.7 Finalising the Dissertation

Irrespective of whether the work is published in journals or not, it is necessary to produce the dissertation in a bound and final form. If the researcher has been writing extensively during the course of the degree, as recommended earlier in this chapter, the compilation of the final dissertation might be only a matter of a few weeks. If the dissertation has to be written from scratch, then writing the final document may take several months and the time needed should not be underestimated.

It is useful for the research candidate to obtain informal reviews of his or her work from friends and colleagues. To this end the candidate should attempt to build up a network of associates consisting of other research candidates and members of academic staff who will be prepared to provide feedback.

When the candidate has received feedback from friends and colleagues the final draft will be presented to the university or business school for examination. Typically there will be at least one internal and one external examiner for whom copies of the dissertation will have to be prepared. However, this is not the final document that will eventually be published, as the examination process itself will inevitably identify areas in which the dissertation needs to be improved. Thus, after the final examination the candidate may often be asked to make some changes or to make additions to the work, even if the dissertation is fully accepted, and these need to be completed as soon as possible while the subject is still fresh in the candidate's mind.

14.8   Summary and Conclusion

Because the issues addressed in this chapter are specific to the particular degree being followed and to the institution at which the work is being conducted, it is difficult to offer general advice on matters of dissertation length, when to finalise it, technical requirements of the dissertation document and so on. The research degree candidate needs to consider these issues carefully, with reference to his or her institution, and his or her supervisor or promoter.

It is always useful for research candidates to start to have their work published in academic refereed journals while pursuing the degree, as papers published in academic journals will generally have a much wider readership than dissertations. This will ensure that the work of the author is widely acknowledged.

Suggested Further Reading

Bell, J. (1993) *Doing Your Research Project: A Guide for First-time Researchers in Education and Social Science*. Second Edn, Open University Press, Milton Keynes.

Blaxter, L., Hughes, C. and Tight, M. (1996) *How to Research*. Open University Press, Milton Keynes.

Collinson, D., Kirkup, G., Kyd, R. and Siocomb, L. (1992) *Plain English*. Second Edn, Open University Press, Milton Keynes.

Easterby-Smith, M., Thorpe, R. and Lowe, A. (1994) *Management Research – An Introduction*. Sage Publications, London.

Fairbairn, G. and Winch, C. (1991) *Reading, Writing and Reasoning – A Guide for Students*. Open University Press, Milton Keynes.

Gill, J. and Johnson, P. (1991) *Research Methods for Managers*. Paul Chapman Publishing Limited, London.

Jankowicz, A. (1995) *Business Research Projects*. Second Edn, Chapman and Hall, London.

Lumley, J. and Benjamin, W. (1994) *Research: Some Ground Rules*. Oxford University Press, Oxford.

Miles, M. B. and Huberman, A. M. (1984) *Qualitative Data Analysis – A Source Book of New Methods*. Sage Publications, Newbury Park, CA.

Orna, L. and Stevens, G. (1995) *Managing Information for Research*. Open University Press, Milton Keynes.

Rudestein, K. E. and Newton, R. R. (1992) *Surviving your Dissertation: A Comprehensive Guide to Content and Process*. Sage Publications, Newbury Park, CA .

Notes

[1] Some universities would regard a masters dissertation of 100 pages to be on the short side. Such institutions would require a document of 150 to perhaps 200 pages. Unfortunately this emphasis on quantity sometimes occurs at the expense of quality.

[2] Some universities and business schools like to have the 500 pages include all the appendices, while others are prepared to accept a dissertation of 500 pages with, say, 100 pages of appendices. The issue of length and quality is indeed a very difficult one. However, especially in a doctorate, it should never be possible to trade quantity for quality.

15

Evaluation of Masters and Doctoral Degrees

True science investigates and brings to human perception such truths and such knowledge as the people of a given time and society consider most important.

(Leo Tolstoy, *What Is Art?*, 1989)

If all economists were laid end to end, they would not reach a conclusion.

(Attributed to George Bernard Shaw, 1856–1950)

15.1 Introduction

This chapter discusses some of the various criteria which examiners generally use to evaluate research dissertations submitted by degree candidates. It provides a checklist for dissertations in business and management studies, for masters and doctoral candidates.

15.2 Background to Evaluation for Doctorates

One of the most frequently asked questions by candidates for research degrees is 'How will my dissertation be evaluated?' There is of course no simple answer to this question, as it will depend to a large extent on the actual degree, the institution, the faculty, the supervisor and the external examiner or examiners concerned. However, this chapter provides some ideas as to how research dissertations are assessed.

As mentioned in Chapter 1 there are various different masters and doctoral degrees and this chapter will discuss each in turn as well as giving general guidelines that apply to all the different types of degrees.

15.2.1 The Doctorate and Original Research

To obtain a doctorate a candidate needs to have undertaken a substantial programme of original research and in so doing produce a dissertation which makes a valuable contribution to the body of knowledge. For this degree to be awarded it is essential that the contribution made by the researcher is regarded by his or her examiners to have added something of value to the discipline which is being researched. However, the contribution to the body of knowledge may in fact be quite small or very modest. It is often said that a doctorate will normally add only a grain of new knowledge to an already established mountain but this does not detract from the value of the degree which owes as much to the process of study as it does to the end result.

It is often said that the doctoral dissertation needs to be original. In this context originality may have taken several forms. The originality may be based on the fact that a new theory is being developed, it may be related to a novel research methodology that has been used in the research programme, or it may be derived from the fact that the domain in which the theory and the methodology is being applied has not previously been approached or studied in this way.

A doctoral candidate will work under the supervision of one or more supervisors. The amount of supervision given varies enormously. In some cases the candidate may see his or her supervisor every day and will in effect work with the supervisor throughout the whole period of the degree. In other cases the supervisor can be remote, with the candidate being given little access to him or her and virtually no help. Whether or not there is extensive access to the supervisor, the candidate is considered to be working on his or her own and is thus entirely responsible for preparing him or herself for the research work as well as for the production of the dissertation.

15.2.2 The Doctorate and Critical Assessment

A doctoral candidate is expected to be fully familiar with all the literature appertaining to the subject area that is being researched, as well as to have a broad knowledge and understanding of the discipline in general. The candidate has to show that he or she has understood and critically assessed all the main issues in the field of study. Arising out of this critical assessment he or she will then extend the body of knowledge by developing a new aspect of the discipline. To achieve this it is essential that the researcher be fully conversant with the wide range of research methodologies available, which are discussed in Chapters 2, 3 and 4 (Hubermann and Miles, 1994). This is because the researcher's claim to have made a contribution to the body of knowledge needs to be justified by demonstrating that a sound approach has been taken to the research. Although some universities offer a course in aspects of research methodology, this does not generally constitute a formal part of the doctorate. The justification of the approach taken in the research has to be made at a philosophical level and perhaps explains why the degree is called a doctor of philosophy.

The following is a short extract from the requirements for a PhD or a doctor of business administration (DBA) from a British university, which indicates the breadth of knowledge the doctoral candidate needs to demonstrate.

> In his/her thesis, the candidate is required to show ability to conduct an original investigation, to test ideas (whether his/her own or those of others) and to demonstrate a broad knowledge and understanding of his or her discipline and of appropriate cognate subjects. He or she should also demonstrate a knowledge of the research techniques appropriate to his/her discipline and show that they have been successfully applied. The dissertation should make a distinct contribution to knowledge and provide evidence of the candidate's originality by the discovery of new facts or the exercise of critical power. The candidate is required to show appropriate ability in the organisation and presentation of his/her material in the dissertation, which should be satisfactory as regards clarity of expression and literary form. It should be in the English language, and should be suitable for publication, either as submitted or suitably abridged.

15.2.3 The Doctorate and the Period of Study

The doctoral degree usually requires a minimum of at least two years full-time registration at a university. However, most candidates take between three and five years to complete their dissertation. Although increasingly unusual, there is still the occasional example of a doctoral student requiring 10 to 15 years to conclude their degree. Such a protracted registration implies that the candidate has been registered on a part-time basis but even so it is important not to let the work drag on for too long.

A doctoral degree will be examined by a panel of experts in the field being researched, as well as by experts in the research process itself. The examination may involve having the dissertation read and commented on in writing, or there may be an oral examination. In some cases both approaches are used. An oral examination, sometimes called a *viva voce,* from the Latin for 'the living voice', is generally regarded as the most challenging test for the candidate. During this examination the candidate needs to demonstrate clearly a full understanding of the subject area, as well as a complete command of all the research methodology issues involved with the work. Furthermore, the candidate may need to defend his or her ideas and conclusions to a sceptical and critical examiner.

15.3 The Traditional Masters Degree by Dissertation

In many ways the traditional masters degree by dissertation is a direct preparation for a doctorate. This degree has many of the same attributes as the doctorate, but the studies are in less depth and with a reduced scope. Thus a masters degree by dissertation requires the candidate to demonstrate a mastery of the subject area being researched, as well as a comprehensive understanding of the research methodology being used. The work does not, however, have to be original in the way that a doctorate needs to be.

The following is based on an extract from the rules for a Master of Commerce and a Masters of Economic Science degree and it illustrates the typical requirements for such a degree.

The candidate is required to show acquaintance with the methods of research in that he or she:

1   understands the nature and purpose of the investigation;
2   is sufficiently acquainted with the relevant research literature;
3   has mastered the necessary techniques;
4   has acquired a thorough understanding of appropriate scientific methods;
5   is capable of assessing the significance of the findings.

The main feature distinguishing a masters degree from an undergraduate degree is that the candidate is working alone to demonstrate an independent ability to produce high quality work. Of course the candidate will have a supervisor, but the help provided will be in terms of advice concerning the direction of the work. The masters research project should be such that it can be completed within a year or, at the most, eighteen months of full-time study. However, as with the doctorate, few candidates complete their masters degree in minimum time.

15.4 New Masters and Doctorates

Since the 1960s, with the popularisation of the Masters of Business Administration degree which was started at Harvard University, there has been a growing trend to incorporate both course work and a smaller amount of research into masters degrees in the UK and elsewhere. This has also begun to happen for doctorates in the UK in the 1990s, with several universities starting to offer the Doctor of Business Administration.

15.4.1 Course Work and the Doctoral Degree

As already mentioned, universities in the US generally require doctoral candidates to undertake a period of intense course work before they commence their research dissertation. In many cases there is a requirement for two years of course attendance with corresponding examinations. This period is seen as preparing the candidate by ensuring that he or she has acquired all the appropriate background required in the subject area and associated disciplines to be able to cope competently with the research work ahead. Thus the course work will focus both on the subject matter as well as on research methodological issues.

The main advantage of this system to the candidate is that the institution takes some of the responsibility for preparing the candidate for the work required for the research degree. When the research begins in earnest the candidate is likely to be in a much stronger position than his or her British counterpart. In recognition of this, dissertations from universities in the US can sometimes be relatively small pieces of work. None the less, the basic requirement, that the doctorate be centred around a piece of research leading to original ideas that add value to the body of knowledge, still applies.

15.4.2 Course Work and the Masters Degree

As previously mentioned there is an increasing trend for masters degrees to be based largely on course work. The rationale for this is that these course work masters degrees are mostly to do with preparing individuals to take a more specialist, or in some cases a more distinguished, role in their profession. These masters degrees are sometimes referred to as mid-career development degrees.

Although there is considerable debate as to how rigorous this research has to be, it is generally agreed that it should go some way to meeting the standards laid down for a dissertation required by the more traditional masters degree. Thus a candidate for this type of degree will still have to be familiar with some of the research methodology issues as well as show a firm grasp of the subject matter being studied.

Of course, the exact research requirements for this type of masters degree not only vary from university to university, but also from one department or faculty to another within the same university. Different supervisors will also have varying views of what is required from the research component of a masters degree by course work. Thus candidates need to be familiar with precisely what is required of them from their own institution.

15.5   The Evaluation of the Research Degree

The evaluation of the research degree is a complex process. The evaluation is undertaken by the supervisor as well as by a number of different examiners. The number of examiners varies substantially depending upon the university, the degree, the subject and the country in which the university is located.

15.5.1   The Supervisor or Promoter

Before discussing the details of evaluation it is important to establish that the dissertation should not be presented for evaluation or examination until it has the full support of the supervisor, or, where there is more than one supervisor, all the supervisors. Although most universities allow a candidate to submit his or her dissertation even though the supervisor does not agree that it is ready, this is usually an ill-advised strategy. In fact, although the supervisor may not be a formal examiner, he or she always acts as a filter and his or her advice should be taken seriously. However the approval of the candidate's supervisor does not necessarily mean that the dissertation will be accepted. Another useful test is the opinion of the candidate's peers. If they feel that the candidate has reached the required standard this is a positive sign that the work may be ready for examination. Candidates may also benchmark their work against other dissertations that have already been awarded a degree. But, most important of all, candidates should not submit their dissertation simply because they are bored or fed up with the work.

15.5.2   Masters versus Doctorate

The basic approaches to the evaluation of a masters degree and a doctoral degree are quite similar. Most universities appoint at least two examiners, one of which may be internal and one external. Sometimes two external examiners are required, especially if the candidate is a member of the staff of the university.

The examiners reports on the dissertation and the oral examination, if this is required, are presented to the examinations board who will then consider the findings of the examiners and provided they are satisfied, recommend to the university senate that the degree be awarded.[1]

The examiners fail few masters or doctoral degrees. If the dissertation is not of sufficient quality or if the candidate does not acquit himself or herself adequately at the oral examination, the examiners usually recommend further work to be undertaken. In such cases candidates may be told that they may not resubmit their dissertation within a prescribed period, such as six months, one year or two years. Sometimes this leads to candidates abandoning their research and thus not obtaining their degree.

15.6 A Holistic Evaluation Approach

Research dissertations are frequently evaluated on a holistic basis, that is to say the examiners decide if the dissertation as a whole meets the objectives laid down by the institution. Here the process of the study may be almost as important as the final output. This is especially true where a doctoral degree is seen as an apprenticeship in research. One of the holistic criteria is that the document needs to stand alone as an account of the work which has been performed, and should be fully understandable in its own right. Thus the dissertation needs to be well written, well argued and illustrated with appropriate figures and tables in order to prove convincingly the case being presented. Thus a high quality of written and pictorial presentation is a prerequisite for success. The central issue is that the findings and recommendations of the research need to be persuasively presented and communicated.

A final holistic issue which examiners consider is the production, presentation and layout of the actual document or book. In the first place all universities have regulations with regards to the format of the dissertation, and the candidate needs to comply with these strictly. Secondly the production of the dissertation needs to have been undertaken to a high standard. Thus the candidate needs to ask the question, 'Is the dissertation ready to go on to the university library shelf?'

15.7 Research Report for a Masters Degree by Course Work

The requirements for the research report at this level vary substantially. Some institutions require a relatively short and simple piece of work, while others ask their candidates to produce a dissertation which is close to that required for a masters degree by dissertation. The main guideline for this group of degrees is that the dissertation or research report be distinctly different from a business or management report written by a consultant or executive for decision-making purposes. Even this relatively modest academic work needs to show some evidence of acquaintance with some part of the literature and the fact that some thought has been given to the approach or method which has been taken to the research. MBA research reports, in particular, are sometimes criticised for being little more than business or management reports. But such a comment would only apply to poorly prepared research reports. A research report as part of a masters degree by course work should be academically sound in its own right, that is, it should be correctly documented and should have a modest research question and an attempt to find a sound answer to that question. Although there is substantial variation, these dissertations or research reports tend to be between 40 and 60 pages in length.

15.8 Evaluating a Masters Degree by Dissertation

For a masters degree by dissertation, the dissertation should clearly demonstrate that the candidate is a master of the subject material,[2] that he or she has a comprehensive understanding of the subject which has been addressed, and also that the candidate has understood the methodological issues associated with the approach taken in the research.

It is not usual for the candidate to have to demonstrate that something has been added to the body of knowledge, and thus the work does not have to show originality. A masters dissertation should clearly demonstrate the candidate's ability to document his or her research to academic standards. The masters dissertation will follow the same general format as the doctoral dissertation described below but the work will not be as rigorously pursued as it would be for the higher degree. A masters dissertation does not have to be a long document. Somewhere between 75 to 100 pages[3] is normally quite acceptable.

15.9 Evaluating a Doctorate Degree

For a doctorate degree the examiners require a deeper treatment of the subject material and the research issues. The central issue in evaluating a doctoral dissertation is whether or not the work has added something of value to the body of knowledge. Expressed slightly differently, the doctoral candidate needs to make a theoretical contribution to the subject that will hold up under the detailed scrutiny of the internal and external examiners. This usually requires an analysis and interpretation of theoretical concepts, the collection of evidence and the creative synthesis of evidence and theory.

Unless a valuable contribution to the body of knowledge can be demonstrated it is unlikely that the candidate will be awarded a doctorate.[4] In the context of business and management research the contribution should also be of practical relevance to business organisations. However, although adding to the body of knowledge is a necessary condition, it is not in its own right sufficient. There are several other criteria that are quite central to the evaluation.

The dissertation of a doctoral candidate should show evidence that he or she is familiar with all the literature and all the arguments relating to the issues being researched. The doctoral dissertation needs to focus on relevant material and synthesise the more important issues.

The candidate should know as much about the topic as anyone else, including the examiners. Thus the candidate's reading needs to be fully up to date. In addition, the candidate must show a distinctly critical faculty in discussing the strengths and weakness of this body of literature.

A doctoral dissertation needs to express clearly a distinct point of view, which some scholars refer to as new insights or a new vision of the subject matter being studied or researched. The researcher should be able to demonstrate convincingly why this point of view should be regarded as important as well as being able to argue for its validity.

A doctoral dissertation in the business and management studies area should directly address the implications of the research for management. It needs to establish that the findings of the research are relevant to current management problems or opportunities.

15.10   Quality versus Quantity

Some doctoral candidates show concern over what constitutes an appropriate length or number of pages for a dissertation. This type of question does not have a simple answer. In some circumstances quite short dissertations are acceptable, while in other circumstances the subject will require a lengthier dissertation to do justice to the subject matter. In general, however, most students will find it challenging to produce a document that is adequately comprehensive and free standing in under 200 pages. On the other hand, documents in excess of 500 pages are generally regarded as being too lengthy and probably verbose. Some students produce dissertations running to 1,000 pages but there is now a tendency to return these documents for shortening as the factor of overwhelming importance is to produce a concise, convincing and well-reasoned argument.

15.11   Details that Examiners Inspect Closely

Besides evaluating holistically, as has been discussed above, examiners also look for a considerable amount of detail in each chapter of a dissertation. Although the detail may be regarded in some institutions as less important than the holistic criteria, it is essential if the candidate is to obtain the degree. The following sections look at each chapter of a dissertation separately and highlight the most important issues.

15.11.1   Introduction

It is important that the introduction captures the imagination of the reader by showing why the subject is important and thus worthy of the award of a degree, be it a masters or a doctorate. Examiners will look for a comprehensive presentation of the background to the problem, which should include a clear and convincing argument that the subject of the research is topical, relevant and important. In business and management research this implies that the work will lead to the development of guidelines which will be of direct use in business and management situations. The introduction should include key definitions, a brief description of the research tasks, indicating the steps to be followed through the dissertation, and an outline of the main conclusions.

15.11.2   Literature Review

The literature review is of considerable importance and needs to be thorough and exhaustive. The references should be taken primarily from the leading academic journals and not from general textbooks. References to relevant textbooks or even to articles in the popular press are acceptable, but these should be kept to a minimum. References should be made to both theoretical and empirical issues pertaining to the research topic. All references cited should be complete and should comply with the convention accepted by the university concerned.

The candidate should not simply regurgitate the ideas from the literature but is expected to evaluate and comment on them critically but constructively. There should not be too many direct quotes from referenced works. This is a central requirement, especially for a doctoral degree.

By the end of the literature review the candidate will probably have prepared a conceptual model which describes the key variables relating to the phenomenon being researched and how these variables are linked to one another. This model could be presented as either a narrative or graphical presentation, or both.

15.11.3 Research Questions

The research questions need to be directly related to the conceptual model developed from the literature review referred to above. They should be couched in a clear way and be easily operationalised (Hubermann and Miles, 1994). Only a limited number of research questions are required and examiners will usually be critical if too many issues are covered; in some circumstances one research question may be perfectly adequate. Research questions should be focused so they will have to lead to a theoretical conjecture or to hypotheses or empirical generalisations.

15.11.4 Methodology

The question of methodology is complex and there are many different views. The traditional approach to business and management studies was to employ methodologies borrowed from the natural sciences and thus much of the work performed in this field relied on the positivist research paradigm. In recent years qualitative research approaches (Patton, 1990) have grown in popularity and today play a important role in research in this field.

It is critical to spell out the philosophical approach being used to underpin the research (Remenyi, 1995). This dictates the research strategy and it is important that it is consistent. The two main philosophical stances used in academic research are positivism and phenomenology and within these there are a number of different research strategies (Galliers, 1992). If an eclectic approach is used this should be carefully justified as many examiners are critical of this approach.

This chapter should include a full description of the process used to gather both primary and secondary evidence, which will normally be both qualitative and quantitative in nature. The methods of evidence collection and proposed analyses should be defined, together with a statement of the limitations of the approach that has been adopted.

15.11.5 Evidence Collection and Analysis

This is one of the most challenging parts of a research degree. The examiners look to see if an appropriate approach has been taken to the actual evidence collection. The questions asked here frequently relate to sampling procedures and instrumentation. Where case studies have been used it is important to state why the particular organisations were chosen to be studied (Yin, 1989). Examiners will consider the rigour[5] with which this has been done. The techniques used to analyse the evidence collected will be closely scrutinised and they need to comply with accepted practice in the discipline being researched. If established practices have not been followed the candidate needs to explain why convincingly.

The results of the interpretation or the analysis need to be presented using traditional presentation techniques, such as tables, graphs etc. The departure point for the analysis is the provision of a profile of the sample that forms the basis for subsequent deeper analysis and generalisations and this needs to be explicitly stated. This aspect of the study is key to assessing the validity of the findings from the research.

Any problems encountered in dealing with the above issues should be stated, together with an explanation as to how they were overcome.

15.11.6   Interpretation

This chapter will discuss the findings in a general way as well as focusing on some specific interpretations of the results.

It is essential that the interpretation or the findings are consistent with the analysis. There needs to be a clear logical path from the original conceptual model, to the evidence, to the analysis, and then to the findings. Examiners look to see if the findings constitute a clear addition to the body of knowledge. The question 'Has the work made a clear contribution to the field of study?' will be asked. In establishing this, the examiners will need to decide if the candidate has made a convincing argument (Collins, 1994). In the business and management field one of the most important criteria is whether the results of the research may be put to some practical use. Thus the question, 'Are the findings useful?', is frequently asked. The questions of validity, bias and generalisability have also to be addressed in this chapter irrespective of whether a quantitative or qualitative approach has been taken. It is not essential that the results are generalisable, but this issue needs to be fully discussed.

Sometimes the evidence collected by the research and the analysis thereof does not support the original conceptual model. This does not mean that the candidate's research has been a failure. Failing to confirm a theory or hypothesis can be just as valuable as confirmation, and it could lead to the development of a new theory. Senior degrees may be awarded even where the candidate has not confirmed his or her hypothesis, provided a contribution has been made to the body of knowledge.

15.11.7   Summary and Conclusion of the Dissertation

The conclusion provides an opportunity to tie up the loose ends, to state the limitations of the research and to suggest where research in the subject should now proceed. The implications of the research for the management and business community in general should also be stated here. If any part of the work of the candidate has already been published then this should be pointed out in support of the findings.

The conclusions should finish with a statement of the positive aspects of the research work, even if the research did not support the original model or beliefs.

15.11.8   The Limitations of the Research

In this final chapter in a dissertation there is the opportunity to reflect on the research and to discuss its strengths and weaknesses. It is sometimes said that this is the place for reflectivity, meaning that the researcher can reflect on the work in a holistic way and make an evaluation of the dissertation him or herself. This is an important chapter and even a relatively weak dissertation can be substantially strengthened by an insightful account of the research at this stage.

15.11.9   Management Guidelines or Recommendations

In this final chapter of a dissertation the findings are restructured in terms of practical guidelines which can be used by managers in order to improve their performance in working situations.

15.12   The Grading of Masters and Doctorates

Some universities only distinguish between dissertations that have earned a pass grade and those which have not. Thus the candidate can either pass or not pass. In the case of the latter, the candidate is frequently encouraged to do more work. However, some other universities do award masters and doctorates *cum laude*, or with distinction. It is difficult to define the requirements for these awards and perhaps all that can be said of a general nature is that outstanding work is required to achieve these accolades.

15.13   A Checklist for Doctoral and Masters Degree Candidates

The following is a checklist of 23 questions which will be directly useful to doctoral candidates but will also have some relevance to masters students, especially those hoping to achieve a distinction, and which they should consult before finally submitting their dissertation. The checklist is broken into two parts: general or holistic issues and detailed issues.

15.13.1   General or Holistic Issues

1   Is the problem identified specified, structured and articulated clearly?
2   Does the work make a valuable contribution to the body of knowledge?
3   Is the argument in the dissertation convincing?
4   Does the supervisor agree that the work is ready for examination?
5   Is the document about the right length?
6   Is the dissertation ready to be placed in the public domain, i.e. university library?
7   Are all the university requirements relating to the format of the dissertation complied with?

15.13.2 Detailed Issues

8   Does the introduction demonstrate that the subject of the research is important?

9   Is the literature review complete and is it sufficiently critical?

10 Has a new conceptual model been developed from the literature review?

11 Is the research question clear and is it directly derived from either personal experience[6] or the literature review?

12 Do the research questions lend themselves to empirical generalisations or hypotheses?

13 Has the philosophical underpinning of the research methodology been stated?

14 Have the details of the research method been explained?

15 Has a sound approach to sampling procedures and evidence collection been demonstrated?

16 Have the analytical techniques used on the evidence, whether they be qualitative or quantitative, been fully justified?

17 Is there a clear logical path from the original conceptual model to the evidence to the analysis and then to the findings?

18 Are the findings generalisable and, if not, what is their importance?

19 Have the issues of validity, reliability or credibility, transferability and bias been adequately addressed?

20 Are the final conclusions sufficiently convincing?

21 Have the limitations of the research been adequately addressed?

22 Have the findings of the research been translated into management guidelines?

23 Does the 'Summary and Conclusions' chapter finish on a positive note?

Only when all of these questions have been satisfactorily answered should the candidate present his or her work for examination.

15.14   Summary and Conclusion

This chapter has reviewed the range of research degrees offered by universities. It has considered masters and doctoral degrees, including those offered by dissertation only and those obtained through a combination of course work and research. It will be noticed that there is a range of degrees available with a substantial diversity in the amount of research required from a candidate in order to qualify. Thus candidates who have a relatively low inclination to research can select degree options where there is a substantial amount of course work.

The principal issues on which examiners focus for the evaluation of the research work have been outlined, both holistically and in the detail required for typical chapters of a dissertation.

Research degree candidates are offered advice as to what is required in their written output in terms of both academic content and technical presentation. A checklist has been provided which, if used to ensure the dissertation is complete, can assist candidates obtain approval for their work.

Although research for masters and doctoral degrees is demanding, many graduates report that the research process has been one of the most satisfactory periods of their career.

Suggested Further Reading

Arbnor, I. and Bjerke, B. (1996) *Methodology for Creating Business Knowledge*. Second Edn, Sage Publications, Thousand Oaks, CA.

Black, T. R. (1993) *Evaluating Social Science Research: An Introduction*. Sage Publications, London.

Hansen, K. J. and Waterman, R. C. (1966) 'Evaluation of research in business education', *National Business Education Quarterly*, no. 35: 81–4.

Jankowicz, A. (1995) *Business Research Projects*. Second Edn, Chapman and Hall, London.

Mowday, R. (1997) 'Reaffirming our scholarly values', *Academy of Management Review*, 22 (2) April: 335–45.

Notes

[1] The procedure by which degrees are awarded differs enormously from university to university. However, in almost all cases the university senate awards the degree, but in some cases it may take advice directly from the examiners without going through a board of examiners or a higher degrees committee.

[2] The scope of the masters degree may be relatively narrow and the candidate is usually not required to have the same depth or breadth of knowledge of related fields as would be required for a doctorate.

[3] Most universities have standing rules and regulations that specify the length of research reports as well as masters and doctoral dissertations. These are usually laid down in terms of the maximum number of words. A minimum number is usually not stated as it is generally agreed that quantity cannot be substituted for quality. There have been instances, particularly in the computational sciences, where masters and doctoral degrees have been obtained on the basis of a dissertation of no more than a dozen or so pages.

[4] If a candidate presents a lesser piece of work he or she may be offered another degree such as an MPhil.

[5] The concept of rigour in research is not an easy one. Rigour relates to thoroughness, to attention to detail, to consistency or to conformation with the chosen research strategy. It will not be easy to find fault with a research dissertation that has rigorously complied with the generally accepted rules of research.

[6] If the research question has been derived from personal experience then it also needs to be, at least to some extent, supported by the literature.

Appendix A

A Note on Academic Degrees

Academic degrees have been awarded by European universities since the second half of the twelfth century when Bologna University in Italy began by awarding a Doctor of Civil Laws Degree. Shortly afterwards the university extended this one subject to include canon law, medicine, grammar, logic and philosophy. Today European universities award a wide range of degrees in a number of different faculties, ranging from the arts to science, to law, to medicine, to business, to architecture and to engineering, to mention only a few. The way a degree is designated varies considerably from institution to institution and the status of the degree is largely dependent on the reputation of the university.

Historically, as a general rule European universities awarded either masters degrees or doctorates with the aim of ensuring that their graduates were qualified or licensed to participate in a particular guild. Members of the faculties of the universities were licensed to teach and the degrees awarded were in effect a professional certification. The masters or doctoral degree took a number of years to complete and thus over time a shorter bachelors degree was introduced as a stage towards the masters or doctoral degree. Soon the bachelors degree became a qualification in its own right and its completion demonstrated that the graduate had fulfilled the first stage of academic life and had made progress towards the final certification.

Initially the masters and doctoral degrees, as well as the title of Professor, were all equivalent. The University of Bologna had initiated the title of Doctor, but the University of Paris preferred the title Master. The Universities of Oxford and Cambridge followed the lead of Paris. Some universities used the title Master in certain faculties while in others the title of Doctor was used. Eventually it became practice for a number of universities to establish the masters as a first degree and then have the student follow on from that level with further study leading to a doctoral degree.

The degrees offered and the way degrees are followed varies considerably from one country to the next. In the Anglo-Saxon world, that is the UK, the US and British Commonwealth countries, students, especially those who are carrying on with their formal education immediately after leaving school, usually start by studying for a bachelors degree which generally takes between three and four years. The university rules for admission to a bachelors degree are often very strict with a pass grade at a public examination or a pass grade at a private entrance examination being required.

Having completed the bachelors degree the masters degree will usually take one or two more years of additional study. Increasingly the masters degree consists of a combination of course work and research and the precise proportions vary considerable for university to university and from faculty to faculty. For example, the MBA[1] is typically 75 per cent to 80 per cent taught and evaluated by examination with 20 per cent to 25 per cent based on research and evaluated by dissertation. The doctoral degree follows on from the masters degree and generally requires a further period of two to five years' study based around a programme of original research. Even at doctoral level some universities in the UK and most, if not all, universities in the US have some element of course work which is examined. However, the doctoral degree is largely a research degree and it is usually examined verbally in front of a small panel of experts and conducted in private.

Increasingly doctoral degrees are being undertaken by students who have not completed a masters degree and thus the masters step is being by-passed. Admission to a masters degree and sometimes to a doctoral degree can be less formal than admission to a bachelors degree, sometimes only requiring the personal approval of the head of the department or the dean of the faculty in which the student proposes to study.

There is an interesting exception to the usual relationship between the bachelors and masters degrees at Oxford and Cambridge. At both these institutions students are awarded a bachelor of arts degree (BA) after three years of successful study. However, after another six or seven years the BA graduate may be awarded a masters of arts degree (MA) without further examination and by simply paying an additional fee. Some other universities in the UK are moving away from the bachelors degree. For example in the aeronautical engineering department at Imperial College, which is part of the University of London, undergraduate students are registered directly for a masters degree. If they do not complete the required course of study they can be offered a bachelors degree as a consolation prize.

The system in continental Europe is quite different and each country has its own national approach. In France, the *baccalauréat* is conferred on students when they qualify for university entrance. University students study for a *licence* or a *maitrise* and there is also a degree referred to as the *agrégation* which qualifies them to teach in a university. Doctoral degrees are also awarded.

In Germany universities only award doctoral degrees. On leaving school, students register at university for a *Diplom* which takes at least four and a half years[2] and which has the status of the masters degree but which is not regarded by some as being a degree as such.[3] Once this is completed the student may continue to the doctorate and after that those wishing to become academics need to complete a *Habilitation*, sometimes referred to as a second doctorate. The German doctorates are not defended in public. In contrast in Portugal universities offer five levels of degrees which include *Bacharelato, Licenciatura, Mestrado, Doutoramento and Agregaçao*, the last degree being a special one, required if a career as a university professor is being undertaken.

In northern European countries such as the Netherlands and Sweden the student is required initially to register for four and a half years to complete a masters before proceeding with his or her doctorate. In Sweden there is an intermediate degree between the masters and the doctorate that is referred to as the *licenciate*. This degree is awarded to those who have made material progress towards the doctorate but who are not necessarily going to complete the senior degree for one reason or another. Doctorates are not examined in private, but by public defence which could be in front of a substantial audience.

More than 1500 different degrees are awarded in the US. These range from degrees awarded by high-quality, high-status and very expensive institutions such as Harvard University, to junior or community colleges where degrees are awarded after two years' study and whose status is rather low. The influence of American thinking on academic degrees is increasing and Europe is likely to adopt more American ideas over the next few years.

In conclusion, the range of degrees offered by universities is enormous and the quality and approach used by different institutions is very diverse.

Notes

[1] Before allowing a candidate to be enrolled for an MBA some business schools insist that the student have a number of years' working experience, usually in some management role. However there are increasing number of institutions which are admitting young graduates without working experience.

[2] In Germany some subject areas award a *Vordiplom* after about two years. This is in recognition of some progress towards the *Diplom*.

[3] The *Encyclopaedia Britannica* 1997 takes the view that this is not a degree.

Appendix B

Measuring Instruments

Questionnaire Example: The Measurement of IS Effectiveness

The following survey has been designed to help assess the effectiveness of the corporate computing system used to support the organisation in achieving its objectives. This type of survey is used extensively in businesses in Europe as well as other parts of the world.

The survey has been divided into five parts. Part A relates to demographic details about your position in the firm. Parts B, C and D use the same set of 38 statements which relate to attributes of the information systems department. Part E contains one specific question as well as an opportunity for you to provide open-ended comment on the service provided by the department.

In Part B you are asked to say, by indicating the extent of your agreement with a statement, what you would expect from the information systems department in an ideal set of circumstances. In Part C you are asked to indicate what your expectations actually are, given the imperfect world in which we all have to work.

Please note that although Part B and Part C look very similar at first glance, they are quite different.

Your responses to the third set of 38 statements in Part D refer to how the information systems department actually performs in terms of these attributes.

Finally, in Part E we would like you to rate your overall opinion of the information systems department, and we would welcome any comments that you would like to make concerning your own experience with regard to its effectiveness.

Please ensure that you respond to all statements by ticking one and only one number, where 1 means you strongly agree and 9 means you strongly disagree.

The questionnaire should not take more than 15–20 minutes to complete. All information supplied by respondents will be treated with the utmost confidence.

Thank you very much for your assistance in this research. Please return your completed questionnaire to the survey administrator.

Professor Dan Remenyi
IT Effectiveness Assessment Services

PART A

Please supply the following information about your position:

1 In which function do you work (Tick one)?

    a) Manager   _____
    b) Accountant   _____
    c) Knowledge Worker   _____
    d) Clerk   _____
    e) Personal Assistant   _____
    f) Secretary   _____
    g) Typist   _____
    h) Marketing   _____
    i) Sales   _____
    j) Distribution   _____
    k) Warehouse   _____
    l) Personnel   _____
    m) Logistics   _____
    n) R&D   _____
    o) Other, please specify

2 How many years have you been working in the organisation?   _____
3 How many years experience have you had working with a PC?   _____
4 How many years experience have you had working with a PC network?   _____
5 How many hours per week do you use a PC or a PC network?   _____

PART B – Expectations Under Ideal Circumstances

Please respond by ticking the number that corresponds to how much you agree or disagree with the following statements of expectation, *given an ideal situation.*

		Strongly Agree							Strongly Disagree	
1	I expect ease of access for users to computing facilities to be excellent.	1	2	3	4	5	6	7	8	9
2	I expect up-to-date hardware.	1	2	3	4	5	6	7	8	9
3	I expect up-to-date software.	1	2	3	4	5	6	7	8	9
4	I expect access to external databases to be excellent.	1	2	3	4	5	6	7	8	9
5	I expect a low percentage of hardware and software downtime.	1	2	3	4	5	6	7	8	9
6	I expect a high degree of technical competence from systems support staff.	1	2	3	4	5	6	7	8	9
7	I expect a high level of user confidence in our systems.	1	2	3	4	5	6	7	8	9
8	I expect users to have a high degree of personal control over their systems.	1	2	3	4	5	6	7	8	9
9	I expect the ISD to be responsive to changing user needs.	1	2	3	4	5	6	7	8	9
10	I expect confidentiality of user's own evidence.	1	2	3	4	5	6	7	8	9
11	I expect a provision for disaster recovery.	1	2	3	4	5	6	7	8	9
12	I expect piracy avoidance procedures to be in place.	1	2	3	4	5	6	7	8	9
13	I expect excellent system's response time.	1	2	3	4	5	6	7	8	9
14	I expect excellent technical training.	1	2	3	4	5	6	7	8	9

15	I expect fast response time by support staff to remedy problems.	1	2	3	4	5	6	7	8	9
16	I expect to participate in the planning of system technology requirements.	1	2	3	4	5	6	7	8	9
17	I expect the flexibility to be able to produce professional reports using graphics and desktop publishing.	1	2	3	4	5	6	7	8	9
18	I expect a positive attitude from support staff to users.	1	2	3	4	5	6	7	8	9
19	I expect users to have a thorough understanding of the system.	1	2	3	4	5	6	7	8	9
20	I expect overall cost-effectiveness of information technology.	1	2	3	4	5	6	7	8	9
21	I expect the use of IT to considerably improve my personal productivity.	1	2	3	4	5	6	7	8	9
22	I expect the use of IT to considerably enrich the working experience of staff.	1	2	3	4	5	6	7	8	9
23	I expect complete standardisation of hardware.	1	2	3	4	5	6	7	8	9
24	I expect excellent documentation to support technical training.	1	2	3	4	5	6	7	8	9
25	I expect a lot of help with database or model development.	1	2	3	4	5	6	7	8	9
26	I expect to be able to conduct computer conferencing with colleagues.	1	2	3	4	5	6	7	8	9
27	I expect users to be willing to find time to learn the system.	1	2	3	4	5	6	7	8	9
28	I expect the use of a service level agreement.	1	2	3	4	5	6	7	8	9

29	I expect the ISD to monitor its performance in delivering a service to the users	1	2	3	4	5	6	7	8	9
30	I expect to be able to use GUI (graphical user interface) software.	1	2	3	4	5	6	7	8	9
31	I expect reports to be readily available and delivered quickly.	1	2	3	4	5	6	7	8	9
32	I expect prompt processing of requests for changes to existing systems.	1	2	3	4	5	6	7	8	9
33	I expect IT to be aligned to the overall corporate plan.	1	2	3	4	5	6	7	8	9
34	I expect there to be short lead times for the development of new systems.	1	2	3	4	5	6	7	8	9
35	I expect systems analysts to know the users' business.	1	2	3	4	5	6	7	8	9
36	I expect a high degree of flexibility in the system with regards evidence and reports.	1	2	3	4	5	6	7	8	9
37	I expect the portfolio of applications to be increased.	1	2	3	4	5	6	7	8	9
38	I expect the benefits derived by users of the system to be measured.	1	2	3	4	5	6	7	8	9

PART C – Expectations Under Actual Circumstances

Please respond by ticking the number that corresponds to how much you agree or disagree with the following statements of expectation, *given the imperfect world in which we all have to work.*

		Strongly Agree							Strongly Disagree	
1	I expect ease of access for users to computing facilities to be excellent.	1	2	3	4	5	6	7	8	9
2	I expect up-to-date hardware.	1	2	3	4	5	6	7	8	9
3	I expect up-to-date software.	1	2	3	4	5	6	7	8	9
4	I expect access to external databases to be excellent.	1	2	3	4	5	6	7	8	9
5	I expect a low percentage of hardware and software downtime.	1	2	3	4	5	6	7	8	9
6	I expect a high degree of technical competence from systems support staff.	1	2	3	4	5	6	7	8	9
7	I expect a high level of user confidence in our systems.	1	2	3	4	5	6	7	8	9
8	I expect users to have a high degree of personal control over their systems.	1	2	3	4	5	6	7	8	9
9	I expect the ISD to be responsive to changing user needs.	1	2	3	4	5	6	7	8	9
10	I expect confidentiality of user's own evidence.	1	2	3	4	5	6	7	8	9
11	I expect a provision for disaster recovery.	1	2	3	4	5	6	7	8	9
12	I expect piracy avoidance procedures to be in place.	1	2	3	4	5	6	7	8	9
13	I expect excellent system's response time.	1	2	3	4	5	6	7	8	9
14	I expect excellent technical training.	1	2	3	4	5	6	7	8	9

15	I expect fast response time by support staff to remedy problems.	1	2	3	4	5	6	7	8	9
16	I expect to participate in the planning of system technology requirements.	1	2	3	4	5	6	7	8	9
17	I expect the flexibility to be able to produce professional reports using graphics and desktop publishing.	1	2	3	4	5	6	7	8	9
18	I expect a positive attitude from support staff to users.	1	2	3	4	5	6	7	8	9
19	I expect users to have a thorough understanding of the system.	1	2	3	4	5	6	7	8	9
20	I expect overall cost effectiveness of information technology.	1	2	3	4	5	6	7	8	9
21	I expect the use of IT to considerably improve my personal productivity.	1	2	3	4	5	6	7	8	9
22	I expect the use of IT to considerably enrich the working experience of staff.	1	2	3	4	5	6	7	8	9
23	I expect complete standardisation of hardware.	1	2	3	4	5	6	7	8	9
24	I expect excellent documentation to support technical training.	1	2	3	4	5	6	7	8	9
25	I expect a lot of help with database or model development.	1	2	3	4	5	6	7	8	9
26	I expect to be able to conduct computer conferencing with colleagues.	1	2	3	4	5	6	7	8	9
27	I expect users to be willing to find time to learn the system.	1	2	3	4	5	6	7	8	9
28	I expect the use of a service level agreement.	1	2	3	4	5	6	7	8	9

29	I expect the ISD to monitor its performance in delivering a service to the users.	1	2	3	4	5	6	7	8	9
30	I expect to be able to use GUI (graphical user interface) software.	1	2	3	4	5	6	7	8	9
31	I expect reports to be readily available and delivered quickly.	1	2	3	4	5	6	7	8	9
32	I expect prompt processing of requests for changes to existing systems.	1	2	3	4	5	6	7	8	9
33	I expect IT to be aligned to the overall corporate plan.	1	2	3	4	5	6	7	8	9
34	I expect there to be short lead times for the development of new systems.	1	2	3	4	5	6	7	8	9
35	I expect systems analysts to know the users' business.	1	2	3	4	5	6	7	8	9
36	I expect a high degree of flexibility in the system with regards evidence and reports.	1	2	3	4	5	6	7	8	9
37	I expect the portfolio of applications to be increased.	1	2	3	4	5	6	7	8	9
38	I expect the benefits derived by users of the system to be measured.	1	2	3	4	5	6	7	8	9

PART D – Performance Assessment

Compared to the level of service you would expect in an excellent organisation, respond by ticking the number which corresponds to how much you agree or disagree with the following statements of performance.

		Strongly Agree							Strongly Disagree	
1	Ease of access for users to computing facilities is excellent.	1	2	3	4	5	6	7	8	9
2	Our hardware is up-to-date.	1	2	3	4	5	6	7	8	9
3	Our software is up-to-date.	1	2	3	4	5	6	7	8	9
4	Access to external databases is excellent.	1	2	3	4	5	6	7	8	9
5	There is a low percentage of hardware and software downtime.	1	2	3	4	5	6	7	8	9
6	There is a high degree of technical competence from systems support staff.	1	2	3	4	5	6	7	8	9
7	There is a high level of user confidence in our systems.	1	2	3	4	5	6	7	8	9
8	Users to have a high degree of personal control over their systems.	1	2	3	4	5	6	7	8	9
9	The ISD is responsive to changing user needs.	1	2	3	4	5	6	7	8	9
10	There is confidentiality of user's own evidence.	1	2	3	4	5	6	7	8	9
11	There is a provision for disaster recovery.	1	2	3	4	5	6	7	8	9
12	There are piracy avoidance procedures in place.	1	2	3	4	5	6	7	8	9
13	There is excellent system's response time.	1	2	3	4	5	6	7	8	9
14	There is excellent technical training.	1	2	3	4	5	6	7	8	9

15	There is fast response time by support staff to remedy problems.	1	2	3	4	5	6	7	8	9
16	Users participate in the planning of system technology requirements.	1	2	3	4	5	6	7	8	9
17	There is flexibility to be able to produce professional reports using graphics and desktop publishing.	1	2	3	4	5	6	7	8	9
18	There is a positive attitude from support staff to users.	1	2	3	4	5	6	7	8	9
19	Users have a thorough understanding of the system.	1	2	3	4	5	6	7	8	9
20	Our information technology is cost effective.	1	2	3	4	5	6	7	8	9
21	The use of IT considerably improves my personal productivity.	1	2	3	4	5	6	7	8	9
22	The use of IT considerably enriches the working experience of staff.	1	2	3	4	5	6	7	8	9
23	There is complete standardisation of hardware.	1	2	3	4	5	6	7	8	9
24	There is excellent documentation to support technical training.	1	2	3	4	5	6	7	8	9
25	There is a lot of help available with database or model development.	1	2	3	4	5	6	7	8	9
26	I am able to conduct computer conferencing with colleagues.	1	2	3	4	5	6	7	8	9
27	Users are willing to find time to learn the system.	1	2	3	4	5	6	7	8	9
28	Service level agreements are used.	1	2	3	4	5	6	7	8	9
29	The ISD monitors its performance in delivering a service to the users.	1	2	3	4	5	6	7	8	9

30	I am able to use GUI (graphical user interface) software.	1	2	3	4	5	6	7	8	9
31	Reports are readily available and delivered quickly.	1	2	3	4	5	6	7	8	9
32	There is prompt processing of requests for changes to existing systems.	1	2	3	4	5	6	7	8	9
33	IT is aligned to the overall corporate plan.	1	2	3	4	5	6	7	8	9
34	There are short lead times for the development of new systems.	1	2	3	4	5	6	7	8	9
35	Systems analysts know the user's business.	1	2	3	4	5	6	7	8	9
36	There is a high degree of flexibility in the system with regards evidence and reports.	1	2	3	4	5	6	7	8	9
37	The portfolio of applications is regularly enhanced.	1	2	3	4	5	6	7	8	9
38	The benefits derived by users of the system are measured.	1	2	3	4	5	6	7	8	9

PART E

	Strongly Agree							Strongly Disagree	
The overall performance of the ISD is excellent.	1	2	3	4	5	6	7	8	9

Please supply any further comments you wish concerning the performance of the ISD.

_____

_____

_____

_____

_____

_____

_____

Appendix C

Further Information on Statistical Analysis

The following is some further information on software for statistical analysis for research purposes at masters and doctorate level.

Statistical Packages

Many statistical packages are available for personal computers, and spreadsheet packages offer basic statistical routines. Using one of these will avoid having to carry out detailed and tedious calculations.

There are two large and powerful packages called SAS and SPSS and there is also a range of medium-sized packages that should be adequate for most needs, and several small packages that are cheap but limited. Some vendors offer cut-down versions at cheap rates for students. Prices for the big packages range up to a thousand pounds and it may be necessary to pay an annual licence fee; for smaller packages one should expect to pay up to several hundred pounds.

It is difficult to make firm recommendations because statistical software packages are developing rapidly. In this age of personal computers, menu-driven software combined with publication-quality, interactive graphics and a reasonable range of standard analytical procedures is essential. Based on the authors' experience, packages to consider include MiniTab, StatGraphics, NCSS, StatView and SyStat.

BASS from Bass Institute Inc., PO. Box Chapel Hill, NC 27514, USA. Telephone (919) 489 0729.

C-Stat from Cherwell Scientific Publishing, 27 Park End Street, Oxford OX1 1HU, UK. Telephone (01865) 794884/794664.

Crunch Statistical Package from Crunch Software, 5335 College Avenue, Suite 27, Oakland, CA 94618, USA. Telephone (415) 420 8660.

CSS from StatSoft, 2325 E 13th Street, Tulsa, OK 74104, USA. Telephone (918) 583 4149.

Evidence Desk from Odesta Corp., 4084 Commercial Avenue, Northbrook, IL 60062. Telephone (800) 323 5423.

Exstatix from Strategic Mapping, 4030 Moorpark Avenue, Suite 250, San Jose, CA 95117, USA. Telephone (408) 985 7400.

GLIM from NAG Ltd., Wilkinson House, Jordan Hill Road, Oxford, UK. Telephone (01865) 511245. Fax (01865) 310139.

Mac SS/Statistica from StatSoft, 2325 E. 13th Street, Tulsa, OK 74104, USA. Telephone (918) 583 4149.

MiniTab Statistical Software from Minitab Inc., 3081 Enterprise Drive, State College, PA 16801, USA. Telephone (800) 448 3555 and CLE Com Ltd, The Research Park, Vincent Drive, Edgbaston, Birmingham B15 2SQ, UK. Telephone (0121) 471 4199.

NWA Statpak from Northwest Analytical Inc., 520 N. W. Davis Street, Portland, OR 97209, USA. Telephone (503) 224 7727.

S-Plus from Statistical Sciences Inc., 1700 Westlake Avenue N, Suite 500, Seattle, WA 98109, USA. Telephone (206) 283 8802. Fax (206) 283 8691 and Statistical Sciences UK Ltd, 52 Sandfield Road, Oxford OX3 7RJ, UK. Telephone (01865) 61000. Fax (01865) 61000.

SAS and *JMP* from SAS Institute, SAS Circle, Box 8000, Cary, NC 27512, USA. Telephone (919) 467-8000 and SAS Software Ltd, Wittington House, Henley Road, Marlow SL7 2EB, UK. Telephone (01628) 486933.

Solo 101 and *BP-90* from BMDP Statistical Software Inc., 1424 Sepulveda Boulevard, Suite 316, Los Angeles, CA 90025, USA. Telephone (213) 479 7799.

SPSS/PC+ from SPSS Inc., 444 N. Michigan Avenue, Chicago, IL 60611, USA. Telephone (312) 329 3300, and SPSS International, PO Box 115, 4200 AC, Gorinchem, The Netherlands. Telephone (31) 1830 367 11. Fax (31) 1830 358 39.

StatGraphics from STGC Inc., 2115 E Jefferson Street, Rockville, MD 20852, USA. Telephone (301) 984 5000, (301) 592 0050.

Statistix II from NH Analytical Software, 1958 Eldridge Avenue, Roseville, MN 55113, USA. Telephone (612) 631 2852.

StatPac Gold from StatPac Inc., 3814 Lyndale Avenue S, Minneapolis, MN 55409, USA. Telephone (612) 822 8252, and Perifernalia, Snoekstraat 69, Alken, B–3570, Belgium. Telephone (32) 11 313754.

Statview II/SuperANOVA and *Statview SE and Graphics* from Abacus Concepts, 1984 Bonita Avenue, Berkeley, CA 94704, USA. Telephone (800) 666 7828; (415) 540 1949.

SyStat/SyGraph from SyStat Inc., 1800 Sherman Avenue, Evanston, IL 60201, USA. Telephone (708) 864 5670.

Appendix D

Useful Web Site Addresses

Web Address	Description
www.niss.ac.uk	UK based National Information Service and Systems. Provides links to libraries and to university departments.
www.yahoo.com	Search engine.
www.yahoo.com/reference/libraries	List of libraries around the world.
www.infoseek.com	Search engine.
www.lycos.com	Search engine.
www.webcrawler.com	Search engine.
www.austin.unimelb.edu.au:800/7m/ac ad/lists/acad	Search directory of scholarly e-conferences.
www.nova.edu/inter-links/cgi-bin/lists	Search list of discussion groups.
www.moondog.usask.ca/hytelnet	Tool to search all the major libraries of the world.
www.pcmag.com	Regularly updated list of 100 most visited sites on Internet.
www.pitt.edu/~malhotra/interest.html	Collection of directories and search engines relevant to theory, research and practice related to business and IT.
www.bbcnc.org.uk/babbage/iap.html	Collection of utilities useful for the research.
www.iTools.com	Well organised site with two useful tools called Find-It! and Research-It!

Appendix E

Software for Qualitative Evidence Analysis

There are now a large number of software packages available to assist with the analysis of qualitative evidence. According to Miles and Weitzman (1996) there are six different categories of software products which may be considered as tools to assist with the analysis of qualitative evidence. These include word processors, text retrievers, database managers, code and retrieval programs, code-based theory builders and conceptual network builders. Obviously the amount of functionality provided by this large range of packages varies greatly, with word processors providing very little assistance other than searching and sorting while code-based theory builders and conceptual network builders provide much more extensive help.

In their software source book Weitzman and Miles (1995) list 24 such software packages. These packages contain a wide range of facilities but they all focus on being able to analyse textual evidence and being able to report on patterns in the evidence. These packages vary in price from a few dollars or pounds to several hundred and consequently the sophistication of their function also varies.

One of the more popular products available to assist researchers is called NUD·IST. NUD·IST is a computer package to help with the qualitative analysis of non-numerical and unstructured data. It is produced by Qualitative Solutions and Research Pty Ltd (QSR) who are based in Melbourne, Australia.

NUD·IST creates an environment in which unstructured data can be stored, and through a process of indexing, searching and theorising the researcher can use his or her knowledge and analytical skills to explore ideas around the data. More specifically NUD·IST helps the user:

- manage, explore and search the text of documents;
- manage and explore ideas about the data;
- link ideas and construct theories about the data;
- test theories about the data;
- generate reports and statistical summaries.

NUD·IST can handle wide-ranging types of data including:

- text in the form of reports, minutes, transcripts of unstructured interviews, evidence transcripts, historical or literary documents, personnel records, field notes, newspaper and article clippings
- non-textual documents such as musical scores, photographs, tape recordings, films, maps and plans.

NUD·IST works by creating a document database for each project in which all the records of textual and non-textual data are stored. The database can then be manipulated by the user to:

- store, edit and retrieve the text of any document;
- record factual information about documents, cases, people, times and dates;
- write and edit memos to record ideas about a document;
- search for words or phrases in the text of a document and automatically index these.

As well as the document database NUD·IST also creates an index database which allows a user to:

- create, record, store and explore categories appropriate to a project;
- index data from the document database within categories;
- manage categories and subcategories using index 'trees';
- edit and search the index system;
- write and edit memos about any index category;
- create new categories for further analysis from the results of searches of a document or index database.

The following is a list of 10 software packages for qualitative evidence analysis together with contact details for the organisations which have developed these products.

AskSam from askSam Systems, PO Box 1428, Perry, FL 32347. Telephone: (800) 800-1997; (904) 584-6590 (support). Fax (904) 584-7481.

ATLAS/ti from Thomas Muhr, Scientific Software Development, Trautnaustr. 12,D-10717 Berlin, Germany. Telephone and fax 49-30-861-1415. E-mail thomas muhr@tu-berlin.de

Inspiration from Inspiration Software, Inc., 2920 SW Dolph Court, Suite 3, Portland, OR 97219. Telephone (503) 245-9011; (800) 775-4292. Fax (503) 246-4292).

Martin from Simonds Center for Instruction and Research in Nursing, School of Nursing, University of Wisconsin-Madison, 600 Highland Avenue, Madison, WI 53792-2455. Telephone (608) 263-5336). Fax (608) 263-5332. E-mail : pwipperf@vms2.macc.wisc.edu.

Metamorph from Thunderstone, Expansion Programs International, Inc., 11115 Edgewater Drive, Cleveland, OH 44102. Telephone (216) 631-8544. Fax (216) 281-0828.

NUD·IST from Qualitative Solutions and Research Pty .Ltd, Box 171, La Trobe University Post Office, Melbourne, Vic. 3083, Australia. Telephone 61-3-459-1699. Fax 61-3479-1441. E-mail tom@qsr.latrobe.edu.au. United States and Canada distributor: Learning Profiles, Inc., Attn. Jim Adams-Berger, 2329 West Main St.#330, Littlejohn, CO 80120-1951. Telephone (303) 797-2660. E-mail: jimab@omni.org.

SemNet from Semnet Research Group, 1043 University Avenue, Suite 215, San Diego, CA 92103-3392.Telephone (619) 232-9334. E-mail: jfaletti@sciences.sdsu.edu

WordKruncher from Johnson & Co, PO Box 6627, Bloomington, IN 47407, Telephone (812) 339-9996. Fax (812) 339-9997.

ZyINDEX from ZylLAB Division, ZYCO International, Inc., 19650 Club House Road, Suite 106, Gaithersburg, MD 20879. Telephone (301) 590-2760; (800) 544-6339. Fax (301) 590-0903.

Appendix F

A Glossary of Terms

A posteriori

Knowledge derived from experience, as opposed to *a priori* knowledge that is independent of observation. The view that knowledge is underpinned by *a posteriori* experiences is the basis of empiricism.

A priori

Reasoning from cause to effect or from a general to a particular instance, independently of any particular observation. This underpins the theoretical approach to research.

Action research

Usually involves a small-scale intervention on the part of the researcher in the phenomenon being studied. In this paradigm the researcher becomes actively involved with the situation or phenomenon being studied.

Alternate hypothesis

The experimental hypothesis used in testing situations, symbolised as H_1 as opposed to H_0.

Anachronism

Representation of someone as existing or something as happening in other than the chronological, proper, or historical order.

Anomaly

Deviation from the common rule.

Bias

Net systematic error that creeps into the research process usually due to the conscious or unconscious views of the researcher.

Central tendency

Location of the bulk of a distribution measured by statistics, such as the arithmetic mean or the median or the mode.

Chi-square (χ^2)

A statistic used to test the degree of agreement between the data actually obtained and that expected under a particular hypothesis (e.g. the null hypothesis).

Concept An abstract or generic idea that will often be a building block of a theory.

Confirmability With phenomenological research the concept of 'confirmability' poses the question, 'does the research confirm general findings or not?' The test is whether the findings of the research can be confirmed by another similar study.

Construct An abstract variable constructed or built or developed from ideas or images, which serves as a higher level explanatory term. Frequently it is a construct that is tested in business and management research.

Construct validation The procedure by which a means for the measurement of a construct is devised and then related to subjects' performance in a variety of other spheres as the construct would predict or imply.

Content analysis A method of categorising subjective information based on frequency of occurrence.

Contingency table A table in which the data are displayed as counts.

Creativity The quality of producing new ideas, usually reliant on the imaginative ability of the researcher. Creativity is one of the most important attributes of a researcher.

Credibility The issue of credibility refers to being able to demonstrate that the research was designed in a manner which accurately identified and described the phenomenon to be investigated. Such a representation of the phenomenon will therefore be valid for that particular study.

Deduction The deriving of a conclusion by logical reasoning in which the conclusion about particular issues follows necessarily from general or universal premises.

Deontology The view that certain actions are categorically immoral or unethical no matter what their consequences.

Dependability	This is similar to reliability in the case of the positivist.
Determinism	The assertion that there are causal laws for behaviours and actions; also called strict determinism when causal laws are presumed for every behaviour or action.
Dialetic	A discussion and reasoning by dialogue as a method of intellectual investigation first proposed by Socrates which he used to expose false beliefs and eliciting truth. Further developed by Plato and Aristotle and then refined in relatively modern times by Hegel. The dialectic involves a thesis, antithesis and a synthesis in order to reach a position of clarity within the argument under review.
Empirical generalisation	A statement similar to a hypothesis, which it is intended will be tested as part of the research process.
Empirical method	Any procedure employing controlled experience, observation, or experiment to map out the nature of reality or realities.
Empiricism	An ensemble of theories of explanation, definition and justification, to the effect that our concepts or knowledge are derived from or justified in terms of *sense-experience*. It was initially a reaction to Platonic and Cartesian doctrines of 'innate ideas' and 'natural intuition', but is characteristic of positivism generally. However, empiricism is also the basis for phenomenological research which relies on the observation of evidence.
Epistemology	The study or a theory of the nature and grounds of knowledge especially with reference to its limits and validity. Epistemological assumptions underpin any approach to research.
Ethics	A sense or understanding of what is right and wrong.
Evidence	An obvious sign or indication that may be taken as furnishing proof. In business and management research the word evidence is sometimes used as an alternative to the words data or fact.

Face validity	The possibility of a construct being valid as a result of a superficial or on the face of it enquiry or inspection.
Factor analysis	The rewriting of a set of variables into a new set of orthogonal factors. Factor analysis requires the use of sophisticated computer software and some knowledge of statistics in order to be able to interpret the results.
Falsifiablity	The principle (advanced by Karl Popper) that a theoretical proposition is 'scientific' only if it is stated in such a way that, if incorrect, it may be seen to be false by empirical tests.
Generalisability	The characteristic of research findings that allow them to be applied to other situations and other populations.
Gnomic present	The use of present tense in relating past events.
Grounded theory	An inductive, theory-discovery methodology that allows the researcher to develop a theoretical account of the general features of a topic while simultaneously grounding the account in empirical observations or evidence (Glaser and Strauss, 1967).
Hawthorne effect	The notion that the mere fact of being observed experimentally can influence the behaviour of those being observed.
Hermeneutics	Study of the methodological principles of interpretation and explanation of written texts. The method of understanding by hermeneutics, similar to that of *Verstehn,* contrasts with the methods usually presupposed to hold in natural science. In the former, understanding comes through 'getting within the object'; in the latter, by subsuming the object within the operation of a more general set of laws. These differences may not be as real as is sometimes supposed.
Heterogeneity	Dissimilarity among the element of a set.
Heuristic	Involving or serving as an aid to learning, discovery, or problem-solving by experimental and especially by trial-and-error methods.

Hypothesis

A research idea that can serve as a premise or supposition to organise certain facts and thereby guide observations.

Hypothesis testing

The use of some technique, usually statistical, to establish whether a hypothesis may be rejected.

Induction

The inference of a generic or generalised conclusion from the observation of particular instances.

Instrumentalism

A doctrine that ideas are instruments of action and that their usefulness is their primary *raison d'être*. Also the view that a scientific theory is nothing more than a device or instrument for yielding correct predictions about the course of nature and that theories must therefore be assessed not as true or false, but only as effective or ineffective as prediction. Some instrumentalists, also known as fictionalists, think that theories are never true. Other instrumentalists think that some scientific theories might possibly be true but since we have no means of deciding whether or not they are we should avoid any debate about the truth of the theories and simply confine attention to questions about their usefulness.

Internal validity

The degree of validity of statements made about whether X causes Y.

Interpretive

combining facts creatively with stimulating explanatory suggestions.

Likert scale

Summated ratings: a method of attitude-scale construction developed by Rensis Likert, which uses item analysis to select the best items.

Logical positivism

Another more formal expression used to describe positivism, which emphasises the use of logic and thus deduction.

Matched pairs

Pairs of observations made on the same sampling units.

Mean

A measure of central tendency calculated by the arithmetic average of a set of scores calculated by summing the scores and then dividing the sum by the number of scores.

Median	When a series of scores or measurers are laid out in size order, the score or measure which is equidistant from the first and the last is the median.
Metaphor	A word or phrase applied to a concept or phenomenon that it does not literally denote. The metaphor describes a phenomenon *as if* it were something else.
Methodology	The procedural framework within which the research is conducted. It describes an approach to a problem which may be operationalised into a research programme or process, which Leedy (1989) formally defines as 'an operational framework within which the facts are placed so that their meaning may be seen more clearly.'
Metonymy	A figure of speech consisting of the use of the name of one thing for that of another.
Model	A model may be described as a representation of an artefact, a construction, a system or an event or sequence of events. The representation may be abstracted into symbols, equations and numbers, i.e. mathematical expectations; it may consist of a picture or a drawing, or a fabricated likeness such as a model aeroplane, or it may be an expression of a situation or relationship in words. A complex model may contain several of these representations simultaneously. The purposes of modelling are many and various, and include developing a fuller understanding of the relationship between the inputs, the process and the outputs of the issue being studied, as well as calculating the likely results of a project.
	Models are primarily used for their explanatory power and to help understand the impact of changes in the assumptions that underpin the suggested project.
Modes	The most frequently occurring score or measure. There may be multiple modes.
Noise (experimental)	The occurrence of experimental errors due to extraneous factors in the experiment or in the

environment, which are not controllable by the researcher.

Nominalism

The view that the world may be understood only through the use of particular or specific named data i.e. those concepts for which there is a name or a word, or facts.

Normal distribution

Bell-shaped curve or distribution that is completely described by its mean and standard deviation.

Null hypothesis

The hypothesis that there is no relation between two or more variables symbolised as H_0.

Observation

An act of recognising and noting or recording an occurrence often involving measurement of some sort. Evidence is normally collected by observation.

Occam's razor

A scientific and philosophical principle established by William of Occam that explanations should be as parsimonious as possible.

Ontology

A branch of philosophy or metaphysics concerned with the nature and relations of being.

Paradigm

A philosophical and theoretical framework of a scientific school or discipline within which theories, laws, and generalisations, and the experiments performed in support of them, are formulated.

Paradox

A statement that appears to be contradictory or opposed to common sense and yet is perhaps correct.

Participant observer

A research tactic in which the researcher joins a group of individuals who are working within the organisation which is being studied and whereby the researcher participates in the phenomenon while recording his or her observations.

Phenomenology

Phenomenology is a theoretical point of view that advocates the study of direct experience taken at face value; and one which sees behaviour as determined by the phenomena of experience rather than by external, objective and physically described reality (Cohen and Manion, 1987).

Polemic	An attack on or refutation of the opinions or principles of another: the art or practice of disputation or controversy.
Population	The universe of elements from which sample elements are drawn, or the universe of elements to which we want to generalise.
Positivism	Positivism was adopted by Comte (1798–1857) to express the idea that phenomena were real, certain, and precise. All knowledge consists in the description and coexistence and succession of such phenomena. It became an extremely influential intellectual trend from the mid-nineteenth century, forming, until very recently, the generally accepted view of science. Positivism is a theory of the nature, omnicompetence and unity of science as understood in the physical world.
Post-modernism	Several movements (as in art, architecture, or literature) that are reactions against the philosophy and practices of modern views and are typically marked by revival of traditional elements and techniques. In research post-modernism suggests a move in emphasis from positivism to phenomenology.
Power of a test	The probability when doing significance testing of not making a Type II error.
Primary data	Refers to data collected from original sources and not already published sources such as directories or databases.
Probability	The mathematical chance of an event occurring.
Probability sampling	In survey sampling, a selection procedure in which every unit in the population has a known non-zero probability of being chosen.
Prolepsis	The anachronistic representation of something as existing before its proper or historical time, as in *the precolonial United States*.
Promoter	The term used by some universities, particularly in continental Europe, for a research students' supervisor. It is increasingly believed that the term

promoter more properly describes the role of the supervisor. Also see Supervisor.

Qualitative research   Research based on evidence that is not easily reduced to numbers. In some cases the evidence cannot be reduced to numbers and any attempt to so do would not be useful. In such cases statistical techniques are not sensible and hermeneutic approaches are preferable.

Random errors   The effects of uncontrolled variables that cannot be specifically identified. It is suggested that such events are, theoretically speaking, self-cancelling in that the average of the errors will probably equal zero.

Random sample   Sample chosen by chance procedures and with known probabilities of selection so that every individual in the population will have the same likelihood of being selected.

Realism   Scientific realism is the thesis that the objects of scientific knowledge exist and act independently of the knowledge of them. More generally 'realism' asserts the existence of some disputed kind of object or thing (e.g. universals, material objects, scientific laws; propositions, numbers, probabilities). Also the assertion that scientific theories give (or probably give) a literally true account of the world; a view associated with Rudolf Carnap, Ronald Giere and Karl Popper.

Regression analysis   Loosely equivalent to correlational analysis; more technically refers to relations of change in level of Y to changes in level X.

Relativism   A theory that knowledge is relative to the limited nature of the mind and the conditions of knowing: a view that ethical truths depend on the individuals and groups holding them.

Reliability   This implies that similar results will be obtained by researchers on different occasions (Easterby-Smith et al., 1994) and the concern is therefore with how replicable the research study is.

Reliability	The degree to which observations or measures are consistent or stable.
Replication	The repeating of an experiment or a research study.
Research	A scholarly enquiry involving a careful and diligent search.
Research design	The plan that the researcher proposes to follow in the conducting of the research.
Research strategy	The basic philosophical orientation of the research. The research strategy may be either theoretical or empirical and within the empirical classification there are the two major options of positivism and phenomenalism.
Rhetoric	The use of writing or speaking as a means of communication or persuasion.
Sample	The subset of the population for whom we have obtained observations.
Sample selection bias	Systematic error resulting from the nature of the sampling units.
Secondary data	Refers to data obtained from already published sources such as directories or databases.
Serendipity	The happy or pleasant occurrence of discoveries in the course of investigations designed for another purpose.
Simulation	A domain of study in which the input variables and the manner in which they interact is generally known to an uncertain level of accuracy. Sometimes referred to as stochastic modelling, simulation is used to investigate situations that do not readily lend themselves to a strictly deterministic or analytical treatment. Sometimes simulation can be used as a substitute for a laboratory or field experiment. Simulation is particularly relevant where there is a requirement for the evaluation of formal mathematical relationships under a large variety of assumptions (Freedman, 1992; Reiman, Simon and Willie, 1992).

Social sciences The study of people and their ways using a rigorous, science-like approach. As in the natural sciences, many of the fundamental aims and ideas of the social sciences can be traced back to antiquity. For a long time the only major sources of secular explanatory principles in the social sciences were essentially mechanistic, being based on the physical and life sciences. Comte broke radically with traditional or religious explanations with his espousal of a purely positive method based on and limited to observable facts, and a substitution of a religion of humanity for that of God. Social science today uses a much wider series of methods including non-positivistic and phenomenological.

Supervisor A suitably qualified individual whose job it is to help a research student successfully conclude his or her research degree. In some countries there is more than one supervisor.

Survey The collection of a large quantity of evidence, usually numeric, or evidence that will be converted to numbers, normally by means of a questionnaire.

Synecdoche A figure of speech by which a part is put for the whole.

Synthesis The joining together or the creative compilation of ideas and concepts into new ideas, concepts or theories.

T-distributions Family of distributions, centred at zero and ranging from negative to positive infinity and which is frequently used with small samples.

Tetrad A group or arrangement of four.

Theoretical conjecture A clear expression of a possible theory that has been compiled by the researcher for the purposes of testing. The theoretical conjecture is in effect the researcher's first attempt at establishing new theory that will then be tested to see if it should be rejected.

Theory A scientifically acceptable general principle or set of principles offered to explain a phenomenon or a group of phenomena.

Transferability

Refers to external validity and is dependent upon the researcher stating the theoretical parameters of the research explicitly. Here it would be important to specify how the specific phenomenon or research setting being investigated ties into a broader case, making clear the specific organisational processes about which transferable or generalisable comments will be made.

Trope

The figurative use of a word or an expression, as metaphor or hyperbole.

T-test

A test of significance employed to judge the tenability of the null hypothesis of no relation between two variables.

Validity

The degree to which what is observed or measured is the same as what was purported to be observed or measured.

Variables

Attributes of sampling units that can take on two or more values.

Weltanschauung

General world outlook or set of values.

References

Aguinis, H. (1993) 'Action research and scientific method: presumed discrepancies and actual similarities', *Journal of Applied Behavioural Science*, 29 (4) Dec.: 416–31.

Al-Arjani, A. H. (1995) 'Impact of cultural issues on the scheduling of housing maintenance in a Saudi Arabian urban project', *International Journal of Project Management*, 13 (6): 373–82.

American Heritage Dictionary of the English Language, Third Edn, 1992, Houghton Mifflin Company. Electronic version licensed from InfoSoft International, Inc.

Aristotle (1976) *Ethics*. Penguin Books, London.

Baker, J. (1993) *Paradigm – The Business of Discovering the Future*. Harper Business, New York.

Baran, P. A. and Sweezy, P. M. (1970) *Monopoly Capital: An Essay on the American Economic Order*. Penguin Books, Harmondsworth.

Baskerville, R. L. and Wood-Harper, A. T. (1996) 'A critical perspective on action research as a method for information systems research', *Journal of Information Technology*, 11 (3) Sep.: 235–46.

Beardon, W. O., Netermeyer, R. G. and Mobley, M. F. (1993) *Handbook of Marketing Scales*. Sage Publications, London.

Becker, H. S. (1970) *Sociological Work*. Aldine, Chicago.

Belbin, R. M. (1981) *Management Teams: Why They Succeed or Fail*. Butterworth-Heinemann, London.

Bell, J. (1993) *Doing Your Research Project: A Guide for First-time Researchers in Education and Social Science*, Second Edn, Open University Press, Milton Keynes.

Bendixon, M. T. (1991) 'Correspondence Analysis', Working paper, Graduate School of Business Administration, University of the Witwatersrand, Johannesburg.

Benzecri, J. P. ed., (1969) 'Statistical analysis as a tool to make patterns emerge from data', in *Methodologies of Pattern Recognition*, New York, Academic Press, pp. 35–74.

Berelson, J. (1980) cited in K. Krippendorff, *Content Analysis*. Sage Publications, Beverly Hills, CA.

Bernstein, P. (1996) *Against the Gods*. John Wiley, New York.

Boland, R. (1985) 'Phenomenology: a preferred approach to research on information systems', in E. Mumford, R. Hirschheim, G. Fitzgerald and T. Wood-Harper (eds), *Research Methods in Information Systems*, Elsevier Science Publishing Company Inc. Amsterdam.

Boland, R. and Hirschheim, R. (1987) *Critical Issues in Information Systems Research*. Wiley Series in Information Systems, Chichester.

Born, M. (1950) cited in H. Margenau, *The Nature of Physical Reality*. McGraw Hill, New York.

Braiden, P., Alderman, N. and Thwaites, A. (1993) 'Engineering design and product development and its relationship to manufacturing: A programme of case study research in British companies', *International Journal of Production Economics*, 30 (31) 1 July.

Brittain-White, K. (1985) 'Perceptions and deceptions: issues for information systems research', in E. Mumford, R. Hirschheim, G. Fitzgerald and T. Wood-Harper (eds), *Research Methods in Information Systems*, Elsevier Science Publishing Company Inc. Amsterdam.

Bryman, A. (1988) *Quantity and Quality in Social Research*. London, Unwin Hyman.

Bryman, A. and Cramer, D. (1992) *Quantitative Data for Social Scientists*. Routledge, London.

Buchanan, D., Boddy, D. and McCalman, J. (1988) 'Getting in, getting on, getting out and getting back', in A. Bryman (ed.), *Doing Research in Organisations*. Routledge, London.

Bulmer, M.G. (1979) *Principles of Statistics*. Dover Publications, New York.

Burrell, G. and Morgan, G. (1979) *Sociological Paradigms and Organisational Analysis – Elements of the Sociology of Corporate Life*. Heinemann, London.

Bussen, W. and Myers, M. D. (1997) 'Executive information systems failure: a New Zealand case study', *Journal of Information Technology*, 12 (2): 145–54, June.

Bynum, W., Browne, E. and Porter, R. (eds) (1982) *Dictionary of the History of Science*. Macmillan Reference Books, London.

Carr, E. H. (1967) *What is History?* Penguin Books, London.

Chand, D. R. (1994) 'An approach for developing applications in Lotus Notes', *Journal of Information Systems Education*, 6 (3): 134–40.

Christensen, C. R. and Hansen, A. J. (1987) *Teaching and the Case Method.* Harvard Business School, Boston, MA.

Churchill, Jr, G. (1987) *Market Research – Methodological Foundations.* Dryden Press, Chicago.

Clarkson, P. (1989) *Gestalt Counselling in Action.* Sage Publications, London.

Clegg, S. and Dunkerley, D. (1980) *Organisation, Class and Control.* Routledge & Kegan Paul, London.

Cohen, L. and Manion, L. (1987) *Research Methods in Education*, Second Edn, Croom Helm, London.

Cohen, M. R. and Nagel, E. (1984) *An Introduction to Logic and Scientific Method.* Harcourt, Brace & World Inc.

Collins, A. and Young, R. A. (1988) 'Career development and hermeneutical inquiry part 2: undertaking hermeneutical research', *Canadian Journal of Counselling*, 22 (4): 191–201.

Collins, H. (1994) A broadcast video on science matters entitled *Does Science Matter?*, Open University, BBC, UK.

Collins, H. and Pinch, T. (1994) *The Golem.* Canto Cambridge University Press, New York.

Collopy, F. and Armstrong, J. (1992) 'Expert opinions about extrapolation and the mystery of the overlooked discontinuities', *International Journal of Forecasting*, 8 (4) Dec.: 575–82.

Cook, T. D., Campbell, D. T. *Quasi-Experimentation – Design and Analysis Issues for Field Settings.* Rand McNally College Publishing.

Creswell, J. (1994) *Research Design – Qualitative and Quantitative Approaches.* Sage Publications, London .

Czarniawska, B. (1997) 'A four times told tale: combining narrative and scientific knowledge', *Organisation Studies*, 4 (1): 7–31.

Denzin, N. (1981) 'Contributions of anthropology/sociology to qualitative research methods', in E. Kuhns and S. V. Martorana (eds), *Qualitative Methods for Institutional Decision-Making*, Jossey Bass, San Francisco.

Dunbar, R. (1996) *The Trouble with Science.* Faber & Faber Ltd, London.

Easterby-Smith, M., Thorpe, R. and Lowe, A. (1994) *Management Research: An Introduction.* Sage Publications, London.

Edge, A. G. and Coleman, D. R. (1986) *The Guide to Case Analysis and Reporting.* System Logistics.

Einstein, A. (1922) *The Meaning of Relativity.* 1978, Chapman and Hall, London.

Einstein, A. (1931) *The World as I See It.* Covici Friede, New York.

Einstein, A. (1936) 'Physics and reality', Journal of the Franklin Institute, reprinted in *Out of my Later Years*, 1950, Philosophical Library, New York.

Einstein, A. (1950) 'The fundamentals of theoretical physics', in *Out of my Later Years*, Philosophical Library, New York.

Einstein, A. (1954) 'Remarks on Bertrand Russell's theory of knowledge', in *Ideas and Opinions*, Bonanza Books, New York.

Einstein, A. Letter to M. Born, 4 December, 1926 in M. Born, *The Born–Einstein Letters* (Walker, New York) 1971, quoted in *Nature* 278 (1979).

Eliot, T. S. (1920) 'The perfect critic', reproduced in *Selected Prose of T. S. Eliot*, ed. by Frank Kermode, 1975, cited in *Columbia Dictionary of Quotations*, 1995, Columbia University Press, New York.

Emory, C. W. and Cooper, D. R. (1991) *Business Research Methods.* Irwin, Burr Ridge, IL.

Ewing, A. C. (1965) *Ethics.* The Free Press, New York.

Feyerabend, P. (1983) *Science in a Free Society.* Verso Edition, London.

Freedman, J. (1992) 'Behind the smoke and mirrors: gauging the integrity of investment simulations', *Financial Analysts Journal*, 48 (6) Nov./Dec.: 26–31.

French, W. L. and Bell, C. H. Jr. (1978) *Organisation Development: Behavioral Science Interventions for Organisation Improvement.* 2nd edn., Prentice-Hall, Englewood Cliffs, NJ.

Gable, G. (1994) 'Integrating case study and survey research methods: an example in information systems', *European Journal of Information Systems*, 3 (2): 112–26.

Galliers, R. (1985) 'In search of a paradigm for information systems research', in E. Mumford, R. Hirschheim, G. Fitzgerald and T. Wood-Harper (eds), *Research Methods in Information Systems,* Elsevier Science Publishing Company Inc. Amsterdam.

Galliers, R. (1992) *Information Systems Research. Issues, Methods and Practical Guidelines.* Alfred Waller Information Systems Series, Henley-on-Thames.

Galliers, R. and Land, F. (1987) 'Choosing appropriate information systems research methodologies', *Communications of the ACM*, 30 (11): 900–2.

Garfield, E. (1989a) 'Art and science. Part 1. The art–science connection', *Current Contents*, 21 (8): 3–10.

Garfield, E. (1989b) 'Art and science. Part 2. Science for art's sake', *Current Contents*, 21 (9): 3–8.

Gersick, C. (1992) 'Time and transition in my work on teams: looking back on a new model of group development', in P. Frost and R. Stablein (eds) (1992*) Doing Exemplary Research*, Sage Publications, Newbury Park, CA: 52–64.

Gill, J. and Johnson, P. (1991) *Research Methods for Managers*. Paul Chapman Publishing Limited, London.

Glaser, B. and Strauss, A. (1967) *The Discovery of Grounded Theory: Strategies for Qualitative Research*. Aldine, New York.

Goldfisher, K. (1992–93) 'Modified Delphi: A concept for new product forecasting', *Journal of Business Forecasting*, 11 (4) Winter: 10–11.

Gould, S. J. (1980a) *Ever Since Darwin*. Penguin Books, Harmondsworth.

Gould, S. J. (1980b) *The Panda's Thumb*. W. W. Norton and Co., London.

Gould, S. J. (1988) *The Mismeasure of Man*. Fourth Edn, Penguin Books, London.

Gould, S. J. (1995) *Adam's Navel*. Penguin Books, London.

Greenacre, M. J. (1984) *The Theory and Applications of Correspondence Analysis*. Academic Press, London.

Guardian Weekly (1988) 'The mathematician who turned down a $150,000 prize' in the 'Le Monde' section, 15 May p.17.

Gummesson, E. (1988) *Qualitative Methods in Management Research*. Chartwell-Bratt, Bickley, Bromley.

Gummesson, E. (1991) *Qualitative Methods in Management Research*. Sage Publications, London.

Habermas, J. (1993) *Postmetaphysical Thinking – Philosophical Essays*, translated by M. Hohengarten, MIT Press, Cambridge, MA.

Haggard, H. R. (1995) *She*, first published in 1887. Wordsworth Classics, Ware, Hertfordshire.

Hammersley, M. (1989) *The Dilemma of Qualitative Method: Herbert Blumer and the Chicago Tradition*. London, Routledge.

Harnett, D. and Soni, A. (1991) *Statistical Methods for Business and Economics*. Addison Wesley, Reading, MA.

Harre, R. (1972) *The Philosophies of Science – An Introductory Survey*. Oxford University Press, Oxford.

Harvey-Jones, Sir J. (1988) *Making it Happen – Reflections on Leadership*. Fontana Collins, London.

Hodges, A. (1992) *Alan Turing the Enigma*. Vintage, London.

Hoffman, D. L. and Franke, G. R. (1986) 'Correspondence analysis: graphical representation of categorical data in marketing research', *Journal of Marketing Research*, no. 23: 213–27.

Holland, J. (1993) 'Bank corporate relations: change issues in the international enterprise', *Accounting and Business Research*, 23 (91) Summer.

Holton, G. (1978*) The Scientific Imagination – Case Studies*. Cambridge University Press, Cambridge.

Howard, K. and Sharp, J. A. (1983) *The Management of a Student Research Project*. Gower, Aldershot.

Hubbard, R. (1979) 'Have only men evolved?' in R. Hubbard, M. S. Henifin and B. Fried (eds), *Women Look at Biology Looking At Women*. cited in *Columbia Dictionary of Quotations*, 1995, Columbia University Press, New York.

Hubermann, A. M. and Miles, M. B. (1994) 'Data analysis and analysis methods', in N. Denzin and Y. Lincoln (eds), *Handbook of Qualitative Research*, Sage Publications, Thousand Oaks, CA.

Hughes, J. (1990) *The Philosophy of Science*. Longman, London .

Ishiwara, J. (1977) Kyoto Lecture, Einstein Koen-Roku, (Tokyo-Tosho, Tokyo,) cited by A. Pais (1982) in *Subtle is the Lord: The Science and the Life of Albert Einstein*. Oxford University Press, Oxford.

Jacques, R. (1997) *Classic Review: The Empire Strikes Out: Lyotard's Postmodern Condition and the Need for a 'Necrology of Knowledge'* 4 (1): 130–43.

Jankowicz, A. (1995) *Business Research Projects*. Second Edn, Chapman and Hall, London.

Jankowski, N. W. and Webster, F. (1991) 'The qualitative tradition in social science inquiry: contribution to mass communication research', in K. B. Jensen and N. W. Jankowski (eds), *A*

Handbook of Qualitative Methodologies for Mass Communication Research, Routledge, London.

Jenkins, T. (1996) A discussion with Professor Trefor Jenkins of the South African Institute of Medical Research in Johannesburg, December.

Jensen, K. B. (1991) 'Introduction: the qualitative turn', in K. B. Jensen and N. W. Jankowski, (eds), *A Handbook of Qualitative Methodologies for Mass Communication Research*, Routledge, London.

Jick, T. D. (1979) 'Mixing qualitative and quantitative methods: triangulation in action', *Administrative Science Quarterly*, 24: 602–11.

Jocher, C. (1928/29) 'The case method in social research', *Social Forces Journal*.

Jones, O. (1992) 'No guru, no method, no teacher: epistemological issues and managerial research', Unpublished paper delivered at BAM Conference, September.

Jung, C. G. (1995) *Memories, Dreams, Reflections*, Fontana, London.

Kallinikos, J. (1997): 'Classic Review: Science, Knowledge and Society: The postmodern condition revisited', *Organisation Studies*, 4 (1): 114–30.

Kant, I. (1948) *The Moral Laws*. Hutchinson, London.

Kaplan, A. (1964) *The Conduct of Inquiry: Methodology for Behavioral Science*. Chandler, Scranton, PA.

Kasanen, E. and Suomi, R. (1987) 'The case method in information systems research, Liiketaloudellinen Aikakauskirja – Foretagsekonomisk', *Finnish Journal of Business Economics*, 8 (3): 120–135.

Kawalek, P. and Leonard, J. (1996) 'Evolutionary software development to support organisational and business process change: a case study account', *Journal of Information Technology*, 11 (3) September: 185–98.

Kayes, P. (1995) 'How ICL used project management techniques to introduce a new product range', *International Journal of Project Management*, 13 (5): 321–8.

Kazdin, A. E. (1980) *Behaviour Modification in Applied Settings*. Dorsey Press, Irwin-Dorsey Ltd, Ontario.

Kaplan, A. (1964) *The Conduct of Inquiry: Methodology for Behavioural Science*. Chandler, Scranton, PA.

Kerlinger, F. N. (1969) *Foundation of Behavioural Research*. Holt, Rinehart & Winston, London.

Keynes, J. M. (1921) *A Treatise on Probability*. London. Macmillan.

King, D. (1996) Equinox 'Dr Satin's Robot', Broadcast by Channel 4 on Sunday 15 December.

Kourrie, D. and Introna, L.(1995) 'What is a good contribution', *South African Computer Journal*, (4): 12, July.

Kuhn, T. (1962) *The Structure of Scientific Revolutions*. University of Chicago Press, Chicago.

Lacey, A. (1982) *Modern Philosophy*. Routledge & Kegan Paul, Boston.

Lakatos, I. (1970) 'Methodology of scientific research programmes in criticism and the growth of knowledge', *Proceedings of the International Colloquium in the Philosophy of Science*, London, edited by I. Lakatos and A. Musgrave, Cambridge University Press, Cambridge.

Lakatos, I. (1978) 'The methodology of scientific research programmes', *Philosophical Papers Volume 1*, Cambridge University Press, Cambridge.

Laudan, L. (1977) *Progress and Its Problems: Towards a Theory of Scientific Growth*. University of California Press, Berkeley, CA.

Ledford, G. and Mohrman, S. (1993) 'Looking backward and forward at action research', *Human Relations*, 46 (11) Nov.: 1349–59.

Lee, A. S. (1989) 'A scientific methodology for MIS case studies', *MIS Quarterly*, 13 (1) 156-172.

Leedy, P. D. (1989) *Practical Research – Planning and Design*, Macmillan Publishing Company, New York.

Lehmann, D. R. (1989) *Marketing Research Analysis*. Third Edn, Richard D. Irwin, Burr Ridge, IL.

Lincoln, Y. and Guba, E. (1995) *Naturalistic Inquiry*. Sage Publications, Newbury Park, CA.

Loveridger, R. (1990) 'Triangulation – or how to survive your choice of business school PhD course', *Graduate Management Research*, 5 (3): 18–25.

Lumley, J. and Benjamin, W. (1994) *Research: Some Ground Rules*. Oxford University Press, Oxford.

Mackenzie, D. (1979) 'Eugenics and the rise of mathematical statistics in Britain', in J. Irvine, I. Miles, and J. Evans (eds.), *Demystifying Social Statistics*, Pluto Press, London.

MacNaughton, R. J. (1996) 'Numbers, scales and qualitative research', *Lancet*, 347, 20 April: 1099–1100.

Maital, S. (1993) 'Oracles at work', *Across the Board*, 30 (5) June: 52–3.

Marsh, C. (1989) *Exploring Data: An Introduction to Data Analysis for Social Scientists*. Blackwell Publishers, Oxford.

Marshall, C. (1990) 'Goodness criteria: are they objective or judgement calls?' in E. Gua (ed.), *The Paradigm Dialogue*. Sage Publications, Newbury Park, CA: 188–97.

Marshall, C. and Rossman, G. (1995) *Designing Qualitative Research*. Sage Publications, Thousand Oaks, CA.

Martin, P. Y. and Turner, B. A. (1986) 'Grounded theory and organisational research', *Journal of Applied Behavioural Science*, 22 (2) NTL Institute.

Marx, K. (1844) 'Economic and philosophic manuscripts of 1844', reprinted in *Karl Marx and Friedrich Engels: Collected Works*, 3, 1975, cited in *Columbia Dictionary of Quotations*, 1995, Columbia University Press., New York.

Mason, D. and Cullen, R. (1996) *Research in the Age of the Internet*. McGraw Hill, Maidenhead.

McCarthy, K. (1992) 'Comment on the "Analytic Delphi Method"', *International Journal of Production Economics*, 27 (2) May: 135–6.

McCutcheon, D. and Meredith, J. (1993) 'Conducting case study research in operations management', *Journal of Operations Management*, 11 (3) September.

McKeon, R., Owen, D. and McKeon, Z. (eds) (1994) *On Knowing – The Natural Sciences*. University of Chicago Press, Chicago.

Mead, G. H. (1934) *Mind, Self and Society*. University of California Press, Berkeley, CA.

Medawar, P. B. (1984) 'Science and literature', in *Pluto's Republic*, Oxford University Press, Oxford.

Medawar, P. B. (1986) *The Limits of Science*. Oxford University Press, Oxford.

Miles, M. B. and Hubermann, A. M. (1984) *Qualitative Data Analysis – A Source Book of New Methods*. Sage Publications, Newbury Park, CA.

Miles, M. B. and Weitzman, E. (1996) 'The state of qualitative data analysis software: what do we need?' *Current Sociology*, 44 (3) Winter: 206–24.

Mill, J. (1863) *Utilitarianism*. Everyman, London.

Millar, R. (1994) A broadcast video on science matters entitled *Does Science Matter?*, Open University, BBC, UK.

Miller, C. (1994) 'Focus groups go where none has been before', *Marketing News*, 28 (14) July.

Mintzberg, H. (1973) *The Nature of Managerial Work*. Harper & Row, New York.

Mintzberg, H. (1996) 'Beyond configuration: forces and forms in effective organisations', in H. Mintzberg, J. B. Quinn and S. Ghoshal (eds), *The Strategy Process*. European Edition, Prentice-Hall, London: 737–54.

Mintzberg, H., Quinn, J. B. and Ghoshal, S. (eds) (1996) *The Strategy Process*. European Edition, Prentice-Hall, London: 605–20.

Molnar, K. K. and Sharda, R. (1996) 'Using the Internet for knowledge acquisition in expert systems development: a case study', *Journal of Information Technology*, 11 (3): 223–34, September.

Morgan, G. (1980) 'Paradigms, metaphors, and puzzle solving in organisation theory', *Administrative Science Quarterly*: 9 (4): 605–20, December.

Moroney, M. (1963) *Facts from Figures*. Penguin, Harmondsworth.

Moser, C. A. (1958) *Surveying Methods in Social Investigation*. Heinemann, London.

Moszkowski, A. (1970) in *Conversations with Einstein*. Horizon, New York.

Nachmias, C. and Nachmias, D. (1989) *Research Methods in the Social Sciences*. Edward Arnold, London.

Nandhakumar, J. (1996) 'Executive information systems development: a case study for a manufacturing company', *Journal of Information Technology*, 11 (3): 199–210, September.

Needham, J. (1988) Interviewed in 'Joseph Needham', Channel 4 television, 13 August.

Nisbet, R. (1976) *Sociology as an Art Form'*. Oxford University Press, London.

Oakley, A. (1981) 'Interviewing women, a contradiction in terms', in H. Roberts (ed.), *Doing Feminist Research*, Heinemann, Oxford, pp. 30–61.

O'Brien, J. (1965) *The Myth of Sisyphus*. Hamish Hamilton, London.

Oppenheim, A. N. (1966) *Questionnaire Design and Attitude Measurement*. Gower, New York.

Parasuraman, A., Zeithaml, A. and Berry, L. (1995) 'A conceptual model of service quality and its implications for future research', *Journal of Marketing* 47, Fall: 41–50.

Parsons, H. (1992) 'Hawthorne: An early OBM experiment', *Journal of Organizational Behaviour Management*, 12 (1): 27–43.

Pascale, R. (1990) *Managing at the Edge*. Penguin Books, London.

Patton, M. (1990) *Qualitative Evaluation and Research Methods.* Sage Publications, Newbury Park, CA.

Pettigrew, A. (1985) 'Contextualist research: a natural way to link theory and practice', in E. E. Lawler (ed.), *Doing Research that is Useful in Theory and Practice,* Jossey Bass, San Francisco.

Pfaffenberger, B. (1988) *Microcomputer Applications in Qualitative Research,* Sage Publications, London.

Philips, H., Broderick, A. and Thompson, P. (1997) 'Perception, selectivity and decision making at the point of sale', *International Review of Retail, Distribution and Consumer Research,* 7 (1): 79–89.

Phillips, E. M. and Pugh, D. S. (1994) *How to Get a PhD,* Second Edn, Open University Press, Milton Keynes.

Popper, K. (1975) *The Rationality of Scientific Revolutions,* ed. I. Hacking, Oxford University Press, Oxford. First given as the Herbert Spencer Lecture, Oxford 1973. First printed in *Problems of Scientific Revolution: Progress and Obstacles to Progress in the Sciences* (1973), Oxford, Clarendon Press.

Quinn, J. B. (1988a) cited in J. B. Quinn, H. Mintzberg, and R. M. James (eds), *The Strategic Process, Concepts, Context and Cases.* Prentice Hall, New Jersey.

Quinn, J. B. (1988b) *Strategies for Change: Logical Incrementalism.* Richard D. Irwin, Burr Ridge, IL.

Ray, M. (1993) 'Introduction: what is the new paradigm in business?', in *The New Paradigm in Business,* G. P. Putnam's Sons, New York.

Redpath, T. (1990) *Ludwig Wittgenstein – A Student's Memoir.* Duckworth, London.

Reiman, M., Simon, B. and Willie, J. (1992) 'Simterpolation: a simulation based interpolation approximation for queuing systems', *Operations Research,* 40 (4) Jul./Aug.: 706–23.

Remenyi, D. (1990a) *Strategic Information Systems: Current Practice and Guidelines.* Unpublished Doctoral Dissertation, Henley Management College, United Kingdom.

Remenyi, D. (1990b) *Strategic Information Systems: Development, Implementation, Case Studies.* NCC Blackwell, Manchester.

Remenyi, D. (1995) 'So you want to be an academic researcher in business and management studies! – Where do you start and what are the key philosophical issues to think about?' *Working Paper Series, Henley Management College,* Henley-on-Thames.

Remenyi, D. (1996) 'Reengineering Charter Life – A case study', *Journal of Business Change and Re-engineering,* 3 (2): 13–25.

Remenyi, D. and Cinnamond, B. (1996) 'Banking 2000? Reengineering at the First National Bank of Southern Africa to create a branch of the future', *Strategic Information Systems,* 5 (4): 293–316.

Remenyi, D. and Williams, B. (1993) 'Some aspects of methodology for research in information systems', accepted for publication in the *Journal of Information Technology.*

Remenyi, D. and Williams, B. (1995) 'Some aspects of ethics and research into artificial intelligence', working paper published by the Department of Information Systems, University of the Witwatersrand, Johannesburg.

Remenyi, D. and Williams, B. (1996) 'Some aspects of ethics and research into the silicon brain', *International Journal of Information Management,* 16 (6): 401–11.

Remenyi, D. and Williams, N. (1995) 'Some aspects of methodology for research in information systems', *Journal of Information Technology,* 10: 191–201.

Remenyi, D., Money, A. and Twite A. (1991) *Measuring and Managing IT Benefits.* NCC-Blackwell, Oxford.

Robinson, J. P. and Shaver, P. R. (1973) *Measures of Social Psychological Attitudes,* Ann Arbor: University of Michigan Institute for Social Research.

Robinson, J. P., Shaver, P. R. and Wrightman, L. S. (1991) *Measures of Personality and Social Psychological Attitudes,* Ann Arbor: University of Michigan Institute for Social Research, Survey Research Centre.

Rosenthal, R. and Rosnow, R. L. (1991) *Essentials of Behavioral Research Methods and Data Analysis,* Second Edn, McGraw-Hill, New York.

Rudestein, K. E. and Newton, R. R. (1992) *Surviving your Dissertation: A Comprehensive Guide to Content and Process.* Sage Publications, Newbury Park, CA.

Russell, B. (1946) *A History of Western Philosophy.* Unwin Hyman, London.

Russell, B. (1976) 'A free man's worship and other essays', cited in *Columbia Dictionary of Quotations,* 1995, Columbia University Press, New York.

Sachs, O. (1986) 'Rebecca', in *The Man Who Mistook his Wife for a Hat*. Pan Books, Gerald Duckworth, London.

Salvi, S. M. (1994) 'Degrassing and wall rock alteration in the rare metal – rich peralkaline granite at Strange Lake Quebec/Labrador', a thesis submitted to the Faculty of Graduate Studies and Research in partial fulfilment of the requirements of the degree of Doctor of Philosophy, Department of Earth and Planetary Science, McGill University, Montreal, Quebec, Canada.

Schramm, W. (1971) 'Notes on case studies of instructional media projects', *Working paper for the Academy for Educational Development*, Washington, DC.

Scudder, S. (1874) 'Look at your fish', cited in D. Erlandson (1993) *Doing Naturalistic Enquiry – Guide to methods*. Sage Publications, London.

Sekaran, U. (1992) *Research Methods for Business – A Skill-Building Approach*. Second Edn, John Wiley & Sons, New York.

Silverman, D. (1994) *Interpreting Qualitative Data: Methods for Analysing Talk, Text and Interaction*. Sage Publications, London.

Silverman, D. (1997) 'Qualitative research', unpublished paper presented at the Second UK Association of Information Systems Conference, 2–4 April, Southampton University.

Singer, P. (1994) *Ethics – Oxford Readers*. Oxford University Press, Oxford.

Singer, P. (1995) *Practical Ethics*. Second Edn, Cambridge University Press, Cambridge.

Smith, N. (1990) 'The case study: a useful research method for information management', *Journal of Information Technology*, no. 5:123–33.

Snee, R. (1995) 'Listening to the voice of the employee', *Quality Progress* 28 (1) Jan.

Storey, D. (1994) *Understanding the Small Business Sector*. Routledge, London.

Subramanian, A. and Lacity, M. C. (1997) 'Management client-server implementations: today's technology, yesterday's lessons', *Journal of Information Technology*, 12 (3) Sep.: 169–86.

Sullivan, J. (1952) *The Limitation of Science*. Mentor Books, New York.

Sutrick, K. (1993) 'Reducing the bias in empirical studies due to limit moves', *Journal of Future Markets*, 13 (5) Aug.: 527–43.

Townsend, R. (1984) *Further up the Organisation*. Knopf, New York.

Trevelyan, G. M. (1993), 'English Social History, Introduction' (1942) in *The Columbia Dictionary*, Columbia University Press.

Tung, L. and Heminger, A. (1993) 'The effects of dialectical inquiry, devil's advocacy, and consensus inquiry methods in a GSS environment', *Information and Management* 25 (1) July: 33–41.

Turner, B. (1981) *Quality and Quantity*. Elsevier Science Publishing Company Inc., Amsterdam.

Underhill, L. G. and Peisach, M. (1985) 'Correspondence and its applications in multi-elemental trace analysis', *Journal of Trace and Microprobe Techniques* 3 (1 and 2): 41–65.

Vitalari, N. (1985) 'The need for longitudinal designs in the study of computing environments', in E. Mumford, R. Hirschheim, G. Fitzgerald and T. Wood-Harper (eds) *Research Methods in Information Systems*, Elsevier Science Publishing Company Inc., Amsterdam.

von Clausewitz, C. (1981) *On War*, Pelican Classics. First published by Vom Kriege, 1832.

Wadeley, A. (1991) *Ethics in Psychological Research and Practice*. British Psychology Society, Leicester.

Walsham, G. (1993) 'Ethical issues in information systems development: the analyst as moral agent', in D. Avison, Kendall and DeGross (eds), *Human, Organizational and Social Dimensions of Information Systems Development*, Elsevier Science Publishing Company Inc., Amsterdam.

Weitzman, E. A. and Miles, M. (1995) *Computer Programs for Qualitative Data Analysis*. Sage Publications, London.

Wells, H. G. (1905) 'A Modern Utopia', chapter 2, section 5 (repr. in *The Works of H. G. Wells*, vol. 9, 1925).

Wessley, S. (1994) A broadcast video on science matters entitled 'Does Science Matter?', Open University, BBC, UK.

Whalen, J. (1994) 'Qualitative research adds the "why?" to measurement', *Marketing*, 28 (10).

Wheatley, M. (1992) *Leadership and the New Science*. Berrett-Koeler Publishers, San Francisco.

Whitehead, A. N. (1928) *Introduction to Mathematics*. Thornton Butterworth, London.

Wiersema, F. (1996) *Customer Intimacy*. Knowledge Exchange, Santa Monica, CA.

Wilde, O. (1891) *The Picture of Dorian Gray*, 'Preface', reprinted in *The Complete Illustrated Stories, Plays and Poems of Oscar Wilde*, 1992, Chancellor Press, London.

Wilkinson, A. and Redman, T. (1994) 'Quality management and the manager: a research note on the findings from an institute of management study', *Employee Relations*, 16 (1).

Wittgenstein, L. (1969) *On Certainty*, section 378, by Anscombe and von Wright (eds), cited in *Columbia Dictionary of Quotations*, 1995, Columbia University Press, New York.

Wood-Harper, T., Miles, R. and Booth, P. (1992) 'Designing research education in information systems: towards a global view', in M. Khosrowpour and K. Loch (eds), *Global Information Technology Education: Issues and Trends*. Harrisburg, PA.

Yin, R. K. (1981) 'The case study crisis: some answers', *Administrative Science Quarterly*, 26 (March): 58–65.

Yin, R. K. (1989) *Case Study Research – Design and Methods*. Sage Publications, Newbury Park, CA.

Yin, R. K. (1993) *Applications of Case Study Research – Design and Methods*. Sage Publications, Newbury Park, CA.

Yontef, G. M. (1993) *Awareness Dialogue and Process: Essays on Gestalt Therapy*. Gestalt Journal Press Inc., New York.

Index

interviews
  case study evidence 126, 176
  grounded theory methodology 76
  in-depth surveys 55, 111-12
  questionnaire administration 157-8
  schedules 55, 111, 112, 173
  structured 126
introductions to dissertations 255

Jankowski, N.W. 101
Johnson, P. 103
journal articles *see* academic papers
judgement samples 194
Jung, C.G. 33, 123, 150

Kaiser-Meyer-Olkin measure 223
Kepler, Johann 29, 90
KMO measure 223
knowledge
  role of observation 73
  use and misuse of 24-5
  see also body of knowledge
Kolb learning cycle 100-1
Kuhn, T. 34

laboratory experiments 56
Lakatos, I. 33
large-scale surveys 56-7
laws, scientific 30-1
  and positivism 32
leading questions 234
learning cycle 100-1
Lee, A.S. 28
length of dissertations 241-2, 254, 255
libraries, bibliographical resources 66
Likert scales 155, 284
limitations of research, recognition of 68-9, 258
literature reviews 65-6, 67, 75, 81, 83
  writing dissertation chapters on 255-6
logical positivism, definition of 284
  see also positivism
long-run frequencies 208
longitudinal research 47-8

MacNaughton, R.J. 102
mailed questionnaires 156
management games 54-5
management guidelines, production of 69, 258
Manion, L. 34, 95
market research *see* commercial research
Marsh, C. 150
Marshall, C. 64, 100, 105, 107, 109, 115
masters degrees
  checklist for candidates 258-9
  course work 15, 18-19, 251-2
  evaluation of 252-4, 255-8
  geographical variations 261-3

grading of 258
history of 261
nature of and requirements for 15, 17-18, 250
research reports for course work degrees 253
Masters of Business Administration
  see MBA degrees
matched pairs, definition of 284
mathematical simulation 53
MBA degrees 15, 18, 251, 261-2
Mead, G.H. 97
mean 210-11, 284
  sample size required to estimate 196-7, 198, 200, 201-2, 202, 203, 204
  standard errors 212, 214-16
measuring instruments *see* questionnaires
Medawar, P.B. 28, 33, 132
median 211, 285
mental models 128-9
methodology *see* research methodology
mid-career development degrees 18, 251
Miles, M.B. 113, 114, 278
Mill, John Stuart 208
Mintzberg, H. 96-7, 163
misconduct within research site, discovery of 235-6
misrepresentation of work 235
  definition of 285
  in deliberate intervention research 85
  in forecasting research 53
  mental models 128-9
  phenomenological and positivist approach to 33, 34, 36-7
  of positivist research process 80, 83, 86
  of qualitative research process 133
  of quantitative research process 135, 136
  role in paradigmatic research 134-5
  stochastic modelling 58-9
  see also integrity of evidence models
Morgan, G. 100, 103
multi-stage sampling 195
multiple case studies 182
multiple-item scales 154, 155
multiple regression analysis 54
multivariate analysis 79, 222-4
Myrdal, G. 117

narrative thinking 127-30
  distinguished from paradigmatic thinking 121-2
narratives
  analysis of 122-4
  case studies as 164, 184-6
  high order narratives 122, 123, 126, 130, 132
  primary narratives 122, 123, 124-5
  role in quantitative research 125-6, 135
  transitions to paradigms from 122-4